TRIBAL DEMOGRAPHY OF INDIA

TRIBAL DEMOGRAPHY OF INDIA

B.R. PANT

Foreword by

INDU KUMAR PANDE

ANAMIKA PUBLISHERS & DISTRIBUTORS (P) LTD.
4697/3, 21A, Ansari Road, Daryaganj, New Delhi 110002
Phone: 23281655, 23270239; Fax . : 011-27868035
E-mail : anamikapublishers@yahoo.co.in

First Published 2010

ISBN 978-81-7975-320-0

PRINTED IN INDIA

Published by Anamika Publishers & Distributors (P) Ltd., 4697/3, 21A, Ansari Róad, Daryaganj, New Delhi 110002. Typeset by Shivani Computer, Ashok Nagar, Delhi 110093 and Printed at Nagri Printers, Delhi.

Contents

इन्दु कुमार पाण्डे
Indu Kumar Pande

मुख्य सचिव
Chief Secretary

उत्तराखण्ड सचिवालय
Uttarakhand Secretariat
4, सुभाष मार्ग, देहरादून
4, Subhash Marg, Dehradun
Phone : (Off.) 0135-2712100
0135-2712200
(Fax) 0135-2712500

Foreword

The study of tribal development is an imperative dimension of the study in the recent years by the social scientists all over the country because the tribal community and their habitat constitute a very significant proportion of the backward populace and regions of this developing country. The community, mentioned as above, encompasses around eighteen percent of country's land and eight percent of its population. However, the steps taken for the development of these tribal communities is too meager in comparison with the yardsticks of expected successes. Uttarakhand has been a fascinating spot for the social scientists, specially, geographers for its varied tribes and cultural heritage. Tribal community in Uttarakhand constitutes three percent of the total population of the State. However, the distribution of tribal population is not uniform across the districts in Uttarakhand (as well as in India).Studies on socio- economic, health and nutrition in tribal population are few. Therefore, the book titled "Tribal Demography of India", written by the renowned academician Dr. B.R. Pant, is an admirable work. Based on large-scale survey, data collected and sample taken related to the tribes, this book contributes an empirical demographic insight about the 'Tharu' tribe, in particular, that is evident in Udham Singh Nagar district in Uttarakhand.

This work is an outcome of Dr. Pant's widespread study and research on tribal demography in India and particularly in Uttarakhand. He has many research papers and articles to his credit. Dr. Pant wrote this book systematically with the facts necessary to support the study. Based on census data of year

2001, he analysed the tribal setting of the country as well as the State. The most important chapter in this book contains the information collected by the sample survey. It includes geographical, historical, cultural and social backgrounds with environmental sanitation, food intake, nutrition status and health; and hygiene patterns of the Tharu population in 445 households in ten sample villages in Sitaganj and Khatima tehsils of Udham Singh Nagar in Uttarakhand State. Such type of systematic and detailed study on Tharu tribe is unavailable.

Present work can be important source of information and guidelines to those who are interested in tribal demography. It not only provides important aspects for general awareness but also apprises researchers about the tribal demography of India and Uttarakhand State, in particular.

A commendable study of such type is an eye-opener and a wake-up call for action at governmental and community level. I hope this book will be useful to those who are interested in tribal scenario and tribal development in India.

(Indu Kumar Pande)

Preface

The tribal community and their habitats constitute very significant proportion of backward people and regions of the country respectively. The tribal community encompasses around 18 per cent of country's land and 8 per cent of its population. In the Uttarakhand State of India, which is spread over the thirteen–two purely plain, two semi-plain and nine purely hilly districts, there are five major tribal communities, namely, the Bhotia, the Jaunsari, the Raji, the Tharu and the Buksa constituting about 3 per cent of the total population of the state. The habitation of a particular tribe is confined to a particular inhospitable location in the Uttarakhand, such as the Tharu and Buksa are confined to once waterlogged land of Tarai-Bhabar region while Bhotia (Shauka, Tolcha, Marcha and Jad) are confined to the higher altitudes of Pithoragarh, Bageshwar, Chamoli and Uttarkashi districts and Raji is confined to Didihat and Dharchula tehsils of Pithoragarh and Champawat tehsil of Champawat district. Likewise, Jaunsari resides in Chakrata and Kalsi block of Dehradun district.

Despite their habitation in different zones, there prevails a few common features in the economic and social life of all the tribal communities with minor variations necessitated to maintain a harmonious coordination between the resource availability and needs of the society. However, agriculture forms the basic livelihood of Tharu, Buksa and Jaunsari tribes while trade is the main source of livelihood of the Bhotia tribe. However, Raji (*Vanraut*) whose population is less than 1300 persons have been mainly depending on animal husbandry and daily wages in various developmental activities.

The tribal ecosystem is perpetuated through culture totally in balance with the production system and social heritage. Besides the traditional productive social economy of the tribal communities is a characteristic manifestation of their interaction through various institutions with nature. The institutions evolve the strategies that make effective use of resources through adaptations.

Despite the record economic growth, Indian social indicators are lagging behind largely because of poor access to good health care and information. Though the various schemes have been launched for the overall development from the First Five Year Plan in 1951, but the impact of these schemes is not visibly reflected in the improvement of the socio-economic wellbeing of the tribal people. The socio-economic level of the society plays dominant role to determine the health and nutrition status of the people. The tribals, particularly Tharus, are the lowest income group people living in abject poverty and are also surviving in shadow of severe under-nutritional conditions prone to several diseases including deficiency-related diseases. An unhealthy person cannot perform the physical as well as mental responsibilities properly.

With a number of physical as well as cultural diversities, Sitarganj and Khatima tehsils (District U.S. Nagar) of Uttarakhand state are selected for appraising the socio-economic and nutritional status of the Tharu tribal populace. This particular tribe of the Uttarakhand (India) is least studied and researched. Similarly, the impact of socio-economic level on health and nutrition status of the tribal communities is hardly known. Among the five major tribes of the region only one tribe – the Tharu as a sample has been selected for the present study.

Remarkably, the present investigation is based on first hand information. In all 445 Tharu sample households from ten sample villages of Sitarganj and Khatima tehsils have been surveyed comprehensively. The present book has been divided into five chapters. The first chapter consists of the research problem, review of literature, objectives, methodology and introduction to the study region. The second chapter is devoted to the tribal demography of India as a whole based on census data. The third chapter is devoted to the physical environment and geographical introduction of Uttarakhand as a whole. The fourth chapter focuses on the Tribal setting of Uttarakhand. The most important section of this book is in fifth chapter. It includes general introduction to the Tharu Habitat (study region) — geographical, historical, cultural, social and economic background; demographic and socio-economic structure, housing and environmental sanitation pattern, role and status of Tharu women, hygiene and food intake pattern, health and nutrition status of the Tharu population in the sample villages. Last chapter concludes the finding of the study.

Grateful acknowledgement is due to the University Grants Commission, New Delhi for financial assistance in the form of Major Research Project during 2005-06.

I deem it my honour that Shri Indu Kumar Pande I.A.S., Chief Secretary of Uttarakhand Government and also Vice-Chancellor of Uttarakhand Open University Haldwani has so kindly written the foreword of this book. I am indebted to him.

I express my deep sense of gratitude to late Padma Shree Prof. M. Shafi, Department of Geography, Aligarh Muslim University, Aligarh, Prof. M.H. Qureshi and Prof. Sudesh Nangia, Jawaharlal Nehru University New Delhi, Mr. Vijendra Paul, Mr. Keshav D. Raju and Mrs. Anjali Prasad, Principal Secretary, Govt. of Uttarakhand, Dehradun, Padma Shree Prof. Shekhar Pathak (Retired), Department of History, Prof. D.S. Jalal (Retired) and Prof. R. Chand, Department of Geography, Kumaun University Nainital, Director Higher Education, Uttarakhand, Dr. S. Mathpal, Dr. R.S. Bhakuni and Y.K. Sharma, P.G. College Rudrapur, Dr. G.C. Joshi, G.B. Pant University of Agriculture and Science and Technology, Pant Nagar, Ms. Sushma Joshi Advocate Nainital and official staff of the various district and state level offices, for their kind help in various ways. I express my deep sense of gratitude to the Principal, Government Post Graduate College, Rudrapur for providing necessary facilities. Thanks are also due to Mr. Surendra Pal, Field Assistant and number of other hired workers of the project for their kind help in various ways during the present research work.

I would like to express my esteemed gratitude towards my late wife Dr. Hemlata Pant who left for her heavenly abode on 23.03.2007 for her kind support even in her critical condition.

I am thankful to my lovely daughter Geetika who supports me in adverse circumstances.

I would like to express my sincere thanks to my family members who support me in my critical time. Thanks are also due to Mr. M.S. Mehra who look my family and provides opportunity for academic and research activities.

I would like to express my sincere thanks to all those, in particular, members of the interviewed families who volunteered the author and field workers at various stages of this work.

I would like to express my thanks to Mr. Anil Sharma for publishing the manuscript with very care and patience.

15th August, 2009 **(B.R. Pant)**
Independance Day
Haldwani

List of Tables

List of Figures

1

Introduction

The tribal community and their habitats constitute very significant proportion of backward people and regions of the country respectively. The tribal community encompasses around 18 per cent of country's land and 8 per cent of its population. In the Uttarakhand State or Himalaya of India, which is spread over the thirteen—two plain, two semi-plain and nine purely hilly districts, there are five major tribal communities, namely, the Bhotia, the Jaunsari, the Raji, the Tharu and the Buksa constituting about 3 per cent of the total population of the state. In the Indian context, a tribe is defined as a group with traditional territory, specific name, common language, strong kin relations, association with clan structure, tribal authority, and rigid inclination to religion and belief. Functional independence, homogeneity, primitive means of exploiting resources, economic backwardness, rich culture and tradition and least desire to change are some of the other characteristics dominant among the tribes (Majumdar and Madan, 1970 and Pati, 1991).

The habitation of a particular tribe is confined to a particular terrible location in the Uttarakhand, such as Tharu and Buksa are confined to once waterlogged land of Tarai-Bhabar region while Bhotia (Shauka, Tolcha, Marcha and Jad) is confined to the higher altitudes of Pithoragarh, Bageshwar, Chamoli and Uttarkashi districts and Raji is confined to Didihat and Dharchula tehsils of Pithoragarh and Champawat tehsil of Champawat district. Likewise, Jaunsari resides in Chakrata and Kalsi block of Dehradun district.

Despite their habitation in different zones, their prevails a few common features in the economic and social life of all the tribal communities with minor variations necessitated to maintain a harmonious coordination between the resource availability and needs of the society. However, agriculture forms the basic livelihood of Tharu, Buksa and Jaunsari tribes while trade is the main source of livelihood of the Bhotia tribe. However, Raji (*Vanrawt)* whose population is lower then 1300 persons are mainly depending on animal husbandry and daily wages in various developmental activities. The qualitative symbiotic relationship of the tribal people with forest is the strenuous outcome of their experiences of different survival (Furer-Haimendorf, 1909 and Bose, 1990).

The tribal ecosystem is perpetuated through culture totally in balance with the production system and social heritage. Besides the traditional productive social economy of the tribal communities is a characteristics manifestation of their interaction through various institutions with nature. The institutions evolve the strategies that make effective use of resources through adaptations. In this process of adaptation, the tribal communities have resorted to eco-cultural adjustments for a harmonious articulation between technologies of the communities and the institutions (Pande, 1998).

Despite the various schemes have been launched for the overall development from the First Five Year Plan in 1951, but the impact of these schemes is not visibly reflected in the improvement of the socio-economic wellbeing of the tribal people. The socio-economic level of the society plays dominant role to determine the health and nutrition status of the people. The tribal, particularly Tharus are the lowest income group people living in absolute poverty and are also surviving in shadow of severe undernutritional conditions inviting several diseases including deficiency-related diseases. An unhealthy person cannot perform the physical as well as mental responsibilities properly.

With a number of physical as well as cultural diversities, Uttarakhand state is selected for appraising the socio-economic and nutritional status of the tribal populace. This is particularly so far the tribe of the Uttarakhand state of India on which little such study has been done. Similarly, the impact of socio-economic level on health and nutrition status of the tribal communities is hardly known. Among the five major tribes of the region only one tribe – the Tharu as a sample will be selected for the present study.

The deduction of proposed research work will entirely be based on descriptive and inferential statistical technique embracing the widely applicable resource utilization, socio-economic structure, housing and environmental sanitation, dietary habits, hygiene pattern, food intake, nutrition status, magnitude of malnutrition, disease pattern to define the present status of tribal community in Tarai region of Uttarakhand state. The present investigation is not only academically sound but also important because it will provide the appropriate strategy for the all-round development of the tribal community. It will investigate the factors responsible for low and slow development. These findings will play an important role at that time when policy will be decided. Therefore, the present study is very significant.

The main objective of this study is to highlight the social, economic, cultural, nutritional, housing and environmental sanitation status of the Tharu tribal society in Udham Singh Nagar district of Uttarakhand state which is quite relevant for the geographers, sociologists, anthropologists, economists and policy-makers. However, few social scientists of these disciplines have already worked on tribes in different parts of the country in their own point of view.

In spite of the crucial importance of the regional dimensions in the proper evaluation of the social phenomena for the better appreciation of the diverse character of the Indian polity, geographical research in the country has tended to ignore it either almost entirely or treated it area of peripheral interest. Despite various incentives available to the researchers in the field, tribes continue to receive scant attention from the social as well as the population geographers. Evidently the social sciences including geography were already seized of the problem of Indian tribes and studies such as those of Singh (1972), Roy Burman (1972), Raza (1972, 1984 and 1986), Raghaviah (1972),

Aggarwal and Mathur (1973), Ashfaq Ali (1972), Aurora (1972), Patnaik (1972), Pratap (1975), Vidyarthi (1974), Majumdar (1973), Despande (1973), Mehdi Raza (1973), Verma (1975), Mukerji (1979), Bhati (1972), Venkatraman (1972), Hasan (1990), Mookharjee (1986), Dash and Ahmad (1985), Goswami (1994), Fernandes (1994), Jafri and Imchen (1994), Gupta and Baghel (1995), Jain (1992), Joshi (1996), Parizanganeh and Rangaswami (1991), Bhole and Bhangale (1999), Chib (1995), Pathak (2001) and Chand (2004) focused on the multifarious problems faced by the tribes in different parts of the country and abroad.

The studies relating to tribal society of Uttarakhand state as a whole are quite negligible. In the beginning there was slow rate of growth of scientific studies because of inhospitable environment. The credit goes to the administrator and explorers who have given some very fascinating account of these people particularly Bhotias of Uttarakhand like Trail (1832), Atkinson (1886), Sherring (1906), Seven Hedin (1913), Pant (1935) and Swami Pranavanand (1950 and 1953). Authors like Pate Ram (1911), Panna Lal (1911), and Pant (1935), etc. have dealt with selected aspects of Bhotias life and culture in considerable detail and precision. But now we have the scholarly contribution from authors like Tiwari (1953), Srivastava (1953), Srivastava (1958), Upreti (1967 and 1968), Sastry (1975), Berreman (1972 and 1983), Hazra (1981), Chand (1981 and 1995), Prasad and Kapoor (1982), Bisht *et al.* (1995), Satyal *et al.* (1999), Samal (1993), Choudhuri and Ghatak (1987), etc. and few others who have enriched the scientific literature on Bhotia.

The review of literature provides a clear vision of the works done by various scholars to find out the social, economic and cultural attributes at micro and macro levels. These studies are mainly confined to Bhotia a particular tribe of particular area and have taken only a limited number of indicators. No geographical study of scheduled tribe population particularly Tharu at micro level has been undertaken in the Udham Singh Nagar district of Uttarakhand State. Therefore it is urgent need to undertake a scientific study of this tribe.

The prime objectives of the present study are:

1. To study the demographic structures of India—Country level
2. To study the demographic structures of Uttarakhand—State level
3. To study the socio-economic and demographic structures;
4. To study the housing and environmental sanitation patterns
5. To study the role and status of Tharu women; and
6. To study the health, hygiene, dietary, food consumption patterns and nutritional status.

The nature of the present study is empirical, about 7% (10) of the total 141 Tharu sample villages has been selected in the Sitarganj and Khatima tehsils of district U.S. Nagar in Uttarakhand state. About 50 percent (445 households of the total 890) Tharu households from each sample village have been selected for detailed study (Tables 5.1 & 5.2). Stratified purposive sampling procedure has been adopted to select the households as well as to collect the authentic and relevant information. The main aim of the statistical sampling is to obtain, representative sampling of the tribal community as possible from each strata, so that the data collection regarding the socio-cultural milieu and economic status, demographic composition, housing and environmental sanitation, dietary habits, hygiene pattern, anthropometric characteristics, food consumption, nutrition intake pattern etc. may closely reflect the situation as it exist in overall tribal population.

The present study is hierarchical in nature taking the region, study area, village and family as components of study.

In selecting the sample villages, the following criteria have been followed:

1. Distance from block headquarters.

2. Available infrastructure in the village itself.
3. Running development programs like, Jawahar Rozgar Yojana.
4. Type of village—purely tribal, mixed, forest village etc.

In selecting the households, the economic status with reference to per capita annual income from all economic activities like primary occupation, secondary, tertiary jobs, and other works like labouring, cattle keeping, and trade have been taken into consideration. The primary survey has been conducted in to two phases—first Pilot survey for selecting the sample household and second detailed survey of the selected households. The detailed investigation has been carried out through collection of data from secondary sources and primary surveys by canvassing specially structured schedules and questionnaires, personal observations and interviewing the head of the households and respondents. Overall information of the region has been gathered from secondary sources—statistical diaries, censuses, Survey of India, Toposheets etc.

Food items taken by the sample population has been measured (weighment method) in local units and then converted into the standard units i.e. kg, gram, and milligram with the help of conversion formula and these items has been converted into various nutrients—energy, protein, fat, minerals, vitamins etc. with the help of food composition tables and then finally percentage departure has been compared with the standard requirement or Recommended Dietary Allowances (R.D.A.) as suggested by the National Institute of Nutrition, Indian Council of Medical Research, Hyderabad (Gopalan *et al.*, 1993 and Nutrition Foundation of India's websites). Height and weight of the samples has been measured with the help of measuring tape and portable balance. Chronic Energy Deficiency (mal-and undernutrition) has been computed with help of the method evolved by James *et al.* (1988).

The Himalaya constitutes one of the greatest and youngest folded mountain systems in the world rising from 200 m to more than

8000 m above sea level. The Himalaya makes the northern boundary of India extended from eastern border of Pakistan to the western border of Myanmar and having length of 2500 km and width varying from 250 to 400 km. The Himalaya encompasses an area of about five lakh km^2 (Fig. 1.1). From east to west it has been divided into four sections 560 km long Punjab Himalaya extends from Indus to Sutlaj, 320 km Kumaun Himalaya extends from the Sutlaj to the Kali (Sharda), 800 km long Nepal Himalaya lies between the Kali and the Tista and 820 km long Assam Himalaya extend from the Tista to the Myanmar (Brahmaputra) or eastern most border of Arunachal Pradesh (Burrared *et al.*, 1933, Pant, 1995, 1998 and 2004).

The Planning Commission of India (1982) has also divided the Himalaya into three broad regions. The Western Himalaya consisting of the States of Jammu & Kashmir and Himachal Pradesh, the Central Himalaya consisting of Kumaun and Garhwal Division (Uttarakhand) and North Eastern Himalaya comprising the states of Sikkim, Manipur, Tripura, Arunachal Pradesh, Nagaland, Mizoram, and hill districts of Assam and West Bengal. (Fig. 1.1) From Northern boundary of Gangetic plain to the extreme north up to the Indian boundary with Tibet (China), the Himalaya is divided into several geo-physical divisions—the Outer Himalaya consisting of the Tarai, Bhabar, Siwaliks and Duns, the densely populated Lesser Himalaya having a number of fertile river valleys, terraces, the Great Himalaya—a zone of high snow peaks, glaciers and a birth region of rivers, and the Trans Himalaya—a region across the Himalaya. These latitudinal divisions are separated from one another by thrusts/faults such as Himalayan Frontal Fault (HFF) exists between the Shiwalik and Bhabar, Main Boundary Thrust (MBT) lies between the Lesser Himalaya and Shiwalik, Main Central Thrust (MCT) separated the Lesser and the Great Himalaya and Trans Himadri Thrust (THT) lies between the Great and the Trans Himalaya (Pant, 1995 and 1998). Total population of Indian Himalaya was about 3.5 crore persons in 2001, accounting 3.6% population of the country. Out of the total 48% are females in the Himalaya. It records about 28% population growth during 1991 to 2001 (Pant, 2003).

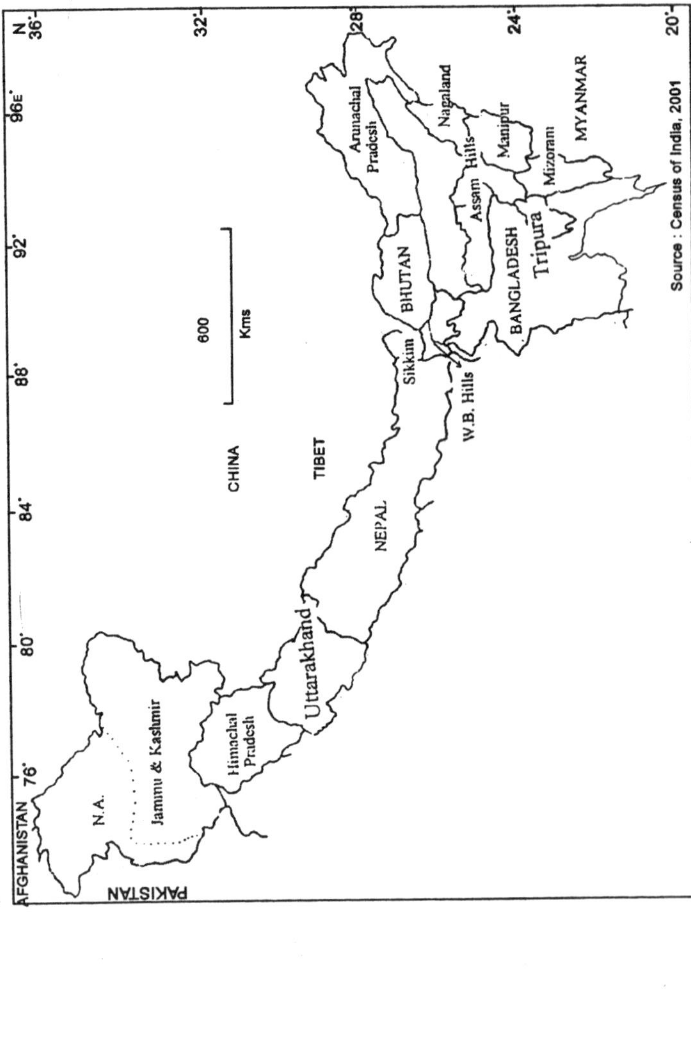

FIG. 1.1 : Indian Himalaya : Administrative Set up

Being a distinct geographical entity Uttarakhand is selected for the present investigation. There are several social and ethnic groups such as Jaunsari, Raj, Bhotia, Tharu and Buksa. Tharu population of U.S. Nagar district of Uttarakhand has been selected for detailed study. Approximately 43% of the total tribal and more than two third of the Tharu tribe reside in the selected district.

The Uttarakhand is considered to be densely forested area, place of God and Goddesses and the home of wild animals and also got recognition to be a confluence of various cultural groups came down from Central Asia in the north Nepal in the east, Himachal in the west and the Gangetic Plain in the south. It extends from the Tons-feeder of Yamuna River in the west to the Kali or Sharda in the east. Its northern boundary is demarcated by Indo-Tibet water parting ridge and southern boundary corresponds almost with the southern limit of Tarai belt separating it from Saharanpur, Bijnor, Moradabad, Rampur, Bareilly, and Pilibhit districts. Administratively, Uttarakhand is one among four new states created after 1991 census. Situated in the Himalayan region, all the districts barring Hardwar and U.S. Nagar of Tarai and Bhabar region are hilly tract. Historically, the region under the present study has been divided into two divisions—Garhwal (Kedarkhand) and Kumaun (Manaskhand)—presently Garhwal includes the districts of Hardwar, Dehradun, Uttarkashi, Tehri, Rudraprayag, Chamoli, and Pauri and Kumaun spreads over the districts of Almora, Bageshwar, Pithoragarh, Champawat, Nainital and U.S. Nagar. Lying between 28°44′ and 31°25′ north latitudes and 77°45′ and 81°1′ east longitudes, it encompasses an area of 53483 km^2 and supports 84.89 lakh persons in 2001 (Fig. 1.2 and 1.3). Approximately 3074 km^2 of land form the Almora district, 2311 km^2 Bageshwar, 3422 km^2 Nainital, 3372 km^2 U.S. Nagar, 7212 km^2 Pithoragarh, 1642 km^2 Champawat, 7626 km^2 Chamoli, 3088 km^2 Dehradun, 5397 km^2 Pauri, 3796 km^2 Rudraprayag, 8016 km^2 Uttarkashi, 1891 km^2 Rudraprayag and 2360 km^2 forms Hardwar district. Out of total population in 2001, there are 12,79,912 in Dehradun, 12,34,548 in U.S. Nagar, 7,62,912 in Nainital, 6,96,851 in Pauri, 4,62,149 in Pithoragarh, 6,04,608 in Tehri, 3,69,198 in Chamoli, 2,94,179 in

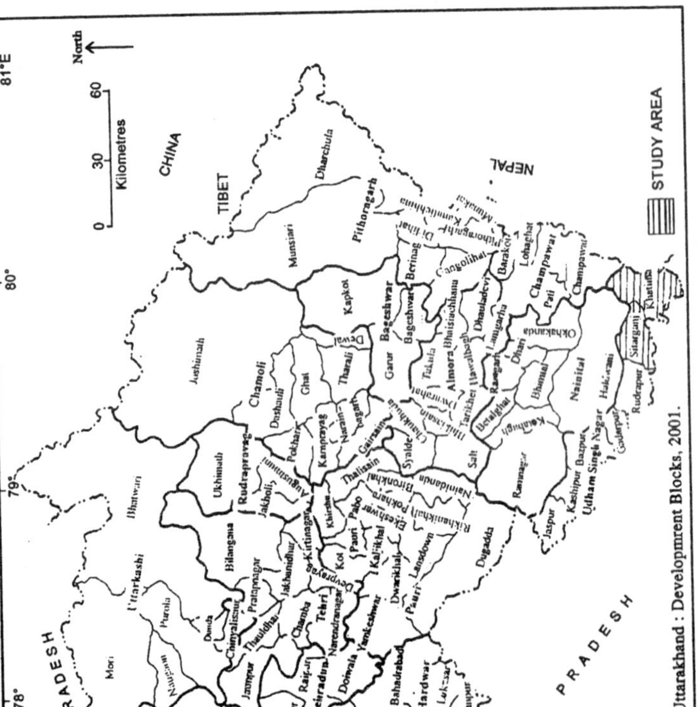

Figure 1.2 : Uttarakhand : Development Blocks, 2001.

FIG. 1.2 : Uttarakhand : Development Blocks, 2001

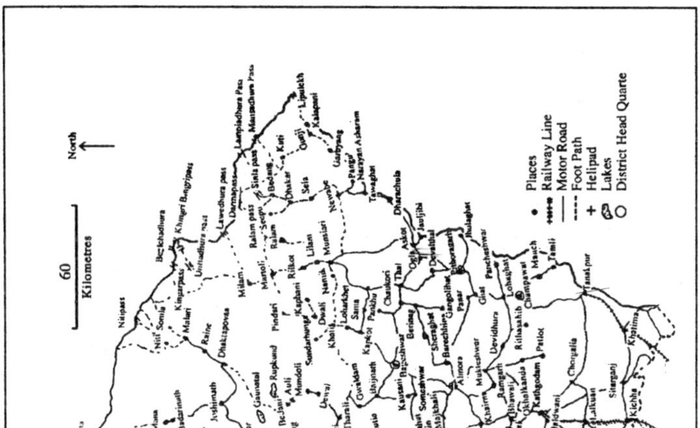

FIG. 1.3 : Transport Network of Uttarakhand

Uttarkashi, 2,49,453 in Bageshwar, 2,27,461 in Rudraprayag, 6,30,446 in Almora, 14,47,187 in Hardwar and 2,24,461 persons in Champawat districts (Anon, 2001b).

For the purpose of detailed study of the tribal society, Tharu tribe of the U.S. Nagar of Uttarakhand state has been selected. The Tharu tribe of the U.S. Nagar has been selected on the following basis—

1. Maximum 75% of the Uttarakhand state's Tharu tribe resides in Sitarganj and Khatima Tehsils as well as Blocks of U.S. Nagar District.
2. About 43% of the state's total tribal populations reside in U.S. Nagar district.
3. In the study region—Sitarganj and Khatima tehsils have 26.8 % and 18.9 % tribal population to the total population, i.e. about one fifth population is tribal.
4. The previous studies on this tribe are very scanty.

The main habitat of Tharus is Sitarganj and Khatima tehsils of U.S. Nagar district in Uttarakhand state. It stretches from the Sharda River on the east to the Kichha Tehsil of the same district on the west and lies between 28°44′ to 29°0′30 "North latitude and 79°28′ to 80° East longitude (Fig. 5.1). It is bounded by the Nainital district on the north, districts Bareilly and Pilibhit on the south, Kichha Tehsil on the west and Nepal on the east. It comprises a narrow strip of the country running for 40 km long and 25 km wide along the foot of the Himalaya with reporting area of 68,206 km^2 supports 3,58,498 totals and 82,385 Tharu population as per census 2001 (Census, 2001b).

2

Tribal Demography of India

Introduction

The tribal community and their habitats constitute very significant parts of backward people and regions of the country respectively. They comprise about the 18.7 per cent of country's land and 8.2 per cent of its population. In the Indian context, a tribe is defined as a group with traditional territory, specific name, common language, strong kin relations, association with clan structure, tribal authority, and rigid inclination to religion and belief. Functional independence, homogeneity, primitive means of exploiting resources, economic backwardness, rich culture and tradition and least desire to change are some of the other characteristics dominant among the tribes (Majumdar and Madan, 1972).

About half of the total tribal population of the world lives in India. The aborigines in Indian language are known as "Adibasi"—*Adi* and *basi* standing for "original" and "inhabitants" respectively. Constitutionally these human groups are known as Scheduled Tribes (S.T.), "Anusuchit Jati", "Vanjati", "Vanbasi", "Pahari", and "Adimjati" etc. According to article 342 of the constitution the Scheduled Tribes are the tribes or tribal communities, which may be notified by the President of India. The census enumerates only such tribal population as are scheduled under the relevant constitutional order in force at the time of the census.

As per 2001 census the tribal population of India was 84326240 persons constituting 8.2% of the country's population. It is worth to mention here that there is a great variation between the

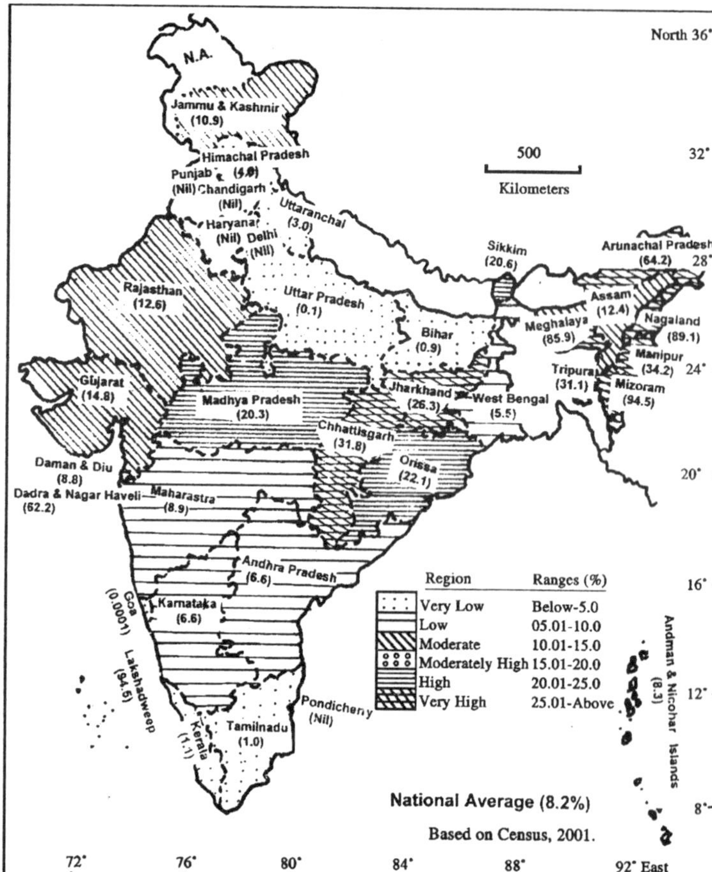

Fig. 2.1 : Distribution of Scheduled Tribe Population in India, 2001.

varieties/type of the Scheduled Tribe in one state/UT to another. It is multicultural and multiracial. It is estimated that the total number of tribal communities in India are more than 1000.

The main characteristic features of Indian tribes are variation in size of the population, inhabit all climatic zones, belong to all in four races—Negrito, Proto-Austroloid, Mongoloid and Caucasoid and use Indo-Aryan, Dravidian and Tibeto-Burman language. The main objective of the paper is to analyses inter-state diversities in selected attributes of tribal population of India. The detailed data released by the census 1991-2001 form the basis of present discussion.

Distribution

The distribution pattern of the population structure differs from one place to another. These aspects are particularly determined by the environmental conditions which have both restrictive and permissive conditions to human activities. The tribal population of India is mostly concentrated in inhospitable regions like rugged mountains, riverine land, extreme climatic zones and dense forest areas. India has the largest tribal population of the World. According to the 2001 census the tribal population of India is enumerated 8,43,26,240 persons which constitutes about 8.2 % of the total population (hereinafter referred to as all castes population) and residing in about 18.7% of the country's geographical area. As per 2001 census country's largest tribal population is found in Madhya Pradesh (14.51%) with 46 tribes (main and sub-tribes). The second largest number of tribal is enumerated in Maharashtra (10.17%) immediately followed by Orissa (9.66%) (Table 2.1). The concentration of country's tribal population has been grouped into five categories—below 0.5 % population, 0.51-1.00 %, 1.01-3.00, 3.01-5.0 and more than 5.01 population respectively termed as very low concentrated, low, moderate, high and very high concentrated zones/regions (Table 2.2 & Fig. 2.1) .Out of total thirty states/UTs (comprising tribal population states/UTs hereinafter referred to states) one third (33.33%) have less than 0.5% country's population. These are Goa, Daman and Diu, Andaman & Nicobar, Lakshadweep, Uttar Pradesh, Sikkim, Dadra & Nagar Haveli, Himachal Pradesh, Uttarakhand and Kerala. Only nine states (30%) possessing more

TABLE 2.1

Distribution of All Castes and Scheduled Tribe (Total) Population in India, 2001

Sl. No.	State/UTs	Total Population (All Castes)	% share to Country Population	House-hold Size (P/HH)	Scheduled Tribes Population	% Share to S.T. Population	% S.T.to State/UT Population	House-hold size (P/HH)	No. of S.Tribes
1.	Jammu & Kashmir	10,143,700	0.99	6.5	1,105,979	1.31	10.9	6.1	12
2.	Himachal Pradesh	6,077,900	0.59	5.0	244,587	0.29	4.0	4.9	8
3.	Punjab	24,358,999	2.37	5.6	Nil	Nil	Nil	Nil	Nil
4.	Chandigarh	900,635	0.09	4.4	Nil	Nil	Nil	Nil	Nil
5.	Uttarakhand	8,489,349	0.83	5.3	256,129	0.30	3.0	6.1	5
6.	Haryana	21,144,564	2.06	5.7	Nil	Nil	Nil	Nil	Nil
7.	Delhi	13,850,507	1.35	5.1	Nil	Nil	Nil	Nil	Nil
8.	Rajasthan	56,507,188	5.49	6.1	7,097,706	8.42	12.6	5.7	12
9.	Uttar Pradesh	166,197,921	16.15	6.5	107,963	0.13	0.1	6.6	5
10.	Bihar	82,998,509	8.07	6.0	758,351	0.90	0.9	5.2	30
11.	Sikkim	540,851	0.05	4.7	111,405	0.13	20.6	4.8	2
12.	Arunachal Pradesh	1,097,968	0.11	5.1	705,158	0.84	64.2	5.3	12
13.	Nagaland	1,990,036	0.19	6.1	1,774,026	2.10	89.1	6.2	5
14.	Manipur**	2,166,788	0.21	5.8	741,141	0.88	34.2	6.0	29
15.	Mizoram	888,573	0.09	5.0	839,310	1.00	94.5	5.4	14
16.	Tripura	3,199,203	0.31	4.8	993,426	1.18	31.1	4.9	19
17.	Meghalaya	2,318,822	0.23	5.5	1,992,862	2.36	85.9	5.6	17
18.	Assam	26,655,528	2.59	5.4	3,308,570	3.92	12.4	5.6	23
19.	West Bengal	80,176,197	7.79	5.1	4,406,794	5.22	5.5	4.8	38
20.	Jharkhand	26,945,829	2.62	5.6	7,087,068	8.40	26.3	5.2	30

....

21.	Orissa	36,804,660	3.58	4.8	8,145,081	9.66	22.1	4.5	62
22.	Chhattisgarh	20,833,803	2.02	5.1	6,616,596	7.86	31.8	4.9	42
23.	Madhya Pradesh	60,348,023	5.87	5.5	12,233,474	14.51	20.3	5.4	46
24.	Gujarat	50,671,017	4.93	5.2	7,481,160	8.87	14.8	5.3	29
25.	Daman & Diu	158,204	0.01	4.4	13,997	0.02	8.8	4.7	5
26.	Dadra & Nagar Haveli	220,490	0.02	4.8	137,225	0.16	62.2	5.3	7
27.	Maharashtra	96,878,627	9.42	4.9	8,577,276	10.17	8.9	5.0	47
28.	Andhra Pradesh	76,210,007	7.41	4.5	5,024,104	5.96	6.6	4.5	33
29.	Karnataka	52,850,562	5.14	5.1	3,463,986	4.11	6.6	5.1	49
30.	Goa	1,347,668	0.13	4.6	566	Negligible	Negligible	3.9	5
31.	Lakshadweep	60,650	Negligible	6.1	57,321	0.07	94.5	6.3	*
32.	Kerala	31,841,374	3.09	4.7	364,189	0.43	1.1	4.3	35
33.	Tamil Nadu	62,405,679	6.07	4.3	651,321	0.77	1.0	4.1	36
34.	Pondicherry	974,345	0.09	4.5	Nil	Nil	Nil	Nil	Nil
35.	Andaman & Nicobar	356,152	0.03	4.6	29,469	0.03	8.3	6.4	6
India		**1,028,610,328**	**100.00**	**5.3**	**84,326,240**	**100.00**	**8.2**	**5.1**	**663**

Source: Census of India, 2001a.

* Throughout the Union Territory. Inhabitants of the Laccadiv, Minicoy and Anindivi Islands who and both of whose parents were born in these Islands.

** excludes Mao Maram, Paomata and Purul sub-divisions of Senapati district of Manipur state.

There is no notified Seheduled Tribes in the States of Delhi,Haryana and Punjab and the Union Territories of Chardigarh and Pondicherry.

TABLE 2.2

Distribution of States/ UTs by Ranges of Percentage Share to Country's Population in India, 2001

Zone/Region	*Ranges of Country's Population*	*All Castes Population*		*Scheduled Tribe Population*		
		(No.)	*(%)*	*(No.)*	*(%)*	*States/Union Territories (UTs)*
Very Low	Below 0.5	14	40.00	10	33.33	Uttar Pradesh, Sikkim, Daman & Diu, Dadra & Nagar Haveli Goa, Lakshadweep, Andman & Nicobar Islands, Himachal Pradesh, Uttara-khand and Kerala
Low	0.51-1.00	3	8.57	5	16.67	Bihar, Arunachal, Manipur, Mizoram and Tamilnadu.
Moderate	1.01-3.00	6	17.14	4	13.33	J. & K., Nagaland, Tripura and Meghalaya.
High	3.01-5.0	3	8.57	2	6.67	Karnataka and Assam.
Very High	Above 5.01	9	25.72	9	30.00	Maharashtra, Andhra Pradesh, Rajasthan, West Bengal, Jharkhand, Orissa, Chhattisgarh, Madhya Pradesh and Gujarat.
Total		**35**	**100**	**30**	**100**	

Source: Anon; 2001a.

than 5 % of the country's tribal population. These are West Bengal, Andhra Pradesh, Chhattisgarh, Jharkhand, Rajasthan, Gujarat, Orissa, Maharastra and Madhya Pradesh. It is evident from the Table 2.1 that only one third state/UTs have less population while two third have more population than the country average (8.2%). It is worth to clear that the states which have more inhospitable geographical area registered more tribal population such as Madhya Pradesh, Jharkhand, Orissa, Chhattisgarh, Rajasthan and north eastern mountainous states of India. Contrary this the states having more fertile land, irrigational and other infrastructural facilities have less tribal population. Even two states—Haryana and Punjab, and three UTs—Delhi, Chandigarh and Pondicherry, have no a notified tribes. But their largest proportion to total state population among all the states is found in Mizoram (94.5%) followed by Nagaland

TABLE 2.3

Distribution of States/UTs by Ranges of Percentage Share to Scheduled Tribe Population to Total Population, 2001

Zone/Region	*Ranges*	*(No.)*	*(%)*	*States/Union Territories (UTs)*
Very Low	Below 5.00	7	23.33	Bihar, Tamilnadu, Himachal Pradesh, Uttarakhand, Goa, Uttar Pradesh and Kerala.
Low	5.01-10.00	6	20.00	Maharashtra, Andhra Pradesh, Daman & Diu, Karnataka, West Bengal and Andaman & Nicobar Islands.
Moderate	10.01-15.00	4	13.33	Jammu & Kashmir, Rajasthan, Gujarat and Assam.
Mode. High	15.01-20.00	Nil	Nil	Nil
High	20.01-25.01	3	10.00	Madhya Pradesh, Orissa and Sikkim.
Very High	Above 25.01	10	33.34	Dadra & Nagar Haveli, Lakshadweep, Nagaland, Tripura, Arunachal Pradesh, Manipur, Mizoram, Jharkhand, Chhattisgarh and Meghalaya.
Total		**30**	**100.00**	

Source: Anon; 2001a.

TABLE 2.4

Distribution of All Castes and Scheduled Tribe (Urban) Population in India, 2001

Sl. No.	State/UTs	Total Population (All Castes) (No.)	% share to Country Population	Household Size (P/HH)	Scheduled Tribe Population	% Share to S.T. Population	% of S.T. to Total Population	Household Size (P/HH)
1.	Jammu & Kashmir	2,516,638	0.88	6.3	51,491	0.74	2.0	4.7
2.	Himachal Pradesh	595,581	0.21	4.2	7,527	0.12	1.3	3.5
3.	Punjab	8,262,511	2.89	5.3	Nil	Nil	Nil	Nil
4.	Chandigarh	808,515	0.28	4.4	Nil	Nil	Nil	Nil
5.	Uttarakhand	2,179,074	0.76	5.2	15,920	0.23	0.7	4.3
6.	Haryana	6,115,304	2.14	5.2	Nil	Nil	Nil	Nil
7.	Delhi	12,905,780	4.51	5.1	Nil	Nil	Nil	Nil
8.	Rajasthan	13,214,375	4.62	5.8	379,876	5.44	2.9	5.0
9.	Uttar Pradesh	34,539,582	12.07	6.4	12,135	0.17	0.0	5.1
10.	Bihar	8,681,800	3.03	6.5	40,649	0.58	0.5	5.0
11.	Sikkim	59,870	0.02	4.6	9,496	0.14	15.9	4.2
12.	Arunachal Pradesh	227,881	0.08	4.6	98,880	1.42	43.4	5.0
13.	Nagaland	342,787	0.12	5.3	230,004	3.29	67.1	5.5
14.	Manipur*	575,968	0.20	5.6	35,229	0.50	6.1	5.7
15.	Mizoram	441,006	0.15	4.9	408,427	5.84	92.6	5.2
16.	Tripura	545,750	0.19	4.4	25,429	0.36	4.7	3.8
17.	Meghalaya	454,111	0.16	5.3	310,192	4.44	68.3	5.5
18.	Assam	3,439,240	1.2	4.8	154,024	2.20	4.5	4.3

19.	West Bengal	22,427,251	7.84	4.9	270,428	3.87	1.2	4.7
20.	Jharkhand	5,993,741	2.09	5.6	587,054	8.40	9.8	5.1
21.	Orissa	5,517,238	1.93	4.9	446,723	6.39	8.1	4.5
22.	Chhattisgarh	4,185,747	1.46	5.1	351,761	5.03	8.4	4.6
23.	Madhya Pradesh	15,967,145	5.58	5.5	787,026	11.26	4.9	4.9
24.	Gujarat	18,930,250	6.62	5.0	614,523	8.79	3.2	4.8
25.	Daman & Diu	57,348	0.02	4.6	2,809	0.04	4.9	4.7
26.	Dadra & Nagar Haveli	50,463	0.02	4.3	9,815	0.14	19.4	5.2
27.	Maharashtra	41,100,980	14.37	4.9	1,090,739	15.62	2.7	4.3
28.	Andhra Pradesh	20,808,940	7.27	4.7	377,181	5.40	1.8	4.5
29.	Karnataka	17,961,529	6.28	4.9	529,456	7.58	2.9	4.8
30.	Goa	670,577	0.23	4.5	376	0.01	0.1	4.3
31.	Lakshadweep	26,967	0.01	6.2	25,112	0.36	93.1	6.5
32.	Kerala	8,266,925	2.89	4.8	14,170	0.20	0.2	4.1
33.	Tamil Nadu	27,483,998	9.61	4.3	100,178	1.43	0.4	4.1
34.	Pondicherry	648,619	0.23	4.5	Nil	Nil	Nil	Nil
35.	Andaman & Nicobar	116,198	0.04	4.4	1,013	0.01	0.9	4.4
India		**286,119,689**	**100.00**	**5.1**	**6,987,643**	**100.00**	**2.4**	**4.8**

Source: Census of India, 2001a.

* Excludes Mao Maram, Paomata and Purul sub-divisions of Senapati distrist of Manipur State.

Nil—There is no notified Seheduled Tribes in the States of Delhi, Haryana and Panjab and the Union Territories of Chandigarh and Pondicherry.

(89.1%), Meghalaya (85.9%), Arunachal Pradesh (64.2%) Manipur (34.2%) Chhattisgarh (31.8%), Jharkhand (26.3%) etc. (Table 2.1). Among the UTs, Lakshadweep (94.5%) ranks first followed by Dadra & Nagar Haveli (62.2%). Table 2.3 shows that out of total about 33% states have more than 25% tribal population to all castes population while 23.33% states have less than 5% tribal population. Out of total tribal population only 2.4% tribal population resides in urban areas (cities and towns).

Maximum urban tribal population is found in Maharashtra (15.62%) followed by Madhya Pradesh (11.26%), Gujarat (8.79%), Jharkhand (8.40%), Karnataka (7.56%) etc. (Table 2.4).

The average household size of the scheduled tribe is 5.1 persons per household (p/hh) which is less than the all castes population average (5.3). The household size varies from minimum of 3.9 p/household in Goa to maximum 6.6 p/household in Uttar Pradesh (Table 2.1). In 2001 census, 40% states are found below and remaining 60% are above the national average (5.1) while in all castes population 62.86% states are found below and only 37.14% are in above from the country average (5.3). Table 2.6 shows that the maximum 26.67% states are falling in group of 5.01 to 5.5 persons/household.

The average urban household size of the tribal population is only 4.8 persons/household which is much lower than that of all castes urban population (5.1). It shows few earning member of tribal family reside in urban areas in comparison to the all castes population. The urban household size varies minimum from 3.5 persons/household in Himachal Pradesh to maximum 6.5 persons/household in Lakshadweep. The urban household size of the 50% states has below while the 10% states are equal and 40% have more than the national average (4.8) (Table 2.7).

Population Growth

The total growth of tribal population of India during the decade of 1991-2001 was 24.45% which is higher than the growth of total population (20.34%). The tribal growth has been computed for the 26 states because in 1991 census could not be conducted in Jammu & Kashmir due to disturbed condition while three

TABLE 2.5

Distribution of States/ UTs by Ranges of Percentage Share to Country Urban Population in India, 2001

Zone/Region	*Ranges of Population*	*All Castes*		*Scheduled Tribe Population*		
		(No.)	*(%)*	*(No.)*	*(%)*	*States/UTs*
Very Low	Below 0.50	15	42.87	12	40.00	Himachal Pradesh, Uttarakhand, Uttar Pradesh, Sikkim, Daman and Diu, Dadra & Nagar Haveli, Lakshadweep, Tripura, Goa, Andaman and Nicobar Islands, Kerala and Manipur.
Low	0.51-1.00	2	5.71	2	6.67	Jammu & Kashmir and Bihar.
Moderate	1.01-3.00	7	20.00	3	10.00	Arunachal Pradesh, Tamil Nadu, and Assam.
High	3.01-5.00	3	8.57	3	10.00	Nagaland, West Bengal and Meghalaya.
Very High	Above 5.01	8	22.85	10	33.33	Maharashtra, Andhra Pradesh, Rajasthan, Karnataka, Mizoram Jharkhand, Orissa, Chhattisgarh, Madhya Pradesh and Gujarat.
Total		**35**	**100.00**	**30**	**100.00**	

Source: Anon; 2001 a.

TABLE 2.6

Distribution of States/ UTs by Ranges of Household Size (Persons/H.H.) in India, 2001

Zone/Region	*Ranges of Household Size(P/H.H)*	*All Castes Population*		*Scheduled Tribe Population*		
		(No.)	*(%)*	*(No.)*	*(%)*	*States/UTs*
Low	Below 4.5	5	14.28	5	16.67	Goa, Tamilnadu, Orissa, Kerala and Andhra Pradesh.
Moderate	4.51-5.00	10	28.57	7	23.33	Himachal Pradesh, Sikkim, Daman & Diu, Tripura, Maharashtra, West Bengal, and Chhattisgarh.
Mod. High	5.01-5.50	10	28.57	8	26.67	Bihar, Arunachal Pradesh, Mizoram, Gujarat, Karnataka, Jharkhand, Madhya Pradesh and Dadra & Nagar Haveli.
High	5.51-6.00	5	14.29	4	13.33	Rajasthan, Manipur, Assam and Meghalaya.
Very High	Above 6.01	5	14.29	6	20.00	Jammu & Kashmir, Nagaland, Uttarakhand, Lakshadweep, Andaman and Nicobar Islands and Uttar Pradesh.
Total		**35**	**100**	**30**	**100.00**	

Source: Anon; 2001.

TABLE 2.7

Distribution of States/UTs by Ranges of Urban Household Size (Persons/H.H.) in India, 2001

Zone/Region	*Ranges of Household Size(P/H.H)*	*All Castes Population*		*Scheduled Tribe Population*		
		(No.)	*(%)*	*(No.)*	*(%)*	*States/UTs*
Low	Below 4.5	0	0.00	2	6.67	Himachal Pradesh and Tripura,
Moderate	4.51-5.00	8	22.86	9	30.00	Uttarakhand, Andaman & Nicobar, Sikkim, Assam, Goa, Andhra Pradesh, Orissa, Kerala and Tamilnadu.
Moder.High	5.01-5.50	12	34.28	11	36.66	Jammu & Kashmir, West Bengal, and Chhattisgarh, Gujarat, Daman & Diu, Karnataka, Bihar, M.P., Maharashtra, Arunachal Pradesh and Rajasthan.
High	5.51-6.00	8	22.86	6	20.00	UP, Meghalaya, Mizoram, Nagaland, Jharkhand, and Dadra & Nagar Haveli.
Very High	Above 6.01	7	20.00	2	6.67	Manipur and Lakshadweep.
Total		**35**	**100.0**	**30**	**100.00**	

Source: Anon; 2001.

states–Jharkhand, Chhattisgarh and Uttarakhand did not exist as a separate states in 1991. The population of newly created states has been included in their parent states. The growth rate varies from minimum 10.08% in Andaman & Nicobar Islands to maximum 80.82% in Karnataka (Table 2.8). Out of total 26 states, 36.64 have registered the growth more than the national average while 65.38% states have recorded less growth then the national average (24.45%). Table 2.9 gives the distribution of the states in India by the ranges of percentage of decadal growth during 1991-2001. Out of total 15.38% states have registered decadal growth less then 15%. These are Andman and Nicobar Islands,

TABLE 2.8

Growth of All Castes and Scheduled Tribe Population in India, (1991–2001) (%)

Sl.No.	*State/UTs*	*Total Population Growth 1991-01*	*S.Ts. Population Growth 1991-2001*
1.	Jammu & Kashmir	29.04	N.A.
2.	Himachal Pradesh	17.53	12.02
3.	Punjab	19.76	Nil
4.	Chandigarh	40.33	Nil
5.	Uttarakhand	19.20	Did not exist in 1991
6.	Haryana	28.06	Nil
7.	Delhi	46.31	Nil
8.	Rajasthan	28.33	29.64
9.	Uttar Pradesh	25.80	26.46
10.	Bihar	28.43	18.57
11.	Sikkim	32.98	22.56
12.	Arunachal Pradesh	26.21	28.13
13.	Nagaland	64.41	67.23
14.	Manipur**	30.02	17.24
15.	Mizoram	29.18	28.42
16.	Tripura	15.74	16.41
17.	Meghalaya	29.94	31.29
18.	Assam	18.85	15.10

Table Contd....

Table Contd....

Sl.No	State/UTs	Total Population Growth 1991-01	S.Ts. Population Growth 1991-2001
19.	West Bengal	17.84	15.70
20.	Jharkhand	23.19	Did not exist in 1991
21.	Orissa	15.94	15.83
22.	Chhattisgarh	25.73	Did not exist in 1991
23.	Madhya Pradesh	24.24	22.41
24.	Gujarat	22.48	21.41
25.	Daman & Diu	55.59	19.39
26.	Dadra & Nagar Haveli	59.20	25.46
27.	Maharastra	22.57	17.20
28.	Andhra Pradesh	13.86	19.64
29.	Karnataka	17.25	80.82
30.	Goa	14.89	50.53
31.	Lakshadweep	17.19	19.01
32.	Kerala	9.42	13.47
33.	Tamil Nadu	11.19	13.43
34.	Pondicherry	20.56	Nil
35.	Andaman & Nicobar	26.94	10.08
	India	**21.34**	**24.45**

Source: Anon; 2001a.

Himachal Pradesh, Tamilnadu and Kerala. About 15.38% states have recorded high growth rate more than 30.01%. These are Nagaland, Goa, Meghalaya, and Karnataka. The highest growth rate in Karnataka is probably due to the inclusion of more castes and more areas in the tribal category (Table 2.9).

Sex Ratio

The number of females/thousand males is termed as sex ratio. It reveals the numerical relationship between women and men. A ratio of one thousand indicates equal balance of males and females in the population, less than one thousand indicates numerical deficit of women (low sex ratio) and above one thousand indicates numerical surplus of women (high sex ratio) in the

TABLE 2.9

Distribution of States/ UTs by Ranges of Percentage Decadal Growth of Population in India, 1991-01

Zone/Region	*Ranges of Decadal Growth (%)*	*All Castes Population*		*Scheduled Tribe Population*		
		(No.)	*(%)*	*(No.)*	*(%)*	*States/UTs*
Very Low	Below 15	3	8.57	4	15.38	H.P., Andman & Nicobar Islands, Kerala and Tamilnadu
Low	15.01-18.00	7	20.00	6	23.09	Manipur, Tripura, Assam, W.B., Maharashtra, and Orissa.
Moderate	18.01-21.00	4	11.43	4	15.38	Daman & Diu, Bihar, Lakshadweep & Andhra Pradesh.
Moder. High	21.01-24.00	3	8.57	3	11.54	Madhya Pradesh, Sikkim and Gujarat.
High	24.01-27.00	5	14.29	2	7.69	Dadra & Nagar Haveli, and Uttar Pradesh
Very High	27.01-30.00	6	17.14	3	11.54	Arunachal Pradesh, Rajasthan and Mizoram.
Very V. High	> 30.01	7	20.00	4	15.38	Nagaland, Goa, Meghalaya and Karnataka
Total		**35**	**100.00**	**26**	**100.00**	

Source: Anon. 2001a.

TABLE 2.10

Sex Ratio of All Castes and Scheduled Tribe Population in India, 2001 (F/1000 M)

Sl. No.	States/UTs	All Castes Total Population		All Castes Urban Population		S.Ts.Total Population		S.Ts.Urban Population	
		Total	Below 6 years	Total	Below 6 years	Total	Below 6 years	Total	Below 6 years
1.	Jammu & Kashmir	892	941	819	873	910	979	799	915
2.	Himachal Pradesh	968	896	795	844	996	955	809	899
3.	Punjab	876	798	849	796	Nil	Nil	Nil	Nil
4.	Chandigarh	777	845	796	845	Nil	Nil	Nil	Nil
5.	Uttarakhand	962	908	845	872	950	955	867	806
6.	Haryana	861	819	847	808	Nil	Nil	Nil	Nil
7.	Delhi	821	868	822	870	Nil	Nil	Nil	Nil
8.	Rajasthan	921	909	890	887	944	950	851	906
9.	Uttar Pradesh	898	916	876	890	934	973	850	994
10.	Bihar	919	942	868	924	929	975	839	958
11.	Sikkim	875	963	830	922	957	964	1024	969
12.	Arunachal Pradesh	893	964	819	980	1003	976	1020	1010
13.	Nagaland	900	964	829	939	943	969	946	954
14.	Manipur**	978	957	1009	961	980	959	1040	965
15.	Mizoram	935	964	948	963	984	966	1012	967
16.	Tripura	948	966	959	948	970	981	921	978
17.	Meghalaya	972	973	982	969	1000	974	1072	974
18.	Assam	935	965	872	943	972	962	929	947
19.	West Bengal	934	960	893	948	982	981	950	979

Table Contd....

Table Contd....

Sl. No.	States/UTs	*All Castes Total Population*		*All Castes Urban Population*		*S.Ts.Total Population*		*S.Ts.Urban Population*	
		Total	*Below 6 years*	*Total*	*Below 6 years*	*Total*	*Below 6 years*	*Total*	*Below 6 years*
20.	Jharkhand	941	965	870	930	987	979	965	975
21.	Orissa	972	953	895	933	1003	979	948	963
22.	Chhattisgarh	989	975	932	938	1013	998	941	975
23.	Madhya Pradesh	919	932	898	907	975	979	912	955
24.	Gujarat	920	883	880	837	974	966	926	918
25.	Daman & Diu	710	926	984	943	947	983	928	911
26.	Dadra & Nagar Haveli	812	979	691	888	1028	1009	973	877
27.	Maharashtra	922	913	873	908	973	965	931	943
28.	Andhra Pradesh	978	961	965	955	972	972	941	950
29.	Karnataka	965	946	942	940	972	961	960	948
30.	Goa	961	938	934	924	893	915	928	900
31.	Lakshadweep	948	959	935	900	1003	957	1006	900
32.	Kerala	1058	960	1058	958	1021	974	1053	945
33.	Tamil Nadu	987	942	982	955	980	945	997	951
34.	Pondicherry	1001	967	1007	967	Nil	Nil	Nil	Nil
35.	Andaman & Nicobar	846	957	185	936	948	956	796	937
	India	**933**	**927**	**900**	**906**	**978**	**973**	**944**	**951**

Source: Census of India, 2001.

** excludes Mao Maram, Paomata and Purul sub-divisions of Senapati distrist of Manipur State.

Nil-There is no notified Seheduled Tribes in the States of Delhi, Haryana and Punjab and the Union Territories of Chandigarh and Pondicherry.

TABLE 2.11

Distribution of States/ UTs by Ranges of Sex Ratio (F/1000 M) of Population in India, 2001

Zone/Region	*Ranges of Household Growth (%)*	*All Castes Population*		*Scheduled Tribe Population*		
		(No.)	*(%)*	*(No.)*	*(%)*	*States/UTs*
Very Low	Below 925	17	48.58	2	6.67	Goa and Jammu & Kashmir.
Low	926-950	6	17.14	7	23.33	Uttarakhand, Andman & Nicobar, Uttar Pradesh, Nagaland, Rajasthan, Daman & Diu, and Bihar.
Moderate	951-975	6	17.14	8	26.67	Sikkim, Assam, Tripura, Gujarat, M.P., Maharashtra, Andhra Pradesh and Karnataka.
High	976-1000	4	11.43	7	23.33	Himachal Pradesh, Jharkhand, Manipur, Mizoram, Meghalaya, West Bengal and Tamilnadu.
Very High	Above1001	2	5.71	6	20.00	Arunachal Pradesh, Orissa, Kerala, Chhattisgarh, Lakshadweep and Dadra & Nagar Haveli.
Total		**35**	**100.00**	**30**	**100.00**	

Source: Anon.2001a.

population. Average sex ratio of the tribal population of India is 978 in 2001 which is higher than the sex ratio of all castes population (Table 2.10). Total sex ratio in tribal population ranges between 893 in Goa to 1028 in Dadra and Nagar Haveli. Out of total 30 states in India 80% states have recorded the low sex ratio below 1000 females per thousand males while only 20% states—Arunachal Pradesh, Orissa, Lakshadweep, Chhattisgarh, Kerala and Dadra and Nagar Haveli, have shown high sex ratio i.e. above one thousand females per thousand males (Table 2.10). The numerical gap between men and women is lower in tribal population than the total population. Likewise total sex ratio in tribal and all castes population, the sex ratio in urban tribal population is higher (944) than that of the total population (906). The ratio in urban population ranges from minimum 851 in Rajasthan to maximum 1072 in Meghalaya. In 2001 census 50% states are found in above the national average (944). It is clear from the table 2.11 that 23.33 % states have recorded high sex ratio i.e. more females than males. These states are Sikkim, Arunachal Pradesh, Manipur, Mizoram, Meghalaya, Lakshadweep and Kerala (Table 2.11).

The sex ratio below the age of 6 years tribal population in India is registered 973 which are also higher from the same segment of total population (927). The sex ratio of this segment varies from minimum 915 in Goa to maximum 1009 in Dadra and Nagar Haveli (Table 2.13). About 43.34% states have registered sex ratio above from the national average The sex ratio below the age of 6 years tribal urban children is found 951 which are higher than all castes population (906). The sex ratio varies from minimum 806 in Uttarakhand to maximum 1001 in Arunachal Pradesh. Fifty percent states have recorded the sex ratio above from the national average. The study of sex ratio shows in tribal population there is no much differentiation between the male and female child. Maximum 56.67 % states are found in the ranges of 951-975 females/1000 males. These are Himachal Pradesh, Uttar Pradesh, Bihar, Uttarakhand, Sikkim, Nagaland, Manipur, Mizoram, Meghalaya, Assam, Gujarat, Maharashtra, Andhra Pradesh, Karnataka, Lakshadweep, Kerala and Andaman & Nicobar Islands (Table 2.13). Table 2.13 shows that there is

TABLE 2.12

Distribution of States/ UTs by Ranges of Sex Ratio (Females/1000 Males) of Urban Population in India, 2001

Zone/Region	*Ranges of Sex Ratio (F/1000M)*	*All Castes Population*		*Scheduled Tribe Population*		
		(No.)	*(%)*	*(No.)*	*(%)*	*States/UTs*
Very Low	Below 850	12	34.30	4	13.33	Jammu & Kashmir, Himachal Pradesh, Uttar Pradesh, Bihar.
Low	851-900	10	28.57	2	6.67	Uttarakhand and Rajasthan.
Moderate	901-950	5	14.28	12	40.00	Tripura, Madhya Pradesh, Nagaland, Assam, West Bengal, Orissa, Chhattisgarh, Gujarat, Daman & Diu, Maharashtra, Andhra Pradesh and Goa.
High	951-1000	5	14.28	5	16.67	Karnataka, Jharkhand, Dadra & Nagar Haveli, Tamilnadu, and Andaman & Nicobar Islands.
Very High	Above1001	3	8.57	7	23.33	Sikkim, Arunachal Pradesh, Manipur, Mizoram, Meghalaya, Lakshadweep and Kerala.
Total		**35**	**100.00**	**30**	**100.00**	

Source: Anon; 2001a.

TABLE 2.13

Distribution of States/ UTs by Ranges of Total Sex Ratio (0-6 Years) in India, 2001

Zone/Region	*Ranges of Sex Ratio (F/1000M)*	*All Castes Population*		*Scheduled Tribe Population*		
		(No.)	*(%)*	*(No.)*	*(%)*	*States/UTs*
Very Low	Below 925	10	28.57	1	3.33	Goa.
Low	926-950	7	20.00	2	6.67	Tamilnadu and Rajasthan.
Moderate	951-975	17	48.57	17	56.67	Himachal Pradesh, Uttar Pradesh, Bihar, Uttarakhand, Sikkim, Nagaland, Manipur, Mizoram, Meghalaya, Assam, Gujarat, Maharastra, Andhra Pradesh, Karnataka, Lakshadweep, Kerala and Andman & Nicobar Islands.
High	976-1000	1	2.86	9	30.00	Jammu & Kashmir, Tripura, West Bengal, Jharkhand, Orissa, Arunachal Pradeah, Chhattisgarh, Madhya Pradesh and Daman & Diu.
Very High	Above 1001	0	0.00	1	3.33	Dadra & Nagar Haveli,
Total		**35**	**100.00**	**30**	**100.00**	

Source: Anon.2001a

TABLE 2.14

Distribution of States/ UTs by Ranges of Urban Sex Ratio (0-6 Years) in India, 2001

Zone/Region	*Ranges of Sex Ratio (F/1000M)*	*All Castes Population*		*Scheduled Tribe Population*		
		(No.)	*(%)*	*(No.)*	*(%)*	*States/UTs*
Very Low	Below 850	5	14.29	1	3.33	Uttarakhand.
Low	851-900	7	20.00	4	13.33	Himachal Pradesh, Dadra & Nagar Haveli, Goa and Lakshadweep.
Moderate	901-950	15	42.86	10	33.33	Rajasthan, Jammu & Kashmir, Assam, Gujarat, Daman & Diu, Maharashtra, Andhra Pradesh, Karnataka, Kerala, and Andman & Nicobar Islands.
High	951-1000	8	22.85	14	46.68	Tamilnadu, Tripura, West Bengal, Jharkhand, Orissa, Uttar Pradesh, Bihar, Sikkim, Chhattisgarh, Madhya Pradesh, Nagaland, Manipur, Mizoram and Meghalaya.
Very High	Above 1001	0	0.00	1	3.33	Arunachal Pradesh
Total		**35**	**100.00**	**30**	**100.00**	

Source: Anon.2001a.

only one—Dadra and Nagar Haveli which has sex ratio above 1001 females/1000 males.

About 30% states have satisfactory sex ratio ranging 976 to 1000. The sex ratio of below the age of six years population is 951 females/1000 males which is more than the all castes population of same segment (906). The sex ratio of this population ranges from minimum 806 in Uttarakhand to maximum 1010 in Arunachal Pradesh. About 47% states are found in the range of 951 to 1000 (Table 2.14).

Literacy Pattern

Literacy is one of the most important social aspect on which information is obtained on every individual in census. For the purpose of census 2001 a person aged seven and above who can both read and write with understanding any language is treated as literate. It denotes the most basic and essential criterion of human development. It is a qualitative indicator of social awakening and cultural advancement of the inhabitants in a geographical unit, whereas a change in literacy reflects the socio-economic and cultural transformation of the society. Keeping in view the significance of literacy the United Nations Development Programme (UNDP) has included in the criteria to determine the Human Development Index (HDI). Lack of literacy can certainly be an impediment in the development progress. Table 2.15 shows the literacy rates by sex of all castes and tribal population of India. As per census 2001 Indian tribal population has registered only 47.1% literacy which is much lower than the literacy of total population at national level (64.8%). The tribal literacy varies minimum from 28.2% in Bihar to maximum 89.3% in Mizoram state (Table 2.15 & Fig. 2.2).

In total 36.67% states have registered less literacy from the national average while 66.33% have recorded high literacy than the country average (Table 2.15). The economically backward states reveals low level of literacy rates which was associated with their inherited old tradition and lack of infrastructural facilities in which little emphasis was placed on education. In tribal literacy point of view the first rank holder state in India is Mizoram where the various educational plans have been launched

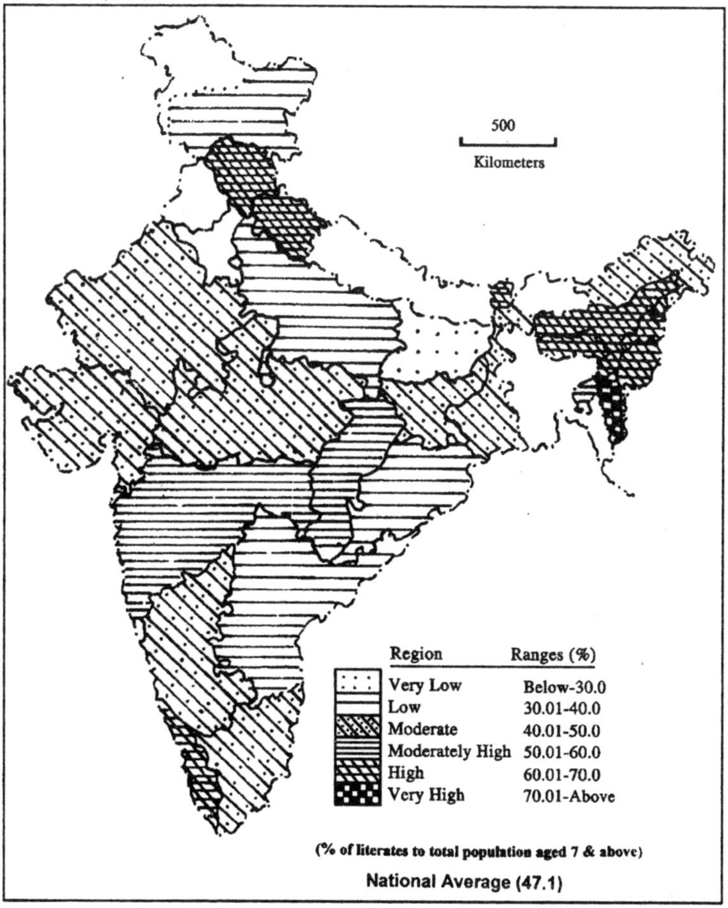

Fig 2.2 : Total Literacy Rate of Scheduled Tribe Population in india, 2001.

TABLE 2.15

Literacy Rates by Sex of All Castes and Scheduled Tribe Population in India, 2001 (%)

Sl. No.	States/UTs	All Castes Total Population			All Castes Urban Population			S.Ts.Total Population			S.Ts.Urban Population		
		Persons	Males	Females	Persons	Males	Females	Persons	Males	Females	Persons	Males	Females
1.	Jammu & Kashmir	55.5	66.6	43.0	71.9	80.0	62.0	37.5	48.2	25.5	70.4	79.0	59.3
2.	Himachal Pradesh	76.5	85.3	67.4	88.9	92.0	85.0	65.5	77.7	53.3	87.2	92.0	81.2
3.	Punjab	69.7	75.2	63.4	79.1	83.0	74.5	Nil	Nil	Nil	Nil	Nil	Nil
4.	Chandigarh	81.9	86.1	76.5	82.6	86.8	77.4	Nil	Nil	Nil	Nil	Nil	Nil
5.	Uttarakhand	71.6	83.3	59.6	81.4	87.1	74.8	63.2	76.4	49.4	85.9	91.5	79.5
6.	Haryana	67.9	78.5	55.7	79.2	85.8	71.3	Nil	Nil	Nil	Nil	Nil	Nil
7.	Delhi	81.7	87.3	74.7	81.9	87.4	75.2	Nil	Nil	Nil	Nil	Nil	Nil
8.	Rajasthan	60.4	75.7	43.9	76.2	86.5	64.7	44.7	62.1	26.2	60.8	75.7	43.0
9.	Uttar Pradesh	56.3	68.8	42.2	69.8	76.8	61.7	35.1	48.4	20.7	51.1	60.6	39.5
10.	Bihar	47.0	59.7	33.1	71.9	79.9	62.6	28.2	39.8	15.5	65.7	74.2	55.3
11.	Sikkim	68.8	76.0	60.4	83.9	87.8	79.2	67.1	73.8	60.2	84.9	89.3	80.6
12.	Arunachal Pradesh	54.3	63.8	43.5	78.3	85.2	69.5	49.6	58.8	40.6	77.4	85.9	69.0
13.	Nagaland	66.6	71.2	61.5	84.7	87.4	81.4	65.9	70.3	61.3	88.7	91.6	85.6
14.	Manipur**	70.5	80.3	60.5	79.3	88.7	70.0	65.9	73.2	58.4	80.9	87.9	74.3
15.	Mizoram	88.8	90.7	86.7	96.1	96.4	95.8	89.3	91.7	86.9	96.8	97.5	96.0
16.	Tripura	73.2	81.0	64.9	89.2	93.2	85.0	56.5	68.0	44.6	92.0	94.5	89.3
17.	Meghalaya	62.6	65.4	59.6	86.3	89.0	83.5	61.3	63.5	59.2	86.7	89.0	84.6
18.	Assam	63.3	71.3	54.6	85.3	89.7	80.2	62.5	72.3	52.4	86.8	92.4	80.6
19.	West Bengal	68.6	77.0	59.6	81.2	86.1	75.7	43.4	57.4	29.2	58.7	68.6	48.2

20.	Jharkhand	53.6	67.3	38.9	79.1	87.0	70.0	40.7	54.0	27.2	67.8	77.8	57.4
21.	Orissa	63.1	75.3	50.5	80.8	87.9	72.9	37.4	51.5	23.4	58.1	69.8	45.8
22.	Chhattisgarh	64.7	77.4	51.9	80.6	89.4	71.1	52.1	65.0	39.3	71.7	82.9	59.8
23.	Madhya Pradesh	63.7	76.1	50.3	79.4	87.4	70.5	41.2	53.5	28.4	57.2	87.5	45.9
24.	Gujarat	69.1	79.7	57.8	81.8	88.3	74.5	47.7	59.2	36.0	61.8	71.0	51.8
25.	Daman & Diu	78.2	86.8	65.6	82.3	91.1	73.4	63.4	74.2	51.9	65.7	75.3	55.4
26.	Dadra & Nagar Haveli	57.6	71.2	40.2	84.4	90.8	74.5	41.2	56.0	27.0	69.2	81.5	56.7
27.	Maharashtra	76.9	86.0	67.0	85.5	91.0	79.1	55.2	67.0	43.1	74.2	83.0	64.7
28.	Andhra Pradesh	60.5	70.3	50.4	76.1	83.2	68.7	37.0	47.2	26.1	56.4	66.2	45.0
29.	Karnataka	66.6	76.1	56.9	80.6	86.5	74.1	48.3	59.7	36.6	64.6	74.4	54.3
30.	Goa	82.0	88.4	75.4	84.4	89.5	79.0	55.9	63.5	47.3	61.4	67.9	54.5
31.	Lakshadweep	86.7	92.5	80.5	88.6	93.8	83.1	86.1	92.2	80.2	87.9	93.3	82.6
32.	Kerala	90.9	94.2	87.7	93.2	95.9	90.6	64.4	70.8	58.1	81.2	85.0	77.7
33.	Tamil Nadu	73.5	82.4	84.4	82.5	89.0	76.0	41.5	50.2	32.8	58.6	66.6	50.7
34.	Pondicherry	81.2	88.6	73.9	84.8	91.2	78.6	Nil	Nil	Nil	Nil	Nil	Nil
35.	Andaman & Nicobar	81.3	86.3	75.2	86.6	90.7	81.5	66.8	73.6	59.6	93.7	97.0	89.5
	India	**64.8**	**75.3**	**53.7**	**79.9**	**86.3**	**72.9**	**47.1**	**59.2**	**34.8**	**69.1**	**77.8**	**59.9**

Source: Census of India, 2001.** excludes Mao Maram, Paomata and Purul sub-divisions of Senapati district of Manipur State.

Nil-There is no notified Seheduled Tribes in the States of Delhi, Haryana and Punjab and the Union Territories of Chandigarh and Pondicherry.

by the Christians during the colonial period. The highest proportion of male tribal literates has been registered in Lakshadweep (92.2%) followed by Mizoram (91.7%). Likewise total tribal literacy the lowest proportion of male tribal literates was recorded in Bihar (39.8%) which is much lower than the national average (59.2%). About 60% states have registered the high male literacy than the national average (59.2%) (Table 2.15). Table 2.15 shows the state-wise female literacy of tribal and all castes population with national average. In tribal female Mizoram with 86.9% literates leads all the states followed by Lakshadweep (80.2%) and Nagaland (61.3%). Average female literacy of India is registered only 34.8% which is too less than the all castes female literacy (53.7%). Bihar has least proportion of female literates (15.5%) followed by Orissa (23.4%). In 2001 census out of the total, 36.67% states have lower total, males and females literacy than the national averages (Table 2.15). Female literacy is one of the most important indicators of socio-economic and infrastructural development. Tables 2.16-2.18 give the spatial distribution of states by the different ranges and categories of all castes and tribal literacy rates for persons, males and females of India as a whole. About 3.33% state (Bihar) of the country where total literacy rate is still below 30% can be recognized as a region with very low level of literacy. The low level of literacy region covers 13.33% states. These are Jammu & Kashmir, Uttar Pradesh, Orissa and Andhra Pradesh. There are 30% states of India with total tribal literacy rates between 40.01-50.0 % can be termed as moderate level literacy zone. About 13.33% states – Goa, Tripura, Maharashtra and Chhattisgarh, have reported moderately high literacy rates (50.01-60.00%). Maximum 33.34% states of India are in the zone of high level of literacy rates while 6.67% (Mizoram and Lakshadweep) has reported very high level of literacy rates above 70.1% (Table 2.16 & Fig. 2.2).

Distribution of states by different ranges of male literacy is presented in table 2.17 and figure 2.3. There is only one state (Bihar) in the country with male literacy below 40% termed as very low literacy region while 10% states (Jammu & Kashmir, Uttar Pradesh and Andhra Pradesh) are found in the region of low literacy level i.e. ranges between 40.01 to 50 %. Only 30% and 6.67% states of the nation have recorded respectively high

TABLE 2.16

Distribution of States/ UTs by Ranges of Literacy Rates (Persons) in India, 2001

Zone/Region	*Ranges of Literacy Rates (%)*	*All Castes Population*		*Scheduled Tribe Population*		
		(No.)	*(%)*	*(No.)*	*(%)*	*States/UTs*
Very Low	Below 30.00	Nil	Nil	1	3.33	Bihar.
Low	30.01-40.00	Nil	Nil	4	13.33	Jammu & Kashmir, Uttar Pradesh, Orissa & A.P.
Moderate	40.01-50.00	1	2.86	9	30.00	West Bengal, Arunachal Pradesh, Rajasthan, Jharkhand, Madhya Pradesh, Dadra & Nagar Haveli, Gujarat, Karnataka and Tamilnadu.
Moder. High	50.01-60.00	5	14.28	4	13.33	Goa, Tripura, Maharashtra and Chhattisgarh.
High	60.01-70.00	14	40.00	10	33.34	Himachal Pradesh, Sikkim, Daman & Diu, Uttarakhand, Manipur, Assam, Meghalaya, Kerala, and Nagaland, Andaman & Niccbar Islands.
Very High	Above 70.01	15	42.86	2	6.67	Mizoram and Lakshadweep.
Total		**35**	**100**	**30**	**100**	

Source: Anon. 2001a.

TABLE 2.17

Distribution of States/ UTs by Ranges of Literacy Rates (Males) in India, 2001

Zone/Region	*Ranges of Household Size(P/H.H)*	*All Castes Population*		*Scheduled Tribe Population*		
		(No.)	*(%)*	*(No.)*	*(%)*	*States/UTs*
Very Low	Below 40.00	Nil	Nil	1	3.33	Bihar.
Low	40.01-50.00	Nil	Nil	3	10.00	Jammu & Kashmir, Uttar Pradesh, and Andhra Pradesh.
Moderate	50.01-60.00	1	2.86	9	30.00	West Bengal, Arunachal Pradesh, Jharkhand, Orissa, Madhya Pradesh, Dadra & Nagar Haveli, Gujarat, Karnataka and Tamilnadu,
Moder. High	60.01-70.00	5	14.28	6	20.00	Rajasthan, Tripura, Goa, Maharashtra, Chhattisgarh and Meghalaya.
High	70.01-80.00	14	40.00	9	30.00	H.P., Sikkim, Daman & Diu, Uttarakhand, Manipur, Assam, Kerala, and Nagaland, and Andaman
Very High	Above 80.01	15	42.86	2	6.67	Mizoram and Lakshadweep,
Total		**35**	**100.00**	**30**	**100.00**	

Source: Anon.2001a.

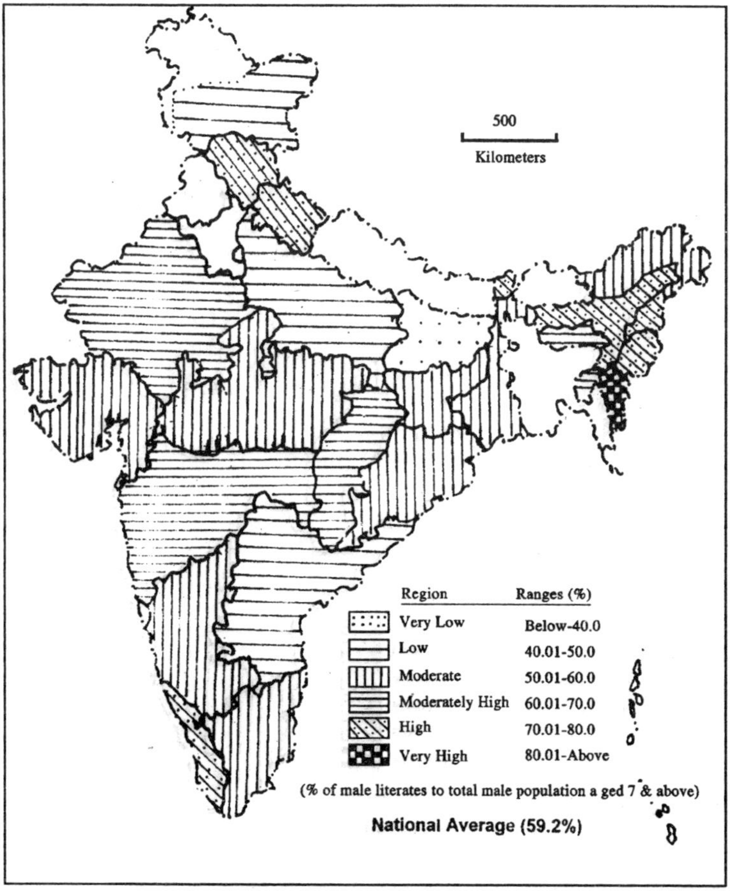

FIG. 2.3 : Male Literacy Rate of Scheduled Tribe Population in India, 2001.

and very high level of literacy i.e. 70.01-80.0% and above 80.01% (Table 2.17). Table 2.18 gives spatial distribution of states by the different ranges and groups of female literacy for India. It is observed that one third (33.33%) states of the country where the female literacy rates are still below 30% can be termed as a region with very low level of female literacy. These states are Bihar, Jammu & Kashmir, Uttar Pradesh, Andhra Pradesh, West Bengal, Jharkhand, Orissa, Rajasthan, Madhya Pradesh and Dadra & Nagar Haveli. The low level of female literacy of these states was associated with the tribal traditions in which proper emphasis was not placed on the education in one hand and economical backwardness on the other. There are 13.33% states (Chhattisgarh, Gujarat, Karnataka and Tamilnadu) of India with female literacy rates between 30.01-40% can be called as low literacy region. Out of total 30 states, 23.33% are in the group of moderately high region (50.01-60%) while only two states—Mizoram and Lakshadweep are in the region of very high level of literacy (Fig. 2.2).

In the census of India 2001, the country has recorded 69.1% rate in overall tribal literacy in urban population which is about 11% points less than the all castes urban population of the country average (79.9%). Maximum urban tribal literacy is registered in Mizoram (96.8%) while minimum literacy rate holder state is Uttar Pradesh (51.1%) which is far below from the national average (Table 2.15). About 43% states are below the national average. These are Uttar Pradesh, West Bengal, Orissa, Madhya Pradesh, Andhra Pradesh, Tamilnadu, Rajasthan, Bihar, Jharkhand, Gujarat, Daman and Diu, Karnataka, and Goa. States having the literacy rates more than 90% are Tripura, Andaman and Nicobar Islands and Mizoram.

About 77.8% male tribes in urban areas are literate which is quite lower than the all castes population (86.3%). The highest proportion of male tribal literates has been registered in Andaman and Nicobar Islands (97%) which is far above from the national average (77.8%) while the minimum literacy has been recorded in the Uttar Pradesh (60.6%). In total 43 % states are the below from the national average while remaining states have attained the more literacy than the national average. One fourth (26.67%)

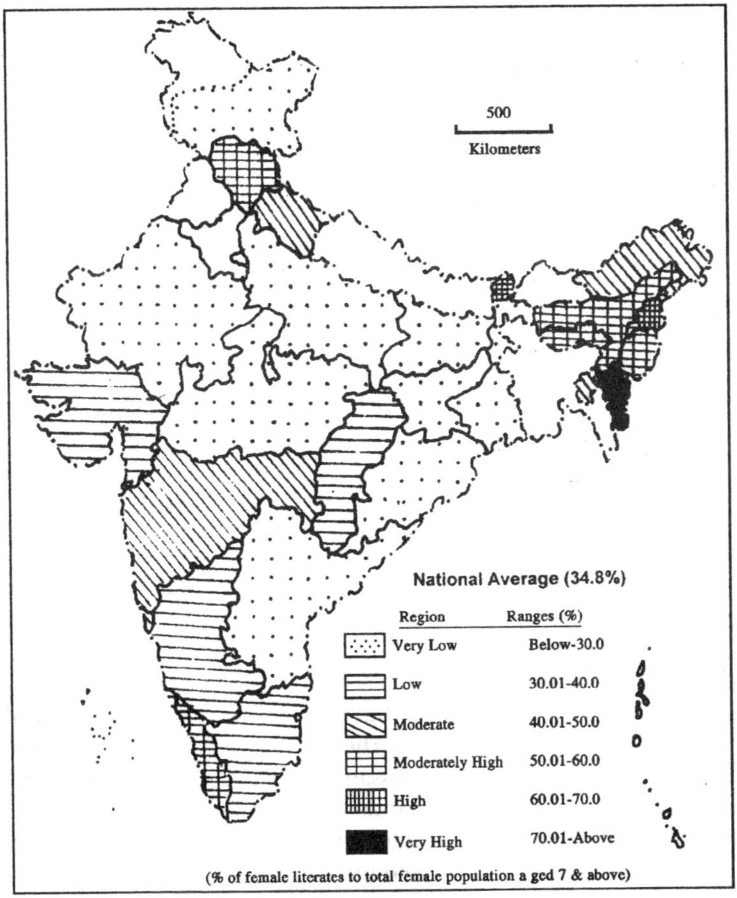

FIG. 2.4 : Female Literacy Rate of Scheduled Tribe Population in India 2001

of the total states has registered more than 90% male literacy which is a good indication to achieve the total literacy goal. About 60% tribal females of urban residents have been registered as literates while females of all castes population have recorded 72.9% literacy rates.

Likewise total tribal and all castes population the female literacy vary from the minimum 39.5% in Uttar Pradesh to maximum 96% in Mizoram followed by Andaman and Nicobar Islands (89.5%). About 53% states have the female below from the national average. The literacy tables reveal that the states which are generally considered as the backward states have less literates than the relatively more developed states.

Tables 2.19 to 2.21 give the spatial distribution of states by different ranges and groups of literacy rates of persons, males and females of urban population. In the total tribal literacy 20% states of the country has still below 60% literacy. These states — Uttar Pradesh, Orissa, West Bengal, Tamilnadu, Madhya Pradesh, and Andhra Pradesh—can be termed as a region with low level of literacy. The moderate level of literacy zone covers 26.67% states of the country. Only 30% and 10% states of the country have reported high and very high level of total tribal literacy rate of 80.01% to 90% and above 90.01% respectively (Table 2.19). There are 23.33% states in the country with the male literacy rates below 70% while in average male literacy of all castes population none of states is found in this category. About 26.67% states of the country have recorded very high level of urban literacy i.e. above 90.01%. These states are Himachal Pradesh, Uttarakhand, Lakshadweep, Assam, Nagaland, Tripura, Mizoram and Andaman & Nicobar Islands (Table 2.20). About 20% states of the country where the female literacy rates in tribal population are still below 50% can be recognized as a region with very low level of female literacy. These are Uttar Pradesh, Rajasthan, Orissa, Madhya Pradesh, Andhra Pradesh and West Bengal (Table 2.21). There are 33.33% states of the country with female literacy in tribal population rates between 50.01 to 60% can be called low literacy region while in all castes population none of states fall below the 60% female literacy. Only one Mizoram state

TABLE 2.18

Distribution of States/ UTs by Ranges of Literacy Rates (Females) in India, 2001

Zone/Region	*Ranges of Literacy Rates (%)*	*All Castes Population*		*Scheduled Tribe Population*		
		(No.)	*(%)*	*(No.)*	*(%)*	*States/UTs*
Very Low	Below 30.00	Nil	Nil	10	33.33	Bihar, Jammu & Kashmir, Uttar Pradesh, Andhra Pradesh, West Bengal, Jharkhand, Orissa, Rajasthan, Madhya Pradesh and Dadra & Nagar Haveli
Low	30.01-40.00	2	5.71	4	13.33	Chhattisgarh, Gujarat, Karnataka and Tamilnadu.
Moderate	40.01-50.00	5	14.29	5	16.67	Uttarakhand, Goa, Arunachal Pradesh, Tripura & Maharashtra.
Moder. High	50.01-60.00	11	31.43	7	23.33	Himachal Pradesh, Daman & Diu, Manipur, Assam, Kerala, Meghalaya and Andaman & Nicobar Islands.
High	60.01-70.00	9	25.71	2	6.67	Sikkim and Nagaland.
Very High	Above 70.01	8	22.86	2	6.67	Mizoram and Lakshadweep,
Total		**35**	**100.00**	**30**	**100.00**	

Source: Anon. 2001a

TABLE 2.19

Distribution of States/UTs by Ranges of Urban Literacy Rates (Persons) in India, 2001

Zone/Region	*Ranges of Literacy Rates (%)*	*All Castes Population*		*Scheduled Tribe Population*		
		(No.)	*(%)*	*(No.)*	*(%)*	*States/UTs*
Very Low	Below 60.00	Nil	Nil	6	20.00	Uttar Pradesh, Orissa, West Bengal, Tamilnadu, Madhya Pradesh and Andhra Pradesh.
Low	60.01-70.00	1	2.86	8	26.67	Rajasthan, Jharkhand, Bihar, Daman & Diu, Goa, Dadra & Nagar Haveli, Gujarat and Karnataka.
Moderate	70.01-80.00	10	28.57	4	13.33	Jammu & Kashmir, Arunachal Pradesh, Maharashtra & Chhattisgarh.
High	80.01-90.00	22	62.86	9	30.00	Himachal Pradesh, Sikkim, Uttarakhand, Manipur, Assam, Meghalaya, Kerala, Nagaland, and Lakshadweep,
Very High	Above 90.01	2	5.71	3	10.00	Tripura, Mizoram and Andaman & Nicobar Islands.
Total		**35**	**100.00**	**30**	**100.00**	

Source: Anon. 2001a.

TABLE 2.20

Distribution of States/ UTs by Ranges of Urban Literacy Rates (Males) in India, 2001

Zone/Region	*Ranges of Literacy Rates (%)*	*All Castes Population*		*Scheduled Tribe Population*		
		(No.)	*(%)*	*(No.)*	*(%)*	*States/UTs*
Low	Below 70.00	Nil	Nil	7	23.33	Uttar Pradesh, Orissa, West Bengal, Tamilnadu, Madhya Pradesh, Andhra Pradesh and Goa.
Moderate	70.01-80.00	3	8.57	7	23.33	Rajasthan, Jharkhand, Bihar, Daman & Diu, Jammu & Kashmir, Gujarat and Karnataka.
High	80.01-90.00	22	62.86	8	26.67	Arunachal Pradesh, Dadra & Nagar Haveli, Manipur, Maharashtra, Chhattishgarh, Sikkim, Kerala and Meghalaya.
Very High	Above 90.01	10	28.57	8	26.67	Himachal., Uttarakhand, Lakshadweep, Assam, Nagaland, Tripura, Mizoram, and Andaman & Nicobar Islands.
Total		**35**	**100.00**	**30**	**100.00**	

***Source*:** Anon. 2001a.

TABLE 2.21

Distribution of States/ UTs by Ranges of Urban Literacy Rates (Females) in India, 2001

Zone/Region	*Ranges of Literacy Rates (%)*	*All Castes Population*		*Scheduled Tribe Population*		
		(No.)	*(%)*	*(No.)*	*(%)*	*States/UTs*
Very Low	Below 50.00	Nil	Nil	6	20.00	Uttar Pradesh, Orissa, West Bengal, Rajasthan, Madhya Pradesh and Andhra Pradesh
Low	50.01-60.00	Nil	Nil	10	33.33	Jammu & Kashmir, Gujarat, Karnataka, Jharkhand, Bihar, Daman & Diu, Goa, Tamilnadu, Chhattisgarh, and Dadra & Nagar Haveli.
Moderate	60.01-70.00	8	22.86	2	6.67	Maharashtra and Arunachal Pradesh.
Moder.High	70.01-80.00	18	51.43	3	10.00	Uttarakhand, Manipur and Kerala.
High	80.01-90.00	7	20.00	8	26.67	Himachal Pradesh, Lakshadweep, Assam, Sikkim, Nagaland, Tripura, and Andaman & Nicobar Islands, And Meghalaya.
Very High	Above 90.01	2	5.71	1	3.33	Mizoram.
Total		**35**	**100.00**	**30**	**100.00**	

Source: Anon. 2001a.

has reported very high level of female literacy in tribal population while in all castes population two states-Kerala and Mizoram have registered more than 90.01% female literacy. It is observed that there are contiguous patches of states with low literacy rates in the tribal population of the country. The states situated in the relatively more rugged topography and adverse climate have also recorded very low literacy rates while states having high literacy associated with comparatively high level of urbanization and high proportion of population in secondary and tertiary jobs. In total population including scheduled tribes of the country have been registered the considerable progress in the literacy rates during the decade 1991-2001.

It is observed that the out of the total literates, more than 60% literates have attained the educational level up to high school standard (Pant, 2004). There is an urgent need to improve the quality of education instead of the quantity the literates.

Gender Gap in Literacy

Table 2.22 depicts that the states having more literacy reflect less gap between male and female literacy. On an average 24.4% points gap between male and female literacy of the total tribal population in the country has been recorded in 2001 census which is slightly higher than the literacy of all castes population (21.6%). The gap between male and female literacy rate varies from minimum 4.3% in Meghalaya followed by Mizoram (4.8%) to maximum 35.9% in Rajasthan. Out of total, 30% states of the country have less male female gap in literacy than the national average. Tables 2.23-2.24 give distribution of states by the ranges of male–female literacy rate gap. There are 30% states of the country having more than 25% male-female literacy gap. These are Uttarakhand, Uttar Pradesh, West Bengal, Jharkhand, Orissa, Chhattisgarh, Madhya Pradesh, Dadra and Nagar Haveli and Rajasthan. Only 10% states have less than 10% gender gap. These are Nagaland, Mizoram and Meghalaya. Net 30% states are found between 25.01 to 30% gap in male-female literacy (Table 2.23). Table 2.24 shows that the gap in male female literacy rates among the urban population is lower than that of total

TABLE 2.22

Gender Gap in Literacy Rates of All Castes and Scheduled Tribe Population in India, 2001 (%) (Anon. 2001a)

Sl.No	States/UTs	All Castes Population		Population Scheduled Tribe	
		Total	Urban	Total	Urban
1.	Jammu & Kashmir	23.6	18.0	22.6	19.7
2.	Himachal Pradesh	17.9	7.0	24.4	10.9
3.	Punjab	11.9	8.6	Nil	Nil
4.	Chandigarh	9.7	9.4	Nil	Nil
5.	Uttarakhand	23.6	12.3	27.0	12.1
6.	Haryana	22.8	14.5	Nil	Nil
7.	Delhi	12.6	12.2	Nil	Nil
8.	Rajasthan	31.8	21.8	35.9	32.8
9.	Uttar Pradesh	26.6	15.0	27.7	21.1
10.	Bihar	26.6	17.3	24.2	18.9
11.	Sikkim	15.6	8.6	13.6	8.7
12.	Arunachal Pradesh	20.3	15.7	18.2	16.9
13.	Nagaland	9.7	6.0	8.9	6.0
14.	Manipur	19.8	18.7	14.7	13.7
15.	Mizoram	4.0	0.6	4.8	1.5
16.	Tripura	16.1	8.2	23.4	5.2
17.	Meghalaya	5.8	5.6	4.3	4.4
18.	Assam	16.7	9.5	19.9	11.8
19.	West Bengal	17.4	10.4	28.2	20.4
20.	Jharkhand	28.4	17.1	26.8	20.4
21.	Orissa	24.8	15.1	28.1	24.0
22.	Chhattisgarh	25.5	18.3	25.7	23.1
23.	Madhya Pradesh	25.8	16.9	25.1	21.6
24.	Gujarat	21.9	13.8	23.2	19.2
25.	Daman & Diu	21.2	17.7	22.3	19.9
26.	Dadra & Nagar Haveli	31.0	16.3	29.0	24.8
27.	Maharashtra	18.9	11.9	23.9	18.3
28.	Andhra Pradesh	19.9	14.4	21.6	20.2
29.	Karnataka	19.2	12.5	23.1	20.1
30.	Goa	13.0	10.5	16.2	13.3
31.	Lakshadweep	12.1	10.6	12.0	10.7
32.	Kerala	6.5	5.3	12.7	7.3
33.	Tamil Nadu	18.0	13.0	17.4	15.9
34.	Pondicherry	14.7	12.6	Nil	Nil
35.	Andaman & Nicobar	11.1	5.2	14.0	7.5
	India	**21.6**	**13.4**	**24.4**	**17.9**

Source: Anon. 2001a.

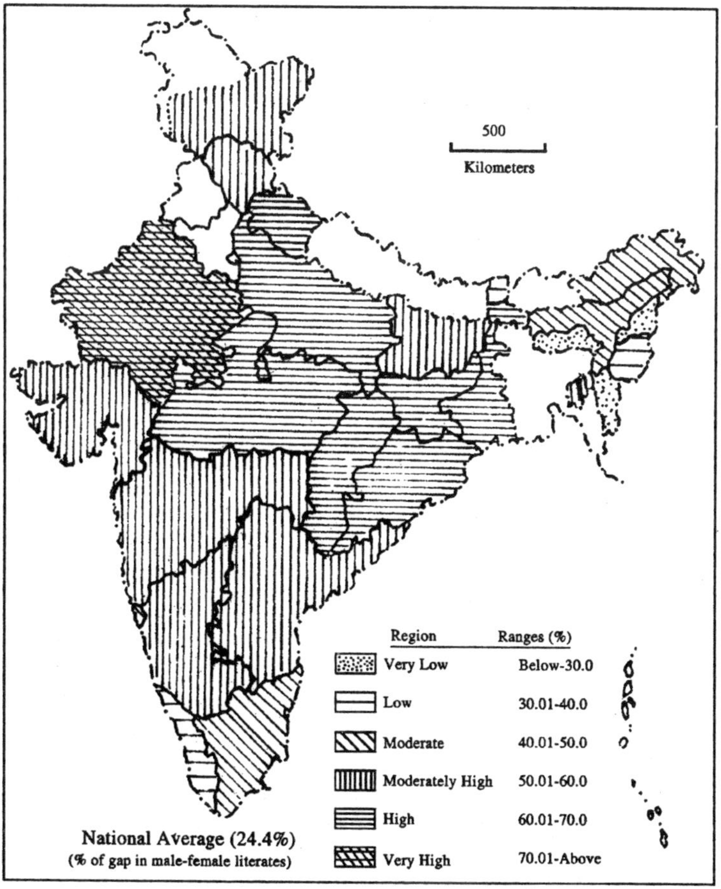

FIG. 2.5 : Gap in Male-Female Literacy Rate of Scheduled Tribe Population in India, 2001.

population. Table 2.22 reveals that 50% states of the nation are below the national average. The gender gap in literacy of urban scheduled tribe population is registered 17.9% which is higher than the all castes urban population (13.4%). The literacy gap in urban tribal population varies from 1.5% in Mizoram to 24.8% in Dadra & Nagar Haveli. Table 2.24 shows the distribution of states by the ranges of male-female literacy rate gap of tribal and all castes urban population (Fig. 2.5). There are 43.33% states having male-female literacy gap below 15%. One third (30% and 3.34%) states of the country are found in the group of 20-25% and above 30.01% points. These are Uttar Pradesh, Orissa, West Bengal, Karnataka, Jharkhand, Chhattisgarh, Madhya Pradesh, Andhra Pradesh; and Dadra Nagar Haveli and Rajasthan. It is observed that the states with high level of total, male and female literacy have registered lower gaps between male and female literacy.

Work Participation Rates

State-wise work participation rates (WPRs) for total and tribal population is depicted in Tables 2.25 & 2.26. The percentage of total workers in tribal population has recorded higher 49.1% in comparison to the total population 39.1% in the country as a whole. The percentage of total workers in the tribal population varies minimum 22.9% in Lakshadweep to maximum 54.9% in Tamilnadu. About 53% tribal males of India are registered as workers in 2001 census while 51.7% males of all castes population are considered as workers. The work participation rate of male tribal population varies minimum 38.6% in Lakshadweep to 60.1% in Tamilnadu. Out of total tribal female population only 44.8% are considered as workers which are higher than the females of all castes population (25.6%). The work participation rates of females vary from minimum 7.10% in Lakshadweep to maximum 52.7% in Himachal Pradesh (Tables 2.25-2.26).

Tables 2.27-2.29 give the spatial distribution of states by the ranges and groups of participation rates of total workers for persons, males and females for the total and tribal population of the country as a whole. These is only one state (Lakshadweep) of the country where the participation rate is below 35% while

TABLE 2.23

Distribution of States/ UTs by Ranges of Male- Female Gap in Literacy Rates (Total) in India, 2001

Zone/Region	*Ranges of Gap in Literacy Rates (%)*	*All Castes Population*		*Scheduled Tribe Population*		
		(No.)	*(%)*	*(No.)*	*(%)*	*States/UTs%%)*
Very Low	Below 10.00	5	14.29	3	10.00	Nagaland, Mizoram and Meghalaya.
Low	10.01-15.00	6	17.14	5	16.67	Lakshadweep, Sikkim, Manipur, Kerala, and Andaman & Nicobar Islands.
Moderate	15.01-20.00	10	28.57	4	13.33	Arunachal Pradesh, Goa, Assam and Tamilnadu.
Moder.High	20.01-25.00	7	20.00	9	30.00	Jammu & Kashmir, Gujarat, Karnataka, Himachal Pradesh, Tripura, Daman & Diu, Andhra Pradesh, Maharashtra and Bihar.
High	25.01-30.00	5	14.29	8	26.67	Uttarakhand, Uttar Pradesh, Orissa, West Bengal, Jharkhand, Chhattishgarh, Madhya Pradesh and Dadra & Nagar Haveli.
Very High	Above 30.01	2	5.71	1	3.33	Rajasthan.
Total		**35**	**100.00**	**30**	**100.00**	

Source: Anon. 2001a.

TABLE 2.24

Distribution of States/ UTs by Ranges of Male- Female Gap in Literacy Rates (Urban) in India, 2001

Zone/Region	*Ranges of Gap in Literacy Rates*	*All Castes Population*		*Scheduled Tribe Population*		
		(No.)	*(%)*	*(No.)*	*(%)*	*States/UTs*
Very Low	Below 10.00	11	31.43	7	23.33	Nagaland, Mizoram, Meghalaya, Sikkim, Kerala, Tripura, and Andaman & Nicobar Islands.
Low	10.01-15.00	13	37.14	6	20.00	Himachal Pradesh, Uttarakhand, Lakshadweep, Manipur, Goa and Assam.
Moderate	15.01-20.00	10	28.57	7	23.33	Arunachal Pradesh, Tamilnadu, Jammu & Kashmir, Gujarat, Daman & Diu, Maharashtra and Bihar.
Moder.High	20.01-25.00	1	2.86	9	30.00	Uttar Pradesh, Orissa, West Bengal, Karnataka, Jharkhand, Chhattis-garh, Madhya Pradesh, Andhra Pradesh and Dadra & Nagar Haveli.
High	25.01-30.00	Nil	Nil	Nil	Nil	Nil
Very High	Above 30.01	Nil	Nil	1	3.34	Rajasthan.
Total		**35**	**100.00**	**30**	**100.00**	

Source: Anon. 2001a.

TABLE 2.25

Work Participation Rates of All Castes Population by Sex, 2001(%)

Sl.No.	States/UTs	Total									Urban								
		Total Workers			Main Workers			Marginal Workers			Total Workers			Main Workers			Marginal Workers		
		P	M	F	P	M	F	P	M	F	P	M	F	P	M	F	P	M	F
1.	Jammu & Kashmir	37.0	50.0	22.5	25.7	41.5	8.0	11.3	8.4	14.5	32.9	51.4	10.4	29.6	48.2	7.0	3.3	3.2	3.4
2.	Himachal Pradesh	49.2	54.6	43.7	32.3	43.2	21.1	16.9	11.4	22.6	37.0	54.2	15.2	34.4	51.4	13	2.5	2.8	2.2
3.	Punjab	37.5	53.6	19.1	32.2	49.5	12.4	5.3	4.1	6.7	33.5	53.1	10.4	31.3	50.7	8.5	2.2	2.4	1.9
4.	Chandigarh	37.8	56.1	14.2	36.5	54.7	13.2	1.3	1.5	1.0	37.1	55.1	14.5	36.0	53.8	13.6	1.2	1.3	0.9
5.	Uttarakhand	36.9	46.1	27.3	27.4	37.9	16.4	9.6	8.3	10.9	29.1	47.4	7.6	26.5	43.6	6.2	2.7	3.7	1.4
6.	Haryana	39.6	50.3	27.2	29.5	43.4	13.4	10.1	6.9	13.8	31.5	49.2	10.6	28.2	45.5	7.7	3.3	3.7	2.9
7.	Delhi	32.8	52.1	9.4	31.2	49.9	8.4	1.6	2.2	1.0	32.9	52.3	9.3	31.3	50.2	8.4	1.6	2.1	0.9
8.	Rajasthan	42.1	50.0	33.5	30.9	43.6	17.0	11.2	6.3	16.5	29.6	47.5	9.5	26.3	43.9	6.5	3.3	3.5	3.0
9.	Uttar Pradesh	32.5	46.8	16.5	23.7	39.2	6.4	8.8	7.6	10.2	26.9	44.6	6.8	23.4	40	4.5	3.5	4.6	2.3
10.	Bihar	33.7	47.4	18.8	25.4	40.5	8.9	8.3	6.9	9.9	25.6	41.7	7.0	22.3	37.7	4.7	3.2	4.0	2.3
11.	Sikkim	48.6	57.4	38.6	39.4	50.8	26.3	9.3	6.6	12.3	40.2	55.5	21.7	37.2	51.5	19.8	3.0	4.0	1.8
12.	Arunachal Pradesh	44.0	50.6	36.5	37.8	46.1	28.5	6.2	4.5	8.0	35.5	50.5	17.2	32.9	48.1	14.3	2.6	2.4	2.8
13.	Nagaland	42.6	46.7	38.1	35.4	40.6	29.6	7.2	6.1	8.4	31.0	43.8	15.6	27.9	40.5	12.7	3.1	3.3	2.9
14.	Manipur**	43.6	48.1	39.0	30.4	39.3	21.4	13.2	8.9	17.6	38.6	44.9	32.2	28.6	38.3	19.0	10.0	6.6	13.3
15.	Mizoram	52.6	57.3	47.5	40.8	49.1	31.9	11.8	8.2	15.6	47.9	54.8	40.5	36.5	46.3	26.1	11.4	8.6	14.4
16.	Tripura	36.2	50.6	21.1	28.5	45.2	10.9	7.7	5.4	10.1	32.5	51.6	12.4	30.1	48.8	10.7	2.3	2.8	1.8
17.	Meghalaya	41.8	48.3	35.1	32.6	41.3	23.7	9.2	7.0	11.4	32.5	43.8	21.0	28.7	40.3	17.0	3.8	3.5	4.0
18.	Assam	35.8	49.9	20.7	26.7	42.5	9.8	9.1	7.4	10.9	33.2	52.9	10.6	30.9	50.2	8.8	2.3	2.7	1.8

Table Contd....

Table Contd....

Sl.No.	States/UTs	Total									Urban								
		Total Workers			Main Workers			Marginal Workers			Total Workers			Main Workers			Marginal Workers		
		P	M	F	P	M	F	P	M	F	P	M	F	P	M	F	P	M	F
19.	West Bengal	36.8	54	18.3	28.7	47.0	9.1	8.1	7.0	9.2	33.9	53.7	11.6	30.8	50.2	9.2	3.0	3.6	2.4
20.	Jharkhand	37.5	48	26.4	23.9	37.0	10.1	13.6	11.0	16.4	25.7	42.4	6.5	22.4	37.8	4.6	3.3	4.5	1.9
21.	Orissa	38.8	52.5	24.7	26.1	42.9	8.7	12.7	9.6	15.9	30.6	49.1	10.0	27.5	45.6	7.3	3.1	3.5	2.7
22.	Chhattisgarh	46.5	52.8	40.0	33.9	45.3	22.3	12.6	7.5	17.7	31.1	47.8	13.2	28.0	44.6	10.2	3.1	3.2	3.0
23.	Madhya Pradesh	42.7	51.5	33.2	31.7	44.7	17.5	11.1	6.8	15.8	30.6	47.4	12.0	27.1	43.6	8.7	3.6	3.8	3.3
24.	Gujarat	41.9	54.9	27.9	33.6	51.1	14.6	8.3	3.8	13.3	33.1	53.9	9.4	31.2	52.3	7.2	1.9	1.6	2.2
25.	Daman & Diu	46.0	65.5	18.6	42.7	63.6	13.2	3.3	1.8	5.4	35.4	53.8	16.7	33.2	52.3	13.9	2.2	1.5	2.9
26.	Dadra & Nagar Haveli	51.8	62.3	38.7	43.6	58.5	25.3	8.1	3.8	13.4	44.7	65.6	14.5	41.9	64.1	9.9	2.8	1.5	4.6
27.	Maharashtra	42.5	53.3	30.8	35.9	48.4	22.2	6.6	4.8	8.6	33.8	52.4	12.6	31.4	49.6	10.5	2.5	2.8	2.1
28.	Andhra Pradesh	45.8	56.2	35.1	38.1	50.5	25.4	7.7	5.7	9.7	32.3	50.8	13.2	29.1	47.1	10.5	3.2	3.7	2.7
29.	Karnataka	44.5	56.6	32.0	36.6	51.7	21.1	7.9	5.0	10.9	35.7	53.8	16.4	32.9	50.8	13.8	2.8	3.0	2.6
30.	Goa	38.8	54.6	22.4	31.6	47.6	14.9	7.2	7.0	7.5	37.0	54.7	18.2	32.9	49.9	14.7	4.2	4.8	3.5
31.	Lakshadweep	25.3	42.4	7.3	19.3	33.0	4.8	6.0	9.4	2.5	27.2	44.6	8.7	21.6	36.4	5.7	5.7	8.2	3.0
32.	Kerala	32.3	50.2	15.4	25.9	41.8	10.8	6.4	8.4	4.5	31.6	50.6	13.6	27.1	44.4	10.7	4.5	6.2	2.9
33.	Tamil Nadu	44.7	57.6	31.5	38.1	51.9	24.0	6.6	5.7	7.5	37.5	55.8	18.9	34.4	52.4	16.2	3.1	3.4	2.8
34.	Pondicherry	35.2	53.1	17.2	32.6	50.4	14.8	2.6	2.8	2.4	33.1	52.5	13.9	31.4	50.4	12.6	1.7	2.0	1.3
35.	Andaman & Nicobar	38.3	56.6	16.6	31.9	50.4	10.0	6.4	6.1	6.6	36.3	55.9	12.2	34.6	53.4	11.5	1.8	2.6	0.8
	India	**39.1**	**51.7**	**25.6**	**30.4**	**45.1**	**14.7**	**8.7**	**6.6**	**11.0**	**32.3**	**50.6**	**11.9**	**29.3**	**47.2**	**9.4**	**3.0**	**3.4**	**2.5**

Source and Notes: As Table-2.1.

TABLE 2.26

Work Participation Rates of Scheduled Tribe Population By Sex, 2001(%)

Sl.No.	States/UTs	Total									Urban								
		Total Workers			Main Workers			Marginal Workers			Total Workers			Main Workers			Marginal Workers		
		P	M	F	P	M	F	P	M	F	P	M	F	P	M	F	P	M	F
1.	Jammu & Kashmir	43.9	50.9	36.1	25.2	37.2	11.9	18.7	13.7	24.1	34.7	47.7	18.5	30	43.5	13.6	4.5	4.2	4.9
2.	Himachal Pradesh	54.6	56.5	52.7	37.0	44.9	29.0	17.6	11.6	23.7	32.6	45.1	17.3	31	43.4	14.7	2.1	1.7	2.6
3.	Uttarakhand	41.1	49.9	31.9	30.0	42.3	17.1	11.1	7.5	14.8	32.1	41.7	21.1	26	36.4	13.5	6.4	5.3	7.7
4.	Rajasthan	47.6	50.1	44.9	31.8	41.3	21.8	15.8	8.9	23.1	31.1	44.5	15.3	25	39.1	8.7	5.9	5.4	6.6
5.	Uttar Pradesh	40.3	49.9	30.1	26.9	39.0	13.9	13.5	10.9	16.2	26.7	41.5	9.4	21	33.8	5.8	5.8	7.7	3.6
6.	Bihar	45.2	52.9	36.9	31.0	43.0	18.1	14.2	9.9	18.7	31.2	44.0	15.9	26	38.1	11.2	5.3	5.8	4.7
7.	Sikkim	48.6	54.6	42.3	37.7	46.5	28.6	10.9	8.1	13.7	39.1	48.7	29.6	37	45.6	27.7	2.5	3.1	2.0
8.	Arunachal Pradesh	43.0	44.8	41.2	36.3	39.8	32.8	6.7	5.0	8.4	28.4	35.4	21.5	26	33.2	18.1	2.8	2.1	3.5
9.	Nagaland	42.3	44.5	40.1	34.8	38.2	31.3	7.5	6.3	8.8	26.2	34.0	18.0	23	31.4	14.8	2.9	2.6	3.2
10.	Manipur**	44.1	46.4	41.8	32.6	37.9	27.2	11.6	8.5	14.6	31.0	37.3	25.0	25	33.1	16.2	6.6	4.3	8.8
11.	Mizoram	51.7	55.3	48.1	39.6	46.8	32.3	12.1	8.6	15.8	46.7	52.2	41.2	35	43.0	26.5	11.9	9.2	14.7
12.	Tripura	42.7	47.6	37.5	29.7	41.2	17.8	13.0	6.5	19.7	32.4	45.3	18.4	31	44.1	17.3	1.2	1.2	1.1
13.	Meghalaya	42.8	47.4	38.3	32.7	39.7	25.7	10.1	7.6	12.5	31.1	38.3	24.3	27	34.2	19.4	4.5	4.1	4.9
14.	Assam	43.2	50.5	35.8	28.2	40.9	15.2	15.0	9.6	20.5	30.0	43.4	15.6	27	40.7	12.2	3.0	2.7	3.3
15.	West Bengal	48.8	53.8	43.7	32.0	42.1	21.8	16.7	11.7	21.9	35.5	48.6	21.6	28	40.4	14.4	7.7	8.2	7.2
16.	Jharkhand	46.3	51.9	40.6	27.5	38.2	16.7	18.8	13.7	23.9	28.0	39.6	15.9	22	32.3	10.9	6.2	7.3	5.0

Table Contd....

Table Contd....

Sl.No.	States/UTs	Total									Urban								
		Total Workers			Main Workers			Marginal Workers			Total Workers			Main Workers			Marginal Workers		
		P	M	F	P	M	F	P	M	F	P	M	F	P	M	F	P	M	F
17.	Orissa	49.0	54.8	43.2	28.1	41.5	14.7	20.9	13.3	28.5	33.9	47.5	19.5	27	41.1	12.4	6.8	6.4	7.1
18.	Chhattisgarh	53.4	56.7	50.2	36.0	47.3	24.9	17.4	9.5	25.3	33.1	46.8	18.5	28	42.1	13.2	5.0	4.6	5.4
19.	Madhya Pradesh	50.5	53.2	47.6	34.2	43.3	25.0	16.2	10.0	22.7	34.9	46.7	22.0	27	39.3	14.1	7.6	7.4	7.9
20.	Gujarat	51.7	55.6	47.7	36.4	48.4	24.0	15.3	7.1	23.7	39.1	53.0	24.1	35	49.4	19.0	4.3	3.6	5.2
21.	Daman & Diu	42.8	54.5	30.4	37.7	5.9	23.7	5.1	3.6	6.6	44.6	53.5	35.1	39	48.0	28.4	6.1	5.5	6.7
22.	Dadra & Nagar Haveli	50.6	53.1	48.1	38.8	47.0	30.9	11.7	6.1	17.2	39.5	51.0	27.6	31	45.8	15.5	8.6	5.2	12.1
23.	Maharashtra	49.7	53.1	46.3	38.3	44.8	31.6	11.5	8.4	14.7	34.6	48.9	19.3	30	43.9	14.3	5.0	5.0	5.0
24.	Andhra Pradesh	53.9	55.7	52.0	42.7	48.0	37.3	11.1	7.7	14.7	35.5	47.3	23.0	30	42.2	17.4	5.3	5.1	5.6
25.	Karnataka	49.4	56.8	41.7	38.4	49.9	26.6	10.9	6.9	15.1	37.6	52.6	21.9	34	48.5	17.8	4.1	4.0	4.2
26.	Goa	44.3	59.2	27.7	38.3	51.8	23.2	6.0	7.4	4.5	39.9	54.9	23.8	35	48.7	21.0	4.5	6.2	2.8
27.	Lakshadweep	22.9	38.6	7.1	16.9	29.2	4.6	6.0	9.4	2.5	24.1	39.9	8.4	18	31.5	5.3	5.7	8.5	3.0
28.	Kerala	46.3	57.5	35.4	30.2	40.7	19.9	16.2	16.8	15.5	39.8	52.1	28.0	32	43.2	21.1	7.9	8.9	6.9
29.	Tamil Nadu	54.9	60.1	49.5	44.6	51.9	37.1	10.3	8.2	12.4	40.9	53.8	28.0	35	47.4	22.2	6.1	6.4	5.8
30.	Andaman & Nicobar	47.0	58.2	35.1	27.0	43.3	9.7	20.0	14.9	25.4	34.0	53.2	9.8	33	51.6	9.8	0.9	1.6	0.0
	India	**49.1**	**53.2**	**44.8**	**33.8**	**43.5**	**23.9**	**15.2**	**9.7**	**20.9**	**34.7**	**46.8**	**21.6**	**29**	**41.3**	**15.5**	**5.8**	**5.5**	**6.1**

Source and Notes: As Table 2.1.

36.67% states are falling in the range of 40.01 to 45%. About 26.67% states have the workers more than 50.01% of the total workers. These are Mizoram, Himachal Pradesh, Tamilnadu, Gujarat, Chhattisgarh, Madhya Pradesh, Andhra Pradesh and Dadra & Nagar Havelli (Table 2.27). Two third states of the country have the participation rates below the national average.

The work participation rate of male tribal is higher than the total tribal population in the country. About 43% states have less male workers than the national average.

Table 2.28 shows that 33.33% states have more than 55.01% male workers. These are Chhattisgarh, Andhra Pradesh, Kerala, Karnataka, Goa, Mizoram, Himachal Pradesh, Tamilnadu, Gujarat and Andaman & Nicobar Islands. Out of the total 30 states having tribal population only 6.67% (Lakshadweep and Goa) have less than 30% female workers while 10% states—Chhattisgarh, Himachal Pradesh and Andhra Pradesh have more than 50.01% female workers. Maximum 30% states are having the ranges between 40.01% to 45% female workers. These are Rajasthan, Sikkim, Orissa, Manipur, West Bengal, Karnataka, Jharkhand, Arunachal Pradesh and Nagaland (Table 2.29). Two third states have less female workers than the national average. In 2001 census 34.7% urban tribal population is considered as workers which are higher than that of all castes urban population (32.3%). The percentage of a tribal urban worker varies from minimum 26.7% in Uttar Pradesh to maximum 46.7% in Mizoram (Table 2.26). Approximately 56% states have more urban workers than the national average.

The work participation rates of urban male workers vary minimum 34% in Nagaland to maximum 53.8% in Tamilnadu. There are 50% states having more urban male workers than the country average. The work participation rate of tribal female in the urban area is 26.6% which is also higher than the female of all castes population in the country (11.9%). The urban tribal female workers rate varies from minimum 8.4% in Lakshadweep to 41.2% in Mizoram state followed by Daman and Diu (35.1%). In total 80% states have less tribal female workers in urban areas than the national average (Table 2.32). Tables 2.30-2.32 give the

TABLE 2.27

Distribution of States/ UTs by Ranges of Work Participation Rates (Persons) in India, 2001

Zone/Region	*Ranges of Work Parti. Rates (%)*	*All Castes Population*		*Scheduled Tribe Population*		
		(No.)	*(%)*	*(No.)*	*(%)*	*States/UTs*
Very Low	Below 35.00	5	14.29	1	3.33	Lakshadweep.
Low	35.01-40.00	13	37.14	Nil	Nil	Nil
Moderate	40.01-45.00	10	28.57	11	36.67	Jammu & Kashmir, Arunachal Pradesh, Uttar Pradesh, Uttarakhand, Manipur, Tripura, Meghalaya, Daman & Diu, Nagaland, Goa and Assam.
High	45.01-50.00	5	14.29	10	33.33	Sikkim, Kerala, Rajasthan, Maharashtra, Bihar, Orissa, West Bengal, Karnataka, Jharkhand, and Andaman & Nicobar Islands.
Very High	Above 50.01	2	5.71	8	26.67	Mizoram, Himachal Pradesh, Tamilnadu, Gujarat, Chhattisgarh, Madhya Pradesh, Andhra Pradesh and Dadra & Nagar Haveli.
Total		**35**	**100.00**	**30**	**100.00**	

Source: Anon. 2001a.

TABLE 2.28

Distribution of States/ UTs by Ranges of Work Participation Rates (Males) of Urban Population in India, 2001

Zone/Region	Ranges of Work Partici-pation Rates	All Castes Population		S. Tribe Population		States/UTs
		(No.)	(%)	(No.)	(%)	
Very Low	Below 35.00	Nil	Nil	1	3.33	Nagaland.
Low	35.01-40.00	Nil	Nil	5	16.67	Arunachal Pradesh, Jharkhand, Meghalaya, Manipur, and Lakshadweep
Moderate	40.01-45.00	7	20.00	5	16.67	Uttarakhand, Rajasthan, Uttar Pradesh, Bihar and Assam.
High	45.01-50.00	6	17.14	11	36.67	Jammu & Kashmir, Tripura, Andhra Pradesh, Sikkim, Chhattisgarh, Himachal Pradesh, West Bengal, Maharashtra, Madhya Pradesh, Orissa and Dadra & Nagar Haveli.
Very High	Above 50.01	22	62.86	8	26.66	Gujarat, Daman & Diu, Tamilnadu, Kerala, Goa, Mizoram, Karnataka and Andaman & Nicobar Islands.
Total		**35**	**100.00**	**30**	**100.00**	

Source: Anon. 2001a.

TABLE 2.29

Distribution of States/UTs by Ranges of Work Participation Rates (Females) of Urban Population in India, 2001

Zone/Region	*Ranges of Work Parti. Rates (%)*	*All Castes Population*		*S. Tribe Population*		*States/UTs*
		(No.)	*(%)*	*(No.)*	*(%)*	
Very Low	Below 15.00	24	68.58	3	10.00	Lakshadweep, Uttar Pradesh, and Andaman & Nicobar Islands.
Low	15.01-20.00	7	20.00	11	36.67	Jammu & Kashmir, Rajasthan, Bihar, Assam, Nagaland, Tripura, Jharkhand, Orissa, Chhattisgarh, Maharashtra and Himachal Pradesh.
Moderate	20.01-25.00	2	5.71	10	33.33	Uttarakhand, Madhya Pradesh, Gujarat, Andhra Pradesh, Arunachal Pradesh, Meghalaya, Manipur, Karnataka, Goa and West Bengal.
High	25.01-30.00	Nil	Nil	4	13.33	Sikkim, Tamilnadu, Kerala and Dadra & Nagar Haveli.
Very High	Above 30.01	2	5.71	2	6.67	Mizoram and Daman & Diu.
Total		**35**	**100.00**	**30**	**100.00**	

Source: Anon. 2001a.

distribution of states by the different ranges and groups of work participation rates for person, males and females of the urban tribal and all caste population of the country as a whole. Maximum 50% states—Jammu & Kashmir, Bihar, Assam, Tripura, Meghalaya, Chhattisgarh, Himachal Pradesh, West Bengal, Maharashtra, Madhya Pradesh, Orissa, Manipur, Uttarakhand, Rajasthan and Andman & Nicobar Islands fall between the ranges of 30.01% to 35% while 16.67% states—Uttar Pradesh, Jharkhand, Arunachal Pradesh, Lakshadweep and Nagaland have less than 30% total tribal workers. Only one state (3.33%) Mizoram has more than 45.01% total tribal workers. It is because Mizoram state has more than 90% tribal population. Among the male tribal workers only one state Nagaland (3.33%) has less than 35% workers while 26.66% states (Gujarat, Daman & Diu, Tamilnadu Kerala, Goa, Mizoram, Karnataka and Andaman & Nicobar Islands) have more than 50.01% male workers (Table 2.31). About 10% states have less than 15% tribal female workers. These are Lakshadweep, Uttar Pradesh and Andaman & Nicobar Islands (Table 2.32). About 70% states have 15-25% female tribal workers. Only 6.67% states (Mizoram and Daman & Diu) have more than 30.01% female tribal workers. Among the total workers percentage 49.1% considered as main, 33.8% are as marginal workers which are more than the all castes population (main—30.4% and marginal—8.7%). Tables 2.25-2.26 show the 43.5% and 9.7% tribal males are in main and marginal category while only 23.9% and 20.9 % female are recorded in these categories respectively.

Work Participation Rates by Occupational Category

Approximately 44% tribals of the total tribal workers are registered as a cultivator which is 10% more than the all castes cultivators (Tables 2.33-2.34). The percentage of tribal cultivator varies nil cultivators in Goa and Lakshadweep to maximum 76.1% in Himachal Pradesh followed by 71.4 % in Nagaland. Out of the total male and female tribal 47.6% males and 41.2% females are registered as cultivators.

Maximum 68.8% male cultivators are recorded in Assam while 13.33% states have below 5% cultivators including Lakshadweep and Goa which have no cultivation. The maximum

TABLE 2.30

Distribution of States/ UTs by Ranges of Work Participation Rates (Persons) of Urban Population in India, 2001

Zone/Region	*Ranges of Work Parti. Rates (%)*	*All Castes Population*		*Scheduled Tribe Population*		
		(No.)	*(%)*	*(No.)*	*(%)*	*States/UTs*
Very Low	Below 30.00	6	17.14	5	16.67	Uttar Pradesh, Jharkhand, Arunachal Pradesh, Lakshadweep and Nagaland.
Low	30.01-35.00	17	48.57	14	46.67	Jammu & Kashmir, Bihar, Assam, Tripura, Meghalaya Chhattisgarh, Himachal Pradesh, Maharashtra, Andhra Pradesh, Orissa, Manipur, Uttarakhand, Rajasthan and Andaman & Nicobar Islands.
Moderate	35.01-40.00	9	25.72	8	26.66	Sikkim, Gujarat, Dadra & Nagar Haveli, Andhra Pradesh, Kerala, Goa, West Bengal and Karnataka
High	40.01-45.00	2	5.71	2	6.67	Daman & Diu, Tamilnadu
Very High	Above 45.01	1	2.86	1	3.33	Mizoram.
Total		**35**	**100.00**	**30**	**100.00**	

Source: Anon. 2001a.

TABLE 2.31

Distribution of States/ UTs by Ranges of Work Participation Rates (Males) of Urban Population in India, 2001

Zone/Region	*Ranges of Work Parti. Rates (%)*	*All Castes Population*		*Scheduled Tribe Population*		
		(No.)	*(%)*	*(No.)*	*(%)*	*States/UTs*
Very Low	Below 35.00	Nil	Nil	1	3.33	Nagaland.
Low	35.01-40.00	Nil	Nil	5	16.67	Arunachal Pradesh, Jharkhand, Meghalaya, Manipur, and Lakshadweep
Moderate	40.01-45.00	7	20.00	5	16.67	Uttarakhand, Rajasthan, Uttar Pradesh, Bihar and Assam.
High	45.01-50.00	6	17.14	11	36.67	Jammu & Kashmir, Tripura, Andhra Pradesh, Sikkim, Chhattisgarh, Himachal Pradesh, West Bengal, Maharashtra, Madhya Pradesh, Orissa and Dadra & Nagar Haveli.
Very High	Above 50.01	22	62.86	8	26.66	Gujarat, Daman & Diu, Tamilnadu, Kerala, Goa, Mizoram, Karnataka and Andaman & Nicobar Islands.
Total		**35**	**100.00**	**30**	**100.00**	

Source: Anon. 2001a.

88.4% female cultivators are found in Himachal Pradesh where mostly women were engaged in fruits cultivation. The study shows that on an average of the nation more male tribals (47.6%) are in cultivation than the female (41.2%) while in all castes population more females (32.9%) are registered as cultivators than males (31.1%). Tables 2.35-2.36 give the distribution of states of India by the ranges total, male and female tribal and all castes cultivators.

Out of the total 23.33% states have less than 30% tribal cultivators while only 10% states have more than 70.1% cultivators (Table 2.35). More than one third states have less than 10% agricultural labourers while 26.67 % states have more than that 50.1% tribal females in agricultural labourers. These are Bihar, Orissa, Gujarat, Maharashtra, Andhra Pradesh, Karnataka and Kerala. Less than 3% tribal workers are found in household industries 4.2%, 3.2% and 6.5% persons, males and females of all castes workers are registered in this occupation. In tribal workers minimum workers as household industries are registered in Daman and Diu (0.3 %) to maximum in Andaman and Nicobar Islands (43.4%). Tables 2. 41-2.43 give the distribution of states by the ranges of total, male and female of all castes and tribal workers in household industries. Maximum states have less than 2% tribal workers engaged in household industries. Similarly more than 40% states are found in below the percentage of national average in these categories.

Out of the total tribal workers 16.3% persons are registered as other workers i.e., these persons are engaged in white collar jobs while in all castes population 37.6% persons are recorded in this category. The percentage of other workers of tribal total workers varies minimum 9.5% in Chhattisgarh to maximum 96.4% in Goa. Out of the total male workers 20.6% males are considered as other workers which are less than the half of all castes male workers. Similarly about 11.1% female workers are registered in other workers category while 21.71% females of all castes population are found in this category. It reflects that the percentage of female workers in both tribal and non-tribal categories is still very low. Tables 2.46-2.48 give the distribution

TABLE 2.32

Distribution of States/ UTs by Ranges of Work Participation Rates (Females) of Urban Population in India, 2001

Zone/Region	*Ranges of Work Parti. Rates (%)*	*All Castes Population*		*S. Tribe Population*		*States/UTs*
		(No.)	*(%)*	*(No.)*	*(%)*	
Very Low	Below 15.00	24	68.58	3	10.00	Lakshadweep, Uttar Pradesh, and Andaman & Nicobar Islands.
Low	15.01-20.00	7	20.00	11	36.67	Jammu & Kashmir, Rajasthan, Bihar, Assam, Nagaland, Tripura, Jharkhand, Orissa, Chhattisgarh, Maharashtra and Himachal Pradesh.
Moderate	20.01-25.00	2	5.71	10	33.33	Uttarakhand, Madhya Pradesh, Gujarat, Andhra Pradesh, Arunachal Pradesh, Meghalaya, Manipur, Karnataka, Goa and West Bengal.
High	25.01-30.00	Nil	Nil	4	13.33	Sikkim, Tamilnadu, Kerala and Dadra & Nagar Haveli.
Very High	Above 30.01	2	5.71	2	6.67	Mizoram and Daman & Diu.
Total		**35**	**100.00**	**30**	**100.00**	

Source: Ancn. 2001a.

TABLE 2.33

Distribution of Total and Urban Workers of All Castes Population by Category, 2001 (%)

Sl.No.	States/UTs	Total												Urban											
		Cultivators			Agri.Labourers			H.H Industries			Other Workers			Cultivators			Agri.Labourers			H.H Industries			Other Workers		
		P	M	F	P	M	F	P	M	F	P	M	F	P	M	F	P	M	F	P	M	F	P	M	F
1.	Jammu & Kashmir	42.4	37.5	54.7	6.6	7.1	5.2	6.2	4.7	10.1	44.8	50.7	30.0	3.8	3.3	7.3	2.3	2.2	2.7	6.7	4.7	19.1	87.2	89.9	70.8
2.	Himachal Pradesh	65.3	49.5	85.8	3.1	3.3	2.9	1.8	2.0	1.4	29.8	45.2	9.8	3.6	2.0	10.9	0.7	0.7	1.0	1.5	1.4	2.1	94.1	96.0	85.9
3.	Punjab	22.6	25.3	13.9	16.3	15.9	17.8	3.7	2.6	7.2	57.4	56.2	61.1	2.4	2.5	1.9	3.5	3.3	4.2	4.1	3.4	8.4	90.1	90.8	85.5
4.	Chandigarh	0.6	0.6	0.8	0.2	0.2	0.2	1.1	0.9	2.5	98.1	98.4	96.6	0.2	0.2	0.3	0.1	0.1	0.1	1.0	0.8	2.1	98.7	98.9	97.4
5.	Uttarakhand	50.1	34.3	77.8	8.3	9.5	6.1	2.3	2.2	2.5	39.3	54.0	13.6	2.2	1.6	6.5	2.4	2.2	3.5	2.5	1.8	6.9	93.0	94.3	83.0
6.	Haryana	36.0	32.5	43.7	15.3	12.5	21.1	2.6	2.3	3.1	46.1	52.7	32.1	3.1	2.7	5.3	2.8	2.1	7.0	3.9	3.2	7.4	90.2	92.0	80.3
7.	Delhi	0.8	0.7	1.8	0.3	0.3	0.8	3.1	2.8	4.7	95.7	96.2	92.7	0.3	0.2	0.5	0.2	0.1	0.4	3.1	2.9	4.7	96.4	96.7	94.4
8.	Rajasthan	55.3	48.1	67.0	10.6	7.2	16.2	2.9	2.9	2.8	31.2	41.9	14.0	5.6	4.0	14.7	2.2	1.4	6.9	5.9	4.5	13.6	86.3	90.1	64.8
9.	Uttar Pradesh	41.1	42.7	36.1	24.8	20.1	39.6	5.6	4.7	8.3	28.5	32.5	16.0	4.4	4.4	5.0	5.0	4.6	8.5	9.3	7.4	23.8	81.2	83.7	62.7
10.	Bihar	29.3	31.5	23.2	48.0	42.6	62.6	3.9	3.2	5.9	18.8	22.6	8.3	5.3	5.3	5.9	12.2	10.2	26.4	6.5	5.2	15.8	75.9	79.4	51.9
11.	Sikkim	49.9	42.3	62.8	6.5	5.3	8.5	1.6	1.7	1.4	42.0	50.7	27.3	0.2	0.2	0.4	0.2	0.2	0.3	1.2	1.1	1.4	98.4	98.5	98.0
12.	Arunachal Pradesh	57.8	46.4	75.5	3.9	3.5	4.5	1.3	1.1	1.5	37.0	49.0	18.5	4.8	2.8	12.0	1.5	1.2	2.6	1.6	1.2	2.8	92.1	94.8	82.6
13.	Nagaland	64.7	55.4	77.5	3.6	3.3	4.2	2.6	1.9	3.5	29.0	39.4	14.9	4.6	2.6	11.2	1.0	0.6	2.1	3.1	1.9	7.1	91.4	94.8	79.6
14.	Manipur**	40.2	40.6	39.6	12.0	9.5	15.2	10	3.9	18.3	37.6	46.0	26.9	13.1	14.3	11.5	9.5	7.3	12.5	13.1	5.3	23.8	64.3	73.1	52.2
15.	Mizoram	54.9	49.6	61.6	5.7	4.9	6.9	1.5	1.3	1.8	37.9	44.2	29.7	23.3	20.2	27.8	8.1	6.5	10.4	2.1	1.7	2.7	66.5	71.6	59.1
16.	Tripura	27.0	26.6	28.1	23.8	19.6	34.6	3.0	1.8	6.2	46.1	52.1	31.1	1.4	1.5	0.7	1.9	2.0	1.6	1.8	1.2	4.5	94.9	95.3	93.2
17.	Meghalaya	48.1	44.9	52.8	17.7	16.0	20.1	2.2	1.6	3.0	32.0	37.5	24.1	4.4	3.4	6.5	4.8	3.7	7.1	1.7	1.5	2.0	89.1	91.4	84.4
18.	Assam	39.1	38.3	41.1	13.2	12.1	16.2	3.6	1.9	7.9	44.0	47.6	34.8	1.6	1.4	2.5	0.9	0.7	1.8	2.7	1.9	7.8	94.8	96.0	87.9
19.	West Bengal	19.2	20.8	14.1	25.0	22.7	32.2	7.4	4.1	17.7	48.5	52.4	36.1	0.9	0.9	1.0	1.6	1.5	2.2	6.0	4.0	16.5	91.5	93.7	80.3
20.	Jharkhand	38.5	36.1	43.0	28.2	22.3	39.6	4.3	3.6	5.6	29.1	38.0	11.8	2.0	1.7	4.4	2.6	2.0	7.7	3.1	2.6	7.5	92.2	93.8	80.5

Table Contd....

Table Contd....

Sl.No.	States/UTs	Total												Urban											
		Cultivators			Agri.Labourers			H.H Industries			Other Workers			Cultivators			Agri.Labourers			H.H Industries			Other Workers		
		P	M	F	P	M	F	P	M	F	P	M	F	P	M	F	P	M	F	P	M	F	P	M	F
21.	Orissa	29.8	34.2	20.1	35.0	26.4	53.9	4.9	3.3	8.5	30.3	36.2	17.5	2.9	3.0	2.6	4.6	3.3	11.2	3.5	2.7	7.7	89.0	90.9	78.4
22.	Chhattisgarh	44.5	44.6	44.5	31.9	22.8	44.1	2.1	2.1	2.0	21.5	30.5	9.4	4.1	3.3	6.8	5.3	2.9	14.7	3.8	2.8	7.6	86.9	91.0	70.9
23.	Madhya Pradesh	42.8	42.5	43.3	28.7	21.7	40.4	4.0	3.2	5.4	24.5	32.6	10.9	6.2	5.6	9.0	5.4	3.5	13.8	6.6	4.3	16.6	81.8	86.6	60.7
24.	Gujarat	27.3	27.0	28.0	24.3	17.3	39.1	2.0	1.7	2.7	46.4	54	30.2	1.7	1.5	2.9	2.8	2.0	8.5	2.7	1.6	9.5	92.8	94.9	79.1
25.	Daman & Diu	5.5	3.3	16.6	1.8	0.6	8.0	1.6	0.6	6.5	91.0	95.5	66.9	0.4	0.3	0.8	0.3	0.2	0.6	3.1	1.3	9.0	96.3	98.3	89.6
26.	Dadra & Nagar Haveli	34.6	23.8	55.9	12.9	7.2	24.3	0.7	0.6	0.9	51.8	68.4	18.9	6.4	4.0	22.2	2.2	1.0	10.1	0.8	0.6	2.1	90.6	94.4	65.6
27.	Maharashtra	28.7	24.9	35.8	26.3	18.3	41.1	2.6	2.1	3.6	42.4	54.7	19.4	1.8	1.5	2.8	3.6	2.3	10.0	3.4	2.1	9.4	91.3	94.1	77.8
28.	Andhra Pradesh	22.5	24.0	20.1	39.6	29.8	55.8	4.7	3.3	7.0	33.1	42.9	17.1	1.5	1.4	2.0	6.7	4.6	14.8	6.0	3.8	15.0	85.8	90.2	68.3
29.	Karnataka	29.2	31.7	24.7	26.5	17.2	43.4	4.1	2.7	6.7	40.2	48.4	25.2	3.1	3.2	2.7	5.1	3.3	11.2	5.7	3.1	14.5	86.1	90.3	71.5
30.	Goa	9.6	6.9	16.7	6.8	4.3	13.4	2.8	2.4	3.9	80.7	86.5	65.9	1.8	1.1	4.0	1.9	1.3	4.0	2.4	2.1	3.6	93.9	95.6	88.4
31.	Lakshadweep	0.0	0.0	0.0	0.0	0.0	0.0	5.9	4.1	17.0	94.1	95.9	83.0	0.0	0.0	0.0	0.0	0.0	0.0	6.3	4.1	18.6	93.7	95.9	81.4
32.	Kerala	7.0	7.8	4.8	15.8	13.9	21.5	3.6	2.5	7.1	73.6	75.9	66.5	1.2	1.2	1.0	4.4	3.7	6.7	3.6	2.7	6.7	90.9	92.4	85.6
33.	Tamil Nadu	18.4	18.0	19.0	31.0	23.5	44.8	5.4	3.6	8.7	45.3	54.9	27.5	3.3	3.0	4.3	10.7	7.9	19.0	6.3	3.9	13.8	79.6	85.2	63.0
34.	Pondicherry	3.2	3.7	1.5	21.1	16.3	35.9	1.8	1.3	3.7	73.9	78.7	58.9	7.0	8.9	2.9	47.1	38.3	67.3	1.7	1.3	2.7	44.1	51.5	27.1
35.	Andaman & Nicobar	15.8	13.7	24.1	3.8	3.7	4.2	5.2	4.3	9.0	75.3	78.3	62.8	0.1	0.1	0.1	0.3	0.3	0.3	1.0	0.9	1.8	98.5	98.7	97.8
	India	**31.7**	**31.1**	**32.9**	**26.5**	**20.8**	**38.9**	**4.2**	**3.2**	**6.5**	**37.6**	**44.9**	**21.7**	**2.8**	**2.5**	**4.1**	**4.7**	**3.4**	**10.7**	**5.2**	**3.6**	**12.8**	**87.3**	**90.4**	**72.5**

Source and Notes: As Table 2.1.

TABLE 2.34

Distribution of Total and Urban Scheduled Tribe Population by Category, 2001(%)

Sl.No.	States/UTs	Total												Urban											
		Cultivators			Agri.Labourers			H.H Industries			Other Workers			Cultivators			Agri.Labourers			H.H Industries			Other Workers		
		P	M	F	P	M	F	P	M	F	P	M	F	P	M	F	P	M	F	P	M	F	P	M	F
1.	Jammu & Kashmir	58.5	58.1	59.0	6.4	8.3	3.5	2.4	1.5	3.8	32.7	32.1	33.7	8.7	6.8	14.9	3.6	3.4	4.3	0.6	0.5	1.2	87.1	89.4	79.7
2.	Himachal Pradesh	76.1	64.7	88.4	1.0	1.1	1.0	1.4	1.4	1.3	21.5	32.8	9.3	2.8	1.9	5.7	0.4	0.5	0.2	1.1	0.9	1.9	95.6	96.6	92.3
3.	Uttarakhand	63.0	61.7	65.3	13.2	13.1	13.3	6.2	2.6	12.1	17.6	22.6	9.3	10.7	7.4	18.2	1.3	1.1	1.7	15.9	4.0	43.1	72.1	87.5	36.9
4.	Rajasthan	69.0	67.3	71.0	14.1	9.6	19.3	0.7	0.7	0.8	16.3	22.5	8.9	12.8	9.3	24.5	5.9	3.6	14.0	1.7	1.2	3.4	79.6	85.9	58.1
5.	Uttar Pradesh	44.6	47.0	40.2	31.4	28.0	37.5	2.4	2.3	2.6	21.6	22.6	19.7	1.7	1.4	3.3	3.0	2.6	5.0	7.7	6.0	16.7	87.6	90.0	75.1
6.	Bihar	21.3	24.7	16.1	62.5	59.0	68.0	4.0	2.4	6.5	12.2	14.0	9.3	2.4	2.6	1.6	25.1	20.3	40.7	2.3	2.2	2.7	70.2	74.8	55.0
7.	Sikkim	56.1	51.5	62.4	5.4	4.8	6.3	1.4	1.2	1.6	37.0	42.5	29.7	0.2	0.3	0.1	0.3	0.3	0.4	1.0	0.7	1.5	98.4	98.7	98.0
8.	Arunachal Pradesh	75.0	68.0	82.6	2.3	2.1	2.5	1.2	1.0	1.5	21.5	28.9	13.4	11.4	7.6	17.4	1.9	1.4	2.7	1.4	0.6	2.8	85.3	90.3	77.1
9.	Nagaland	71.4	65.0	79.0	3.5	3.2	3.9	2.6	1.9	3.5	22.4	29.9	13.6	7.3	4.8	12.5	1.2	0.8	2.0	3.9	2.1	7.3	87.6	92.2	78.2
10.	Manipur**	64.9	63.5	66.4	7.4	6.4	8.5	5.7	2.9	8.8	22.0	27.2	16.3	7.1	7.5	6.6	3.6	2.8	4.8	5.5	2.0	10.6	83.7	87.7	78.1
11.	Mizoram	58.1	54.7	62.1	5.9	5.2	6.8	1.5	1.3	1.8	34.5	38.8	29.3	25.3	23.1	28.1	8.7	7.4	10.4	2.1	1.7	2.6	63.9	67.9	58.8
12.	Tripura	41.6	43.7	38.9	36.2	30.7	43.5	2.1	1.1	3.5	20.0	24.5	14.2	1.7	2.3	0.3	2.6	3.1	1.0	0.9	0.8	1.3	94.8	93.8	97.4
13.	Meghalaya	52.9	51.6	54.5	18.6	17.3	20.3	2.1	1.6	2.8	26.4	29.6	22.4	6.3	5.5	7.3	6.9	6.0	8.2	1.6	1.5	1.8	85.3	87.0	82.7
14.	Assam	67.7	68.8	66.2	11.6	9.0	15.4	3.7	1.3	7.1	17.0	20.9	11.4	8.6	7.9	10.7	2.1	1.6	3.4	3.0	1.1	9.0	86.3	89.4	77.0
15.	West Bengal	19.5	25.0	12.6	53.2	46.1	62.0	3.0	1.7	4.7	24.2	27.1	20.6	2.9	2.8	3.1	14.2	10.7	22.5	1.6	1.2	2.7	81.2	85.2	71.7
16.	Jharkhand	52.6	54.7	49.9	31.0	25.7	37.8	3.0	2.6	3.4	13.5	17.1	8.8	4.8	4.7	5.2	7.3	5.9	10.9	1.9	1.4	3.0	86.0	88.0	80.9
17.	Orissa	33.3	42.4	21.9	46.9	37.2	59.1	4.8	2.1	8.1	15.0	18.3	10.9	4.5	5.0	3.2	12.3	9.2	20.1	3.1	1.7	6.9	80.1	84.1	69.8
18.	Chhattisgarh	56.6	61.9	50.7	32.7	24.3	42.1	1.2	1.1	1.2	9.5	12.7	6.0	8.2	7.3	10.8	10.4	6.4	21.0	2.5	1.5	5.1	78.9	84.8	63.1
19.	Madhya Pradesh	46.8	50.0	43.1	42.1	35.9	49.2	1.1	0.9	1.3	10.0	13.2	6.3	6.0	5.5	7.2	20.2	14.8	32.6	2.1	1.5	3.5	71.7	78.2	56.7

20. Gujarat	37.6	41.6	32.9	43.6	35.6	53.3	0.8	0.8	0.8	18.0	22.0	13.1	2.7	2.2	3.8	12.8	10.1	19.1	0.9	0.7	1.4	83.6	86.9	75.6
21. Daman & Diu	3.8	4.2	3.0	9.2	5.0	17.1	0.3	0.3	0.3	86.7	90.5	79.5	0.2	0.3	0.2	1.5	1.0	2.3	0.6	0.4	0.8	97.7	98.3	96.6
22. Dadra & Nagar Haveli	54.3	47.4	61.7	19.8	14.2	25.8	0.5	0.6	0.4	25.4	37.9	12.1	31.3	25.6	42.2	9.7	6	16.8	0.3	0.3	0.3	58.6	68.1	40.6
23. Maharashtra	30.6	31.5	29.4	50.7	43.3	59.3	1.3	1.1	1.6	17.5	24.1	9.8	1.6	1.5	1.9	14.7	9.9	27.9	3.1	1.8	6.5	80.5	86.7	63.7
24. Andhra Pradesh	34.3	38.8	29.4	49.3	41.0	58.4	3.0	2.5	3.5	13.5	17.7	8.7	1.6	1.6	1.6	17.2	13.1	26.4	6.4	4.6	10.3	74.8	80.7	61.8
25. Karnataka	30.8	37.6	21.3	43.2	31.6	59.4	2.6	1.8	3.8	23.4	29.0	15.5	6.4	6.9	5.1	15.3	10.6	27.0	6.3	3.8	12.6	72.0	78.7	55.3
26. Goa	0.0	0.0	0.0	0.0	0.0	0.0	3.6	4.5	1.4	96.4	95.5	98.6	0.0	0.0	0.0	0.0	0.0	0.0	2.7	3.7	0.0	97.3	96.3	100.0
27. Lakshadweep	0.0	0.0	0.0	0.0	0.0	0.0	6.8	4.7	17.7	93.2	95.3	82.3	0.0	0.0	0.0	0.0	0.0	0.0	7.6	5.0	19.7	92.4	95.0	80.3
28. Kerala	11.2	12.7	8.7	47.1	45.0	50.5	3.1	1.4	5.9	38.6	40.9	34.9	0.7	0.9	0.4	12.6	13.2	11.6	2.3	1.5	3.8	84.3	84.5	84.1
29. Tamil Nadu	36.3	37.8	34.6	37.8	32.8	43.9	2.4	1.9	2.9	23.6	27.6	18.6	3.6	3.5	3.9	22.6	18.9	29.8	4.2	2.9	6.7	69.6	74.8	59.6
30. Andaman & Nicobar	0.4	0.3	0.6	0.1	0.1	0.2	43	44.1	42.2	56.0	55.5	57.0	0.0	0.0	0.0	0.0	0.0	0.0	0.0	0.0	0.0	100.0	100.0	100.0
India	**44.7**	**47.6**	**41.2**	**36.9**	**30.3**	**44.8**	**2.1**	**1.5**	**2.9**	**16.3**	**20.6**	**11.1**	**6.5**	**5.6**	**8.7**	**12.4**	**9.2**	**19.8**	**2.9**	**1.9**	**5.2**	**78.2**	**83.4**	**66.3**

Source and Notes: As Table 1.

TABLE 2.35

Distribution of States/ UTs by Ranges of Cultivators (Persons) of Total Population in India, 2001

Zone/Region	*Ranges of Cultivators (%)*	*All Castes Population*		*Scheduled Tribe Population*		
		(No.)	*(%)*	*(No.)*	*(%)*	*States/UTs*
Very Low	Below 30.00	18	51.43	7	23.33	Bihar, Goa, West Bengal, Daman & Diu, Kerala, Lakshadweep and Andaman & Nicobar Islands.
Low	30.01-40.00	4	11.43	6	20.00	Orissa, Maharashtra, Gujarat, Andhra Pradesh, Karnataka and Tamilnadu.
Moderate	40.01-50.00	7	20.00	3	10.00	Uttar Pradesh, Tripura and Madhya Pradesh.
Moder. High	50.01-60.00	4	11.43	7	23.33	Jammu & Kashmir, Sikkim, Mizoram, Meghalaya, Jharkhand, Chhattis-garh and Dadra & Nagar Haveli.
High	60.01-70.00	2	5.71	4	13.34	Uttarakhand, Rajasthan, Assam and Manipur.
Very High	Above70.01	Nil	Nil	3	10.00	Nagaland, Arunachal Pradesh and Himachal Pradesh.
Total		**35**	**100.00**	30	**100.00**	

Source: Anon. 2001a.

TABLE 2.36

Distribution of States/ UTs by Ranges of Cultivators (Males) of Total Population in India, 2001

Zone/Region	*Ranges of Cultivators (%)*	*All Castes Population*		*Scheduled Tribe Population*		
		(No.)	*(%)*	*(No.)*	*(%)*	*States/UTs*
Very Low	Below 30.00	16	45.71	7	23.33	Bihar, Goa, West Bengal, Daman & Diu, Kerala, Lakshadweep and Andaman & Nicobar Islands.
Low	30.01-40.00	8	22.86	4	13.33	Maharashtra, Andhra Pradesh, Karnataka, and Tamilnadu.
Moderate	40.01-50.00	10	28.57	6	20.00	Uttar Pradesh, Tripura, Orissa, Gujarat, Madhya Pradesh and Dadra & Nagar Haveli.
High	50.01-60.00	1	2.86	5	16.67	Jammu & Kashmir, Sikkim, Mizoram, Meghalaya and Jharkhand.
Very High	Above 60.01	Nil	Nil	8	26.67	Uttarakhand, Rajasthan, Assam, Manipur, Chhattisgarh, Nagaland, Arunachal Pradesh and Himachal Pradesh.
Total		**35**	**100.00**	**30**	**100.00**	

Source: Anon. 2001a.

TABLE 2.37

Distribution of States/ UTs by Ranges of Cultivators (Females) of Total Population in India, 2001

Zone/Region	*Ranges of Cultivators (%)*	*All Castes Population*		*Scheduled Tribe Population*		
		(No.)	*(%)*	*(No.)*	*(%)*	*States/UTs*
Very Low	Below 30.00	17	48.57	11	36.67	Bihar, Goa, West Bengal, Daman & Diu, Kerala, Orissa, Maharashtra, Andhra Pradesh, Karnataka, Lakshadweep and Andaman & Nicobar Islands.
Low	30.01-40.00	3	8.57	3	10.00	Tripura, Gujarat and Tamilnadu.
Moderate	40.01-50.00	5	14.29	4	13.33	U.P., Madhya Pradesh, Chhattisgarh & Jharkhand.
Moder. High	50.01-60.00	3	8.57	2	6.67	Jammu & Kashmir, Meghalaya.
High	60.01-70.00	3	8.57	6	20	Uttarakhand, Assam, Manipur, Sikkim, Mizoram, and Dadra & Nagar Haveli.
Very High	Above 70.01	4	11.43	4	13.33	Rajasthan, Nagaland, Arunachal Pradesh & H.P.
Total		**35**	**100.00**	**30**	**100.00**	

TABLE 2.38

Distribution of States/ UTs by Ranges of Agricultural Labourers (Persons) of Total Population in India, 2001

Zone/Region	*Ranges of Work Parti. Rates (%)*	*All Castes Population*		*S. Tribe Population*		*Scheduled Tribes Population*
		(No.)	*(%)*	*(No.)*	*(%)*	*States/UTs*
Very Low	Below 10.00	13	37.14	11	36.66	Jammu & Kashmir, Sikkim, Himachal Pradesh, Goa, Nagaland, Arunachal Pradesh, Manipur, Mizoram, Daman & Diu, Andaman & Nicobar Islands and Lakshadweep.
Low	10.01-20.00	8	22.86	5	16.67	Uttarakhand, Assam, Rajasthan, Meghalaya, and Dadra & Nagar Haveli.
Moderate	20.01-30.00	9.	25.71	Nil	Nil	Nil
Moder. High	30.01-40.00	4	11.43	5	16.67	Tripura, Tamilnadu, Uttar Pradesh, Jharkhand, and Chhattisgarh
High	40.01-50.00	1	2.86	6	20.00	Kerala, Orissa, Madhya Pradesh, Gujarat, Karnataka, and Andhra Pradesh.
Very High	Above 50.01	Nil	Nil	3	10.00	Bihar, West Bengal and Maharashtra.
Total		**35**	**100.00**	**30**	**100.00**	

Source: Anon. 2001a.

TABLE 2.39

Distribution of States/ UTs by Ranges of Agricultural Labourers (Males) of Total Population in India, 2001

Zone/Region	*Ranges of Agri. Labo. (%)*	*All Castes Population*		*S. Tribe Population*		*States/UTs*
		(No.)	*(%)*	*(No.)*	*(%)*	
Very Low	Below 10.00	16	45.71	13	43.34	Jammu & Kashmir, Sikkim, Himachal Pradesh, Goa, Nagaland, Arunachal Pradesh, Manipur, Mizoram, Daman & Diu, Andaman & Nicobar Islands Lakshadweep, Rajasthan and Assam.
Low	10.01-20.00	10	28.57	3	10.00	Uttarakhand, Meghalaya and Dadra & Nagar Haveli.
Moderate	20.01-30.00	8	22.86	3	10.00	Uttar Pradesh, Jharkhand and Chhattisgarh.
Moder. High	30.01-40.00	Nil	Nil	6	20.00	Tripura, Tamilnadu, Madhya Pradesh, Gujarat, Karnataka, and Orissa.
High	40.01-50.00	1	2.86	4	13.33	Kerala, Andhra Pradesh, West Bengal and Maharashtra.
Very High	Above 50.01	Nil	Nil	1	3.33	Bihar.
Total		**35**	**100.00**	**30**	**100.00**	

Source: Anon. 2001a.

TABLE 2.40

Distribution of States/ UTs by Ranges of Agricultural Labourers (Females) of Total Population in India, 2001

Zone/Region	*Ranges of Agri. Labo. (%)*	*All Castes Population*		*S. Tribe Population*		*States/UTs*
		(No.)	*(%)*	*(No.)*	*(%)*	
Very Low	Below 10.00	13	37.14	10	33.33	Jammu & Kashmir, Sikkim, Himachal Pradesh, Goa, Nagaland, Arunachal Pradesh, Manipur, Mizoram, Andaman & Nicobar Islands and Lakshadweep.
Low	10.01-20.00	4	11.43	3	10.00	Daman & Diu, Uttarakhand, and Assam.
Moderate	20.01-30.00	4	11.43	3	10.00	Rajasthan, Meghalaya and Dadra & Nagar Haveli.
Moder. High	30.01-40.00	6	17.14	2	6.67	Uttar Pradesh and Jharkhand.
High	40.01-50.00	5	14.29	4	13.33	Tripura, Tamilnadu, Madhya Pradesh and Chhattisgarh.
Very High	Above 50.01	3	8.57	8	26.67	Gujarat, Karnataka, Orissa, Bihar, Kerala, Andhra Pradesh, West Bengal and Maharashtra.
Total		**35**	**100.00**	**30**	**100.00**	

Source: Anon. 2001a.

TABLE 2.41

Distribution of States/ UTs by Ranges of Household Industries Workers (Persons) of Total Population in India, 2001

Zone/Region	*Ranges of H.H.I. (%)*	*All Castes Population*		*S. Tribe Population*		*States/UTs*
		(No.)	*(%)*	*(No.)*	*(%)*	
Low	Below 2.00	9	25.71	12	40.00	Himachal Pradesh, Rajasthan, Sikkim, Mizoram, Arunachal Pradesh, Chhattisgarh, Madhya Pradesh, Gujarat, Daman & Diu, Maharashtra, Andhra Pradesh, and Dadra & Nagar Haveli.
Moderate	2.01-4.00	15	42.86	13	43.33	Jammu & Kashmir, Goa, Nagaland, Tripura, Tamilnadu, Kerala, Assam, West Bengal, Karnataka, Bihar, Uttar Pradesh, Meghalaya and Jharkhand.
High	4.01-6.00	8	22.86	2	6.67	Manipur and Orissa.
Very High	Above 6.01	3	8.57	3	10.00	Andaman & Nicobar Islands, Lakshadweep and Uttarakhand.
Total		**35**	**100.00**	**30**	**100.00**	

Source: Anon. 2001a.

TABLE 2.42

Distribution of States/ UTs by Ranges of Household Industries Workers (Males) of Total Population in India, 2001

Zone/Region	*Ranges of H.H.I (%)*	*All Castes Population*		*Scheduled Tribe Population*		
		(No.)	*(%)*	*(No.)*	*(%)*	*States/UTs*
Low	Below 2.00	13	37.14	21	70.00	Himachal Pradesh, Rajasthan, Sikkim, Mizoram, Arunachal Pradesh, Chhattisgarh, Madhya Pradesh, Gujarat, Daman & Diu, Maharashtra, Andhra Pradesh, Dadra & Nagar Haveli, Meghalaya, Nagaland, Kerala, Jammu & Kashmir, Tripura, Tamilnadu, Karnataka,
Moderate	2.01-4.00	17	48.57	6	20.00	Uttarakhand, Uttar Pradesh, Orissa, Manipur, Bihar and Jharkhand.
High	4.01-6.00	5	14.29	2	6.67	Lakshadweep and Goa
Very High	Above 6.01	Nil	Nil	1	3.33	Andaman & Nicobar Islands.
Total		**35**	**100.00**	**30**	**100.00**	

Source: Anon. 2001a.

of states by the ranges of other total, male and female workers of all castes and tribal population.

Table 2.44 shows that 20% states have less than 15% other workers to total tribal workers. About 26.67% states have more than 35.01% males other worker while 26.67 states have more than 25% female of other workers category (Tables 2.45 and 2.46).

One third states have more female other workers than the national average. Out of total tribal workers in Indian urban centres about 6.5 % persons are registered as cultivators which are higher than the all castes cultivators (2.8%). It also reflects that more tribals in urban areas are still in cultivation. The percentage of urban tribal cultivators varies from nil in Goa, Lakshadweep, Andaman and Nicobar Islands to maximum 31.3% in Dadra and Nagar Haveli. Female tribal cultivators in urban areas are more (8.7%) than the male (5.6%) cultivators Tables 2.47-2.59 give the distribution of states of India by the ranges of persons, males and female tribal and all castes urban cultivators. More than 50% cultivators have less than 6% persons, males and females cultivators in urban workers. Out of the total tribal workers in urban areas of the country 12.4, 9.2 and 19.8 % persons, males and females are respectively recorded as agricultural labourers which are also higher than the all castes population in the same category.

The maximum tribal agricultural labourers in urban areas are found in Bihar state. Tables 2.50-2.52 give the distribution of states of India by the ranges of total, male and female tribals and all castes urban agricultural labourers. More than 70% states have less agricultural population than the national average. Similarly more than 50% states have less than 5% urban tribal labourers engage in cultivation.

Tables 2.53-2.55 reflect that the participation of tribal population is lower in the household industries than the all castes population. About 2.9 % urban tribal population is registered as workers of household industries while 5.2% of all castes urban population is engaged in same profession. Table 2.55

TABLE 2.43

Distribution of States/ UTs by Ranges of Household Industries Workers (Females) of Total Population in India, 2001

Zone/Region	*Ranges of H.H.I (%)*	*All Castes Population*		*Scheduled Tribe Population*		
		(No.)	*(%)*	*(No.)*	*(%)*	*States/UTs*
Low	Below 2.00	6	17.14	12	40.00	Himachal Pradesh, Rajasthan, Sikkim, Mizoram, Arunachal Pradesh, Chhattisgarh, Madhya Pradesh, Gujarat, Daman & Diu, Maharashtra, Goa and Dadra & Nagar Haveli.
Moderate	2.01-4.00	10	28.57	9	30.00	Jammu & Kashmir, Tripura, Tamil-nadu, Karnataka, Uttar Pradesh, Jharkhand, Meghalaya, Andhra Pradesh, and Nagaland.
High	4.01-6.00	4	11.43	2	6.67	Kerala and West Bengal.
Very High	Above 6.01	15	42.86	7	23.33	Assam, Lakshadweep, Uttarakhand, Orissa, Manipur, Andaman & Nicobar Islands and Bihar.
Total		**35**	**100.00**	**30**	**100.00**	

Source: Anon, 2001a.

TABLE 2.44

Distribution of States/ UTs by Ranges of Other Workers (Persons) of Total Population in India, 2001

Zone/Region	*Ranges of Other. Work (%)*	*All Castes Population*		*Scheduled Tribe Population*		
		(No.)	*(%)*	*(No.)*	*(%)*	*States/UTs*
Very Low	Below 15.00	Nil	Nil	6	20.00	Bihar, Orissa, Andhra Pradesh, Jharkhand, Chhattisgarh, and Madhya Pradesh.
Low	15.01-20.00	1	2.86	6	20.00	Rajasthan, Uttarakhand, Assam, Tripura, Maharashtra, and Gujarat.
Moderate	20.01-25.00	2	5.71	8	26.66	Himachal Pradesh, Uttar Pradesh, Arunachal Pradesh, Karnataka, Manipur, West Bengal, Nagaland and Tamilnadu.
Moder.High	25.01-30.00	4	11.43	2	6.67	Meghalaya and Dadra & Nagar Haveli.
High	30.01-35.00	3	8.57	2	6.67	Jammu & Kashmir and Mizoram.
Very High	Above 35.01	25	71.43	6	20.00	Sikkim, Daman & Diu, Goa, Kerala, Lakshadweep, and Andaman & Nicobar Islands.
Total		**35**	**100.00**	**30**	**100.00**	

TABLE 2.45

Distribution of States/ UTs by Ranges of Other Workers (Males) of Total Population in India, 2001

Zone/Region	*Ranges of Other Work (%)*	*All Castes Population*		*Scheduled Tribe Population*		
		(No.)	*(%)*	*(No.)*	*(%)*	*States/UTs*
Very Low	Below 15.00	Nil	Nil	3	10.00	Bihar, Chhattisgarh and Madhya Pradesh.
Low	15.01-20.00	Nil	Nil	3	10.00	Orissa, Andhra Pradesh and Jharkhand.
Moderate	20.01-25.00	1	2.86	7	23.33	Rajasthan, Uttarakhand, Assam, Tripura, Maharashtra, Uttar Pradesh and Gujarat.
Moder.High	25.01-30.00	Nil	Nil	7	23.33	Arunachal Pradesh, Nagaland, Meghalaya, Karnataka, Manipur, West Bengal, and Tamilnadu.
High	30.01-35.00	3	8.57	2	6.67	Himachal Pradesh and Jammu & Kashmir.
Very High	Above 35.01	31	88.57	8	26.67	Sikkim, Daman & Diu, Goa, Kerala, Lakshadweep, Mizoram, Dadra & Nagar Haveli and Andaman and Nicobar Islands.
Total		**35**	**100.00**	**30**	**100.00**	

Source: Anon. 2001a.

TABLE 2.46

Distribution of States/ UTs by Ranges of Other Workers (Females) of Total Population in India, 2001

Zone/Region	*Ranges of Other Work (%)*	*All Castes Population*		*Scheduled Tribe Population*		
		(No.)	*(%)*	*(No.)*	*(%)*	*States/UTs*
Very Low	Below 10.00	3	8.57	9	30.00	Uttarakhand, Rajasthan, Bihar, Chhattisgarh, Jharkhand, Madhya Pradesh, Andhra Pradesh, Maharashtra and Himachal Pradesh.
Low	10.01-15.00	5	14.29	7	23.33	Arunachal Pradesh, Nagaland, Assam, Tripura, Orissa, Gujarat and Dadra & Nagar Haveli.
Moderate	15.01-20.00	6	17.14	4	13.33	Uttar Pradesh, Karnataka, Manipur and Tamilnadu.
High	20.01-25.00	1	2.86	2	6.67	Meghalaya and West Bengal.
Very High	Above 25.01	20	57.14	8	26.67	Sikkim, Daman & Diu, Kerala, Lakshadweep, Mizoram, J. & K., Goa and Andaman & Nicobar Islands.
Total		**35**	**100.00**	**30**	**100.00**	

Source: Anon. 2001a.

TABLE 2.47

Distribution of States/ UTs by Ranges of Cultivators (Persons) of Urban Population in India, 2001

Zone/Region	*Ranges of Cultivators (%)*	*All Castes Population*		*Scheduled Tribe Population*		
		(No.)	*(%)*	*(No.)*	*(%)*	*States/UTs*
Very Low	Below 3.00	19	54.29	14	46.67	Himachal Pradesh, Uttar Pradesh, Bihar, Sikkim, Tripura, West Bengal, Daman & Diu, Goa, Lakshadweep, Kerala, Maharashtra, Andhra Pradesh, Gujarat and Andaman & Nicobar Islands.
Low	3.01-6.00	12	34.29	4	13.33	Jharkhand, Madhya Pradesh, Orissa and Tamilnadu.
Moderate	6.01-9.00	2	5.71	7	23.34	Jammu & Kashmir, Nagaland, Assam, Meghalaya, Karnataka, Manipur and Chhattisgarh.
High	9.01-12.00	Nil	Nil	1	3.33	Uttarakhand.
Very High	Above 12.01	2	5.71	4	13.33	Rajasthan, Arunachal Pradesh, Mizoram and Dadra & Nagar Haveli.
Total		**35**	**100.00**	**30**	**100.00**	

Source: Anon, 2001a.

TABLE 2.48

Distribution of States/ UTs by Ranges of Cultivators (Males) of Urban Population in India, 2001

Zone/Region	*Ranges of Cultivator (%)*	*All Castes Population*		*Scheduled Tribe Population*		
		(No.)	*(%)*	*(No.)*	*(%)*	*States/UTs*
Very Low	Below 3.00	24	68.57	14	46.67	Himachal Pradesh, Uttar Pradesh, Bihar, Sikkim, Tripura, West Bengal, Daman & Diu, Goa, Lakshadweep, Kerala, Maharashtra, Andhra Pradesh, Gujarat and Andaman & Nicobar Islands.
Low	3.01-6.00	9	25.72	6	20.00	Jharkhand, Madhya Pradesh, Orissa, Tamilnadu. Nagaland and Meghalaya.
Moderate	6.01-9.00	Nil	Nil	7	23.33	Jammu & Kashmir, Assam, Uttarakhand, Karnataka, Manipur, Arunachal Pradesh and Chhattisgarh.
High	9.01-12.00	Nil	Nil	1	3.33	Rajasthan.
Very High	Above 12.01	2	5.71	2	6.67	Mizoram and Dadra & Nagar Haveli.
Total		**35**	**100.00**	**30**	**100.00**	

Source: Anon. 2001a.

shows that the participation rate of female workers in both the segments is higher than their male counterpart. It reflects that the more female are engaged in cottage industries which are established at home.

Samples are recorded as other worker which is lower than all castes population (72.5%). The percentage of other workers in urban population varies from 58.6% in Dadra and Nagar Haveli to maximum 100% in Andaman and Nicobar Islands. Ninety percent all castes urban males are other workers. The percentage of household industries workers in urban area varies from nil in Andaman and Nicobar Islands to 15.9 % in Uttarakhand state. Similarly highest 43.1% urban tribal females of Uttarakhand are engaged in woollen/cottage industries which are established in the houses. These industries are generally situated in Pithoragarh, Chamoli, Bageshwar and Uttarkashi district of the state.

The participation rate of other workers in urban areas is more in all castes population than tribal population. About 78.2% urban tribals are registered as other workers which is lower than the all castes other workers (87.3%). On an average of the country, only 66.3% urban female registered as other workers while 83.4 % of male tribals are in the same category.

Tables 2.56-2.58 give the distribution of states by the ranges of other workers (person, male and female) of tribal and all castes population. More than 73.33, 76.67 and 63.33% states have respectively more persons, males and females of urban tribal workers than the national averages. About 16.67% states have more than 95% other workers in urban tribal population. Table 2.34 shows that only Pondicherry has more agricultural labourers (47.1%) in all castes population than other workers (44.1%) in the urban areas. It is due to impact of agricultural colonization. About 69.6% urban tribal workers are registered as other workers in Pondicherry.

Summary

The tribal community and their habitats constitute very significant part of backward people and regions of the country respectively. They comprise about 18 per cent of country's land

TABLE 2.49

Distribution of States/ UTs by Ranges of Cultivators (Females) of Urban Population in India, 2001

Zone/Region	*Ranges of Cultivators (%)*	*All Castes Population*		*Scheduled Tribe Population*		
		(No.)	*(%)*	*(No.)*	*(%)*	*States/UTs*
Very Low	Below 3.00	17	48.57	10	33.33	Bihar, Sikkim, Tripura, Daman & Diu, Goa, Lakshadweep, Maharashtra, Andhra Pradesh, Kerala and Andaman & Nicobar Islands.
Low	3.01-6.00	6	17.14	8	26.67	Himachal Pradesh, Uttar Pradesh, West Bengal, Gujarat, Jharkhand, Orissa, Tamilnadu and Karnataka.
Moderate	6.01-9.00	5	14.29	3	10.00	Madhya Pradesh, Manipur and Meghalaya.
High	9.01-12.00	4	11.43	2	6.67	Assam and Chhattisgarh.
Very High	Above 12.01	3	8.57	7	23.33	Nagaland, Jammu & Kashmir, Uttarakhand, Rajasthan, Arunachal Pradesh, Mizoram and Dadra & Nagar Haveli.
Total		**35**	**100.00**	**30**	**100.00**	

Source: Anon. 2001a.

TABLE 2.50

Distribution of States/ UTs by Ranges of Agricultural Laborers (Persons) of Urban Population in India, 2001

Zone/Region	*Ranges of Agri. Labo. (%)*	*All Castes Population*		*Scheduled Tribe Population*		
		(No.)	*(%)*	*(No.)*	*(%)*	*States/UTs*
Very Low	Below 5.00	26	74.29	16	53.32	Nagaland, Jammu & Kashmir, Uttarakhand, Sikkim, Arunachal Pradesh, Tamilnadu, and, Uttar Pradesh, Manipur, Tripura, Daman & Diu, Goa, Lakshadweep, Kerala, Assam, Himachal Pradesh and Andaman & Nicobar Islands.
Low	5.01-10.00	7	20	5	16.67	Rajasthan, Mizoram, Dadra & Nagar Haveli, Meghalaya and Jharkhand.
Moderate	10.01-15.00	2	5.71	5	16.67	West Bengal, Orissa, Chhattisgarh, Gujarat and Maharashtra.
High	15.01-20.00	Nil	Nil	2	6.67	Andhra Pradesh and Karnataka.
Very High	Above 20.01	Nil	Nil	2	6.67	Bihar and Madhya Pradesh.
Total		**35**	**100.00**	**30**	**100.00**	

Source: Anon. 2001a.

TABLE 2.51

Distribution of States/ UTs by Ranges of Agricultural Labourers (Males) of Urban Population in India, 2001

Zone/Region	*Ranges of Agri. Labo. (%)*	*All Castes Population*		*Scheduled Tribe Population*		
		(No.)	*(%)*	*(No.)*	*(%)*	*States/UTs*
Very Low	Below 5.00	31	88.57	17	56.67	Nagaland, Jammu & Kashmir, Uttarakhand, Sikkim, Rajasthan, Arunachal Pradesh, Tamilnadu, and Uttar Pradesh, Manipur, Tripura, Daman & Diu, Goa, Lakshadweep, Kerala, Assam, Himachal Pradesh and Andaman & Nicobar Islands.
Low	5.01-10.00	3	8.57	6	20.00	Mizoram, Dadra & Nagar Haveli, Meghalaya, Jharkhand, Orissa and Maharashtra.
Moderate	10.01-15.00	1	2.86	6	20.00	West Bengal, Chhattisgarh, Gujarat, Madhya Pradesh, Andhra Pradesh and Karnataka.
High	15.01-20.00	Nil	Nil	Nil	Nil	Nil
Very High	Above 20.01	Nil	Nil	1	3.33	Bihar.
Total		**35**	**100.00**	**30**	**100.00**	

Source: Anon. 2001a.

TABLE 2.52

Distribution of States/ UTs by Ranges of Agricultural Labourers (Females) of Urban Population in India, 2001

Zone/Region	Ranges of Agri. Labo. (%)	All Castes Population		Scheduled Tribe Population		
		(No.)	(%)	(No.)	(%)	States/UTs
Very Low	Below 5.00	16	45.71	14	46.67	Nagaland, Jammu & Kashmir, Uttarakhand, Sikkim, Assam, Arunachal Pradesh, Tripura, Daman & Diu, Goa, Lakshadweep Uttar Pradesh, Manipur, Himachal Pradesh and Andaman & Nicobar Islands.
Low	5.01-10.00	9	25.71	1	3.33	Meghalaya.
Moderate	10.01-15.00	8	22.86	4	13.33	Mizoram, Rajasthan, Jharkhand and Kerala.
High	15.01-20.00	1	2.86	2	6.67	Dadra & Nagar Haveli and Gujarat.
Very High	Above 20.01	1	2.86	9	30.00	Orissa, Maharashtra, West Bengal, Chhattisgarh, Madhya Pradesh, Tamilnadu, Bihar, Andhra Pradesh and Karnataka.
Total		**35**	**100.00**	**30**	**100.00**	

Source: Anon. 2001a.

TABLE 2.53

Distribution of States/ UTs by Ranges of Household Industrial Workers (Persons) of Urban Population in India, 2001

Zone/Region	*Ranges of H.H. Ind. W. (%)*	*All Castes Population*		*Scheduled Tribe Population*		
		(No.)	*(%)*	*(No.)*	*(%)*	*States/UTs*
Low	Below 2.00	9	25.71	13	43.33	Jammu & Kashmir, Sikkim, Himachal Pradesh, Meghalaya, Arunachal Pradesh, Tripura, Daman & Diu, Gujarat, Dadra & Nagar Haveli, Andaman & Nicobar Islands, Rajasthan, West Bengal and Jharkhand.
Moderate	2.01-4.00	14	40.00	10	33.33	Nagaland, Assam, Goa, Mizoram, Kerala, Bihar, Orissa, Maharashtra, Chhattisgarh and M.P.
High	4.01-6.00	5	14.29	2	6.67	Manipur and Tamilnadu.
Very High	Above 6.01	7	20	5	16.67	Uttarakhand, U.P., Andhra Pradesh, Karnataka, Lakshadweep.
Total		**35**	**100.00**	**30**	**100.00**	

Source: Anon. 2001a.

and 8.2 per cent of its population. As per 2001 census country's largest tribal population is found in Madhya Pradesh (14.51%). Out of total thirty states, one third (33.33%) have less than 0.5% country's population. But their largest proportion to total state population among all the states is found in Mizoram (94.5%). The average household size of the scheduled tribe in India is 5.1 persons per household which is less than the all castes population average (5.3). The household size varies from 3.9 persons/ household in Goa to 6.6 persons/household in Uttar Pradesh. Average sex ratio of the tribal population of India is 978 in 2001 which is higher than the sex ratio of all castes population. Total sex ratio in tribal population ranges between 893 in Goa to 1028 in Dadra and Nagar Haveli in 2001. India has registered 20.34 % growth of population during the decade 1991-2001 which is lower than the total growth of tribal population in the same decade (24.45%). Total sex ratio in tribal population ranges between 893 in Goa to 1028 in Dadra and Nagar Haveli in 2001. The sex ratio below the age of 6 years tribal population in India is registered 973 which are too high from the same segment of total population (927). The sex ratio of this segment varies from minimum 915 in Goa to maximum 1009 in Dadra and Nagar Haveli. As per census 2001 Indian tribal population has registered only 47.1% literacy which is much lower than the literacy of total population at national level (64.8%). The tribal literacy varies minimum from 28.2% in Bihar to maximum 89.3% in Mizoram state. The highest proportion of male tribal literates has been registered in Lakshadweep (92.2%) followed by Mizoram (91.7%). Likewise total tribal literacy the lowest proportion of male tribal literates was recorded in Bihar (39.8%) which is much lower than the national average (59.2%). About 60% states have registered the high male literacy than the national average (59.2%). Average female literacy of India is registered only 34.8% which is too less than the all castes female literacy (53.7%). Bihar has least proportion of female literates (15.5%). It is observed that there are contiguous patches of states with low literacy rates in the tribal population of the country. The states situated in the relatively more rugged topography and adverse climate have also recorded very low literacy rates while states having high literacy associated with comparatively high level of

TABLE 2.54

Distribution of States/ UTs by Ranges of Household Industrial Workers (Males) of Urban Population in India, 2001

Zone/Region	*Ranges of H.H. Ind.W (%)*	*All Castes Population*		*Scheduled Tribe Population*		
		(No.)	*(%)*	*(No.)*	*(%)*	*States/UTs*
Low	Below 2.00	15	42.86	21	70.00	Jammu & Kashmir, Sikkim, Himachal Pradesh, Meghalaya Arunachal Pradesh, Tripura, Daman & Diu, Gujarat, Dadra & Nagar Haveli, Andaman & Nicobar Islands, Rajasthan, West Bengal, Mizoram, Kerala, Assam, Jharkhand, Orissa, Maharashtra, Chhattisgarh, Madhya Pradesh, and Manipur,
Moderate	2.01-4.00	13	37.14	6	20.00	Nagaland, Goa, Bihar, Uttarakhand, Karnataka and Tamilnadu.
High	4.01-6.00	6	17.14	3	10.00	Uttar Pradesh, Andhra Pradesh and Lakshadweep.
Very High	Above 6.01	1	2.86	Nil	Nil	Nil
Total		**35**	**100.00**	**30**	**100.00**	

Source: Anon. 2001a.

TABLE 2.55

Distribution of States/ UTs by Ranges of Household Industrial Workers (Females) of Urban Population in India, 2001

Zone/Region	*Ranges of H.H.Ind.W (%)*	*All Castes Population*		*Scheduled Tribe Population*		
		(No.)	*(%)*	*(No.)*	*(%)*	*States/UTs*
Low	Below 2.00	3	8.57	10	33.33	Jammu & Kashmir, Sikkim, Himachal Pradesh, Meghalaya, Tripura, Daman & Diu, Gujarat, Dadra & Nagar Haveli, Goa, and Andaman & Nicobar Islands.
Moderate	2.01-4.00	6	17.15	8	26.67	Arunachal Pradesh, Rajasthan, West Bengal, Mizoram, Kerala, Jharkhand, Madhya Pradesh and Bihar.
High	4.01-6.00	3	8.57	1	3.33	Chhattisgarh.
Very High	Above 6.01	23	65.71	11	36.67	Nagaland, Uttarakhand, Karnataka, Orissa, Maharashtra, Uttar Pradesh, Andhra Pradesh, Lakshadweep, Assam, Tamilnadu and Manipur.
Total		**35**	**100.00**	**30**	**100.00**	

Source: Anon. 2001a.

TABLE 2.56

Distribution of States/ UTs by Ranges of Other Workers (Persons) of Urban Population in India, 2001

Zone/Region	*Ranges of Other Work (%)*	*All Castes Population*		*Scheduled Tribe Population*		
		(No.)	*(%)*	*(No.)*	*(%)*	*States/UTs*
Very Low	Below 75.00	2	5.71	8	26.66	Madhya Pradesh, Bihar, Uttarakhand, Karnataka, Mizoram, Andhra Pradesh, Tamilnadu and Dadra & Nagar Haveli.
Low	75.01-80.00	2	5.71	2	6.67	Chhattisgarh and Rajasthan.
Moderate	80.01-85.00	2	5.71	6	20.00	Orissa, West Bengal, Manipur, Maharashtra, Kerala and Gujarat.
Mode. High	85.01-90.00	7	20	7	23.33	Jharkhand, Jammu & Kashmir, Uttar Pradesh, Nagaland, Arunachal Pradesh, Meghalaya and Assam.
High	90.01-95.00	17	48.58	2	6.67	Tripura and Lakshadweep, Sik-
Very High	Above 95.01	5	14.29	5	16.67	kim, Himachal Pradesh, Andman & Diu, Goa and Andaman and Nicobar Islands.
Total		35	100.00	30	100.00	

Source: Anon. 2001.

TABLE 2.57

Distribution of States/ UTs by Ranges of Other Workers (Males) of Urban Population in India, 2001

Zone/Region	*Ranges of Other Work (%)*	*All Castes Population*		*Scheduled Tribe Population*		
		(No.)	*(%)*	*(No.)*	*(%)*	*States/UTs*
Very Low	Below 75.00	2	5.71	4	13.33	Mizoram, Dadra & Nagar Haveli, Bihar and Tamilnadu.
Low	75.01-80.00	1	2.86	2	6.67	Madhya Pradesh and Karnataka.
Moderate	80.01-85.00	1	2.86	4	13.33	Andhra Pradesh, Chhattisgarh, Orissa and Kerala.
Mode. High	85.01-90.00	3	8.57	11	36.67	Jharkhand, Jammu & Kashmir, U.P., Uttarakhand, Goa, Rajasthan, West Bengal, Manipur, Mahara shtra, Gujarat, Meghalaya and Assam.
High	90.01-95.00	18	51.43	4	13.33	Arunachal Pradesh, Nagaland, Tripura and Lakshadweep.
Very High	Above 95.01	10	28.57	5	16.67	Sikkim, Himachal Pradesh, Daman & Diu, Goa and Andaman and Nicobar Islands.
Total		**35**	**100.00**	**30**	**100.00**	

Source: Anon. 2001a.

TABLE 2.58

Distribution of States/ UTs by Ranges of Other Workers (Females) of Urban Population in India, 2001

Zone/Region	*Ranges of Other Work (%)*	*All Castes Population*		*Scheduled Tribe Population*		
		(No.)	*(%)*	*(No.)*	*(%)*	*States/UTs*
Very Low	Below 60.00	3	8.57	8	26.67	Uttarakhand, Rajasthan, Madhya Pradesh, Karnataka, Mizoram, Dadra & Nagar Haveli, Bihar and Tamilnadu.
Low	60.01-70.00	6	17.14	4	13.33	Andhra Pradesh, Chhattisgarh, Orissa and Maharashtra.
Moderate	70.01-80.00	7	20.00	8	26.67	Jammu & Kashmir, Uttar Pradesh, Gujarat, Manipur, Arunachal Pradesh, Nagaland, West Bengal and Assam.
High	80.01-90.00	14	40	4	13.33	Jharkhand, Kerala, Meghalaya and Lakshadweep.
Very High	Above 90.01	5	14.29	6	20.00	Tripura, Sikkim, Himachal Pradesh, Daman & Diu, Goa and Andaman & Nicobar Islands.
Total		**35**	**100.00**	**30**	**100.00**	

Source: Anon. 2001a.

urbanization and high proportion of population in secondary and tertiary jobs. There is an urgent need to improve the quality of education than the quantity of the literates. Average 24.4% points gap between male and female literacy of the total tribal population in the country has been registered in 2001 census which is slightly higher than the all castes population (21.6%). The gap between male and female literacy rate varies from minimum 4.3% in Meghalaya followed by Mizoram (4.8%) to maximum 35.9% in Rajasthan. It is observed that the states with high level of total, male and female literacy have registered fewer gaps between male and female literacy.

The percentage of total workers in tribal population has recorded higher 49.1% in comparison to the total population 39.1% in the country as a whole. The percentage of total workers in the tribal population varies minimum 22.9% in Lakshadweep to maximum 54.9% in Tamilnadu. Similarly the work participation rates of male population varies minimum 38.6% in Lakshadweep to 60.1% in Tamilnadu about 53% tribal males of India are registered as a workers in 2001 census while 51.7% males of all castes population are considered as workers. Out of total tribal female population only 44.8% are considered as workers which are higher than the females of all castes population as 25.6%. The work participation rates of females vary from minimum 7.10% in Lakshadweep to maximum 52.7% in Himachal Pradesh. Out of the total tribal workers of the country 36.9%, 30.3% and 19.8% persons, males and females are respectively registered as agriculture labourers. Less than 3% tribal workers are found in household industries while 4.2%, 3.2% and 6.5% person, males and females of all castes workers are registered in this occupation. Out of the total tribal workers 16.3% person are registered as other workers. Out of the total male workers 20.6% males are considered as other workers which are less than the half of all castes male workers. Similarly about 11.1% female workers are registered in other workers category while 21.71% females of all castes population are found in this category. It reflects that the percentage of female workers in both tribal and non-tribal categories is still very low. Study concludes that the plans for the development of tribal population should be launched at grass root level. Educational and infrastructural facilities should be provided in the tribal areas. There is an urgent need of political will to ensure the grass root people participation in implementation of tribal welfare programmes.

NOTE

1. There is confusion on exact number about the varieties/types of tribes in the country, the reason being there is no single list at the central level and each state/UT has its own list. Just adding the numbers of tribes that have been scheduled in each state/ UT does not serve the purpose and the total number thus arrived should not be taken as total number of tribes in the country. For example, Santhals have been notified in Orissa, Bihar and West Bengal, similarly, Bhils, has been notified in Gujarat, Rajasthan, Maharashtra, Madhya Pradesh etc. Likewise Bhotia, Buksa, Tharu, Jaunsari, Gonds, and many other tribes have been notified in more than one state. Therefore, there is lot of multiple counting. There are five states/UTs like Haryana, Punjab, Chandigarh, Delhi and Pondicherry, where no tribes have been notified as scheduled. However, there are about 250-300 major tribal groups in the country.

3

Physical Setting of Uttarakhand

Physiography

Uttarakhand comprises of all the five latitudinal physiographic-geological zones i.e., the Tarai-Bhabar, the Shiwalik with duns, the Lesser Himalaya, the Great Himalaya and the Trans-Himalaya. The northern fringe of Indo-Gangetic plains, waterlogged in older times is knows as Tarai. Due to the availability of fertile soil, hot climate coupled with abundant water, this 10-25 km. wide, once densely forested Tarai belt has been the home land of Tharus, Buksas and Gujjars, and is largely reclaimed for agriculture. Due to introduction of new agrarian techniques by the enterprising hardworking refuges from Pakistan and Bangladesh, retired army personnel and freedom fighters of Uttarakhand, the Tarai today is one of the most developed parts of the country. In the Tarai, Bhabar, Dun and adjoining Siwalik belts, there are about 13% of rural settlements and 60% of urban centres including Dehradun, Rishikesh, Kotdwar, Kalagarh, Ramnagar, Kashipur, Haldwani-cum-Kathgodam, Tanakpur, Khatima, Rudrapur, Sitarganj, Gadarpur, Kichha, Bajpur, Jaspur, Pantnagar, (Nagla) etc. There are several water reservoirs Nanaksagar, Bahgul, Haripura, Tumeria and Kalagarh.

With an altitude varying from 700 to 1200 m, the Shiwalik, like the Bhabar region, is sparsely inhabited because of thick vegetal cover and water scarcity. The gravel filled, almost plain latitudinal areas in the Shiwalik domain are known as Duns. There are five duns, namely, *Dehradun* between Yamuna and Ganga, *Chaukhamba* and *Kothari* duns between Ganga and Western Ramganga, *Patlidun* between Western Ramganga and Kosi, and *Kotadun* between Kosi and Baur. Course gravels in which all streams

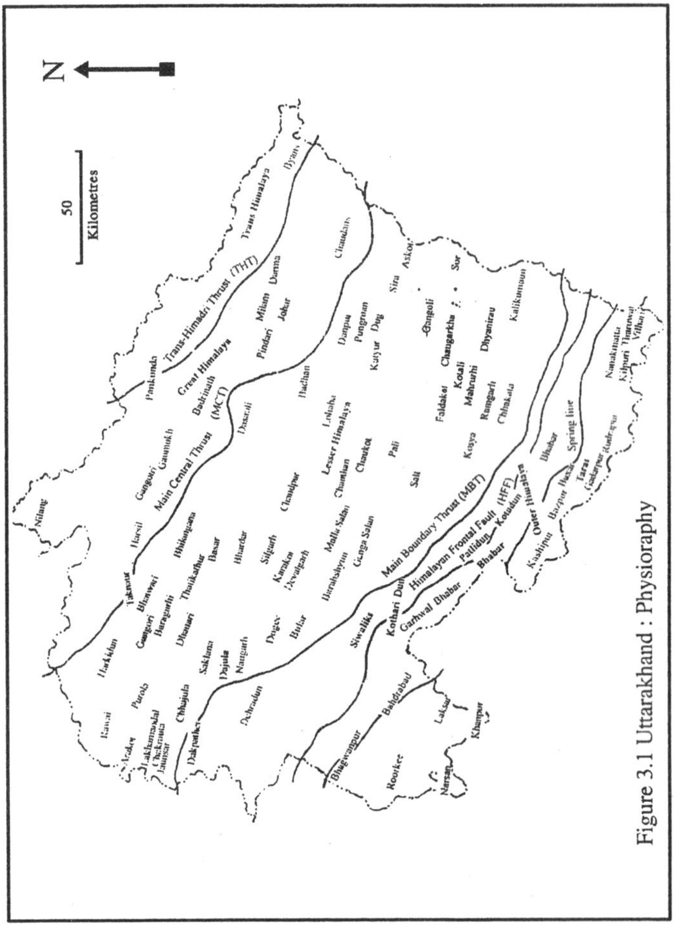

Figure 3.1 Uttarakhand : Physiorаphy

FIG. 3.1 : Uttarakhand : Physiorophy

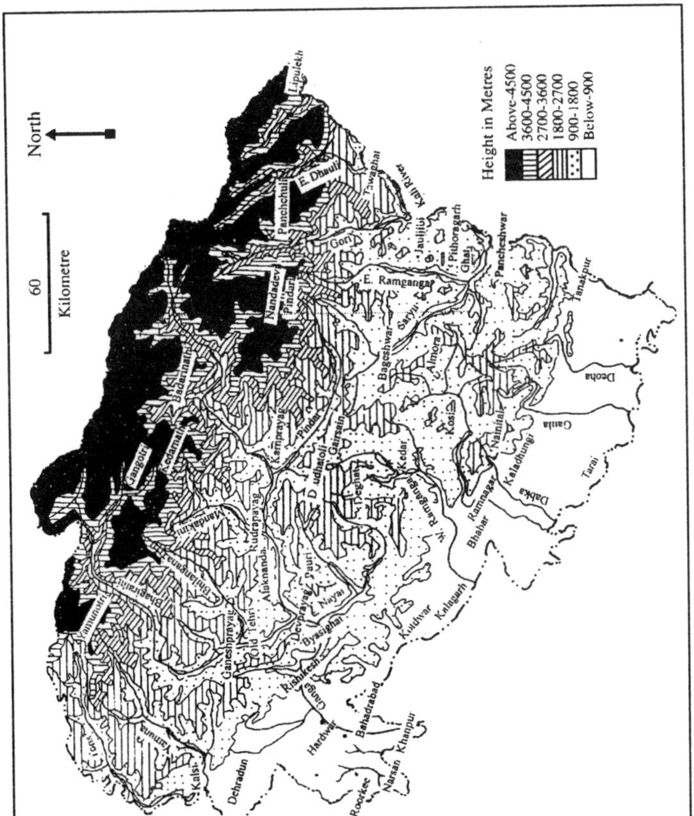

FIG. 3.2 : Uttarakhand : Relief

disappear form a 10-20 km wide belt between the Shiwalik and Tarai known as Bhabar. Consequently, the belt faces acute problem of water scarcity.

North of the Shiwalik hills the 70-km wide Lesser Himalaya having relatively milder terrain. This is the densely populated belt of Uttarakhand. The urban centres (37%) of Dwarahat, Ranikhet, Almora, Bageshwar, Dharchula, Pithoragarh, Lohaghat, Champawat, Bhimtal, Bhawali, Nainital, Lansdown, Narendranagar, Pauri, Srinagar, Tehri, Uttarkashi, Chamba, Mussoorie, Gopeshwar, Joshimath, Karnaprayag, Rudraprayag, Barkot, Purola etc. are located in the Lesser Himalaya. There are about 81% of the rural settlements in the Lesser Himalaya.

The Great Himalayan region in the north is a belt of very high peaks from 3000 m to more than 7000 m in altitude, and of glaciers. It ranges in width from 30 to 50 km. The important peaks include Nandadevi, Panchchuli, Trishul, Kedarnath, Chaukhamba, Badrinath, Bandarpunch and Kamet. Among the glaciers Pindari, Milam, Gangotri and Khatling are the important ones. The harsh and rigorous climatic conditions together with extremely rugged topography are perhaps responsible for scanty habitation. Consequently, there are less than 70 seasonal settlements in the river valleys and *bugyals* (alpine pasture).

The Trans-Himalaya belt is 40 km wide. This is a rain shadow zone, as southeastern monsoon clouds cannot cross the Great Himalaya. The belt is sparsely populated, there being just 20-30 temporary villages of the Bhotia tribes.

Geology

From the geological point of view, the Uttarakhand or Kumaun Lesser Himalaya is divided into five lithotectonic units. These units are demarcated by several thrusts and faults. Most of these faults/thrusts are active. The brief description of the geology/structure is based on Valdiya (1980 and 1988).

1. The Outer Himalaya

The foothill belt of the Lesser Himalaya is made of sandstone, mudstone and subordinate conglomerates of the Middle Miocene

TADLE 3.1

Litho-Tectonic Succession in Uttarakhand

Northern Belt		*Southern Belt*	
Jungbwa Ultrabasics			
——Jungbwa Thrust——			
Kiogarhophiolitic Melange			
—— Kiogarh Thrust ——			
Tethyan Succession			
(Late Precambrian- Late Cetaceous			
—— Trans-Himadri (Malari) Thrust——			
Vaikrita Group			
(Precambrian)			
—Main Central (Vaikarita) Thrust—		Almora Group	
Munsyari Formation		(with 550 + 50 m.y. granite)	
(Early Precambrian)			
—— Munsyari Thrust—		—Almora Thrust—	
(Schuppen Zone)		Ramgarh Group	
Bhatwari- Barkot Formations		(with 1900 + 100 m.y.porphyroids)	
— Bhatwari- Barkot Thrust—		——Ramgarh Thrust——	
Berinag Formation		Krol Succession	
(Precambrian)		(Late Precambrian- lower Cambrian)	
		Subhathu Fm	
		Unidenthu Paleocene (Singtail)	Sirmur Group
		Tal Fm	
		Krol Fm	Mussoorie Group
		Balini Fm	
		Nagthat Fm	Jaunsar Group
		Chandpur Fm	
——Berinag Thrust—		—— Krol or Main Boundary Thrust—	
Tejam Gr.	Mandali Fm.	Siwalik Group	
	Daoban Fm.	(Late Tertiary)	
Damtha Gr.	Rautgara Fm.		
	Chakrata Fm.		
(Precambrian)			
Base not exposed		——Himalayan Front Fault——	
		Ganga plain with Bhabar Fan	
		(Quaternaey Recent)	

Source: Valdiya (1980 and 1988).

to Early Pleistocene age. The Lower Shiwalik consists of fine grained calcareous sub greywacke and sub litharentic alternating with dominant horizons of maroon mudstone and rare Para conglomerates while the Middle Shiwalik consists of predominant coarse-grained sub-litharentic and subordinate Para conglomerate. The Upper Shiwalik sediments comprising boulder conglomerate with maroon mudstone and sandstone. Himalayan Front Fault (HFF) separates Siwalik from the Bhabar. The gravel filled synclinal valleys are known as Duns—Dehra, Chaukhamba, Kothari, Patli and Kota. It include two lithotectonic units—(1) Tarai and Bhabar, and (2) Siwalik.

Lying between the MBT in the south and MCT in the north, the Lesser Himalayan terrain is made of three lithotectonic units:

2. *The Lesser Himalaya*

1. The autochthonous succession of the Precambrian strata forming the larger part of the inner belt.
2. Late Precambrian to early Paleozoic sedimentary rocks formation forming the Krol Nappe includes slates, phylites sandstone, and limestone.
3. The Precambrian metamorphic injected was granite body.

In summing up there are seven main lithological groups namely-Krol Succession, Ramgarh group, Almora Group, Damtha-Tejam group, Bhatwari-Barkot formation, Berinag Formation and Munsyari.

3. *The Great Himalaya*

The Great Himalaya is made of high-grade metamorphic-the Vaikrita group of Precambrian age and intruded extensively by mid Tertiary granite. However, Jhingran referred it Central Crystalline Zone.

4. *The Trans-Himalaya*

Trans-Himadri Thrust-separates the Trans-Himalaya from the Great Himalaya. The rock formations are shattered mylonolized or otherwise complexly folded.

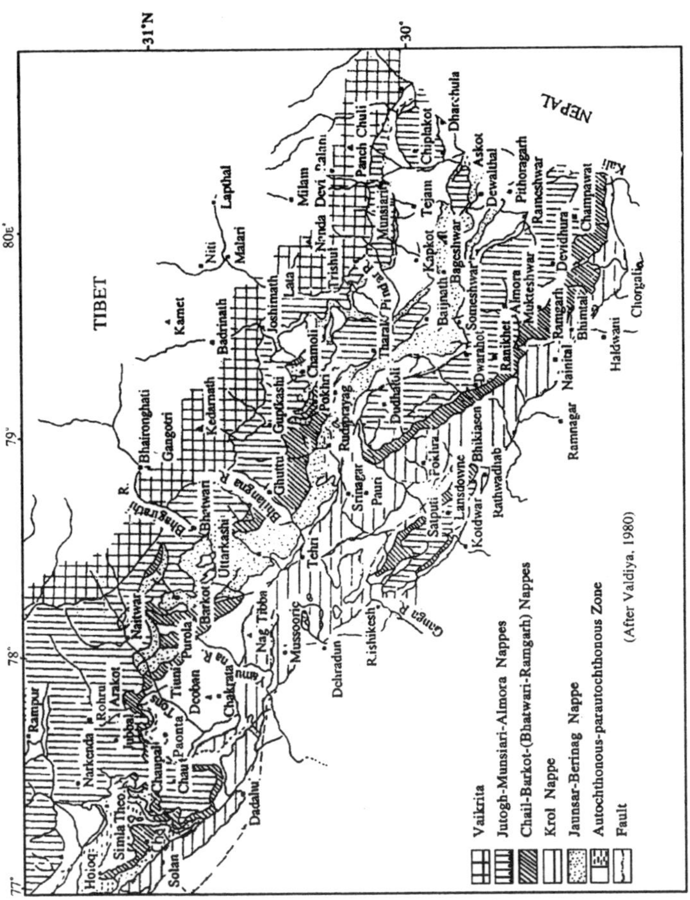

FIG. 3.3 : Uttarakhand : Geology

Peaks

In the Higher Himalayan area there are number of known and unknown important peaks. Some important known peaks are following.

Peaks	*Height (m)*	*District*
Bandarpunch	6316	Uttarkashi
Gangotri	6614	Uttarkashi
Kedarnath	6940	Rudraprayag
Chaukhamba	7318	Chamoli
Kamet	7756	Chamoli
Nandadevi	7816	Chamoli
Dunagiri	7066	Chamoli
Trishul	7120	Chamoli
Nandakot	6861	Chamoli
Srikanth	6728	Chamoli
Badrinath	7140	Chamoli
Meru	6660	Chamoli
Bhrigupanth	6772	Chamoli
Satopanth	7075	Chamoli
Gauri Parvat	6590	Chamoli
Hathi Parvat	6727	Chamoli
Nar	5831	Chamoli
Narayan	5965	Chamoli
Panchchuli	6910	Pithoragarh
Kuti Shangtang	6480	Pithoragarh

Passes

Passes	*Height*	*District*
Chirbatia La	5454	Chamoli
Niti	5070	Chamoli
Shalshal	5000	Chamoli

Belchadhura	5348	Pithoragarh
Kingri Bingri La	5564	Chamoli
Lawedhura	5564	Pithoragarh
Lampiadhura	5533	Pithoragarh
Lipulekh	5122	Pithoragarh
Ralam	6750	Pithoragarh
Keodhura	5439	Pithoragarh
Mansadhura	5600	Pithoragarh
Mana	5450	Chamoli
Muling La	5669	Uttarkashi
Nuwedhura	5650	Pithoragarh
Untadhura	5450	Pithoragarh
Sinla	6600	Pithoragarh
Trail Pass	4530	Bageshwar

Glaciers

There are number of famous glaciers in Uttarakhand. Among them some important and magnificent glaciers are as follows—

Alkapuri, Pindari, Gaumukh, Gangotri, Yamunotri, Ralam, Bamras, Milam, Namik, Khatling, Poting, Arwa, Bhagatkharak, Satopanth, Raktavarna, Swetvarna, Nilamber, Pilapani, Chaturangi, Kedarnath, Kosa, Tata and Sarasut, Ramani, Kurmtoli, Shankapa, Chaulugee, Baling, Nauphe, Guna, Burfu and Syutapani.

Lakes

Nainital, Khurpatal, Bhimtal, Sattal, Naukuchiatal, Punatal, Nal Damyantital, Garurtal, Sariatal, Malwatal, Harishtal, Lokhamtal, Taragtal, Thamorital, Gangapani, Diurital, Dodital, Roopkund, Hemkund, Basukital, Chorbarital, Satopanthtal, Gonatal, Sahastratal, Jaraltal, Masartal, Parvatital, Parital and Aoncharital.

Springs

Badrinath, Madmheshwar, Tapovan, Gaurikund, Kulseni,

Yamunotri, Gangnani, Ralam Kund, Shandaliya Kund and Surya Kund.

Drainage

Uttarakhand is mainly drained by the Ganga and the Kali systems. The Yamuna originates from the Yamunotri hot spring and Saptrishikund on the southwestern slope of the Bandarpunch ridge and flows through the district of Uttarkashi and Dehradun. The Tons is the largest river in respect of volume of water flowing. Bhagirathi and Alaknanda join at Devprayag to make the Ganga River. The Bhilangana is the main tributary of the Bhagirathi that rises from Khatling glacier. Western Dhauli originates at Untadhura and Niti pass on the Indo-Tibet water divide, and joins the Vishnuganga at Vishnuprayag. Saraswati, emanating near Mana Pass, makes the headwaters of the Alaknanda. Pindar (originating from Pindari glacier) and Mandakini (rising in the Kedarnath ridge) are the main tributaries of the Alaknanda. Nayar joining the Ganga from the west at Byasighat, drains the Dudhatoli—Pauri region.

Kali is the largest river in Kumaun both in respect of volume of water as well as extent of the catchment area. It is also largest river in Uttarakhand in respect of length. The Kali originates at Kalapani near the Lipulekh pass and is fed by Kuti, Eastern Dhauli, Gori, Saryu, Lohawati and Ladhiya rivers. Gori emanates from the Milam glacier and Eastern Ramganga from Namik glacier. Eastern Ramganga and Panar are the principal tributaries of the Saryu. Saryu joins the Kali at Pancheswar. Entering the plain at Baramedeo mandi, the Kali known is as Sharda River.

The Western Ramganga rises from the northeast slope of Dudhatoli ridge in Pauri district. Binau the headwater of Western Ramganga takes its rise from the Binsar spring located on the southern slope of Dudhatoli range. It joins the Masangaddi and Western Ramnagar at Deghat and Kedar, respectively. Rising from the Bhatkot ridge, Gagas joins the W. Ramganga at Bhikiasain. The Kosi River rises on the southern slope of Bhatkot-Kausani range and leave Kumaun near Sarkara eventually to join the Western Ramganga.

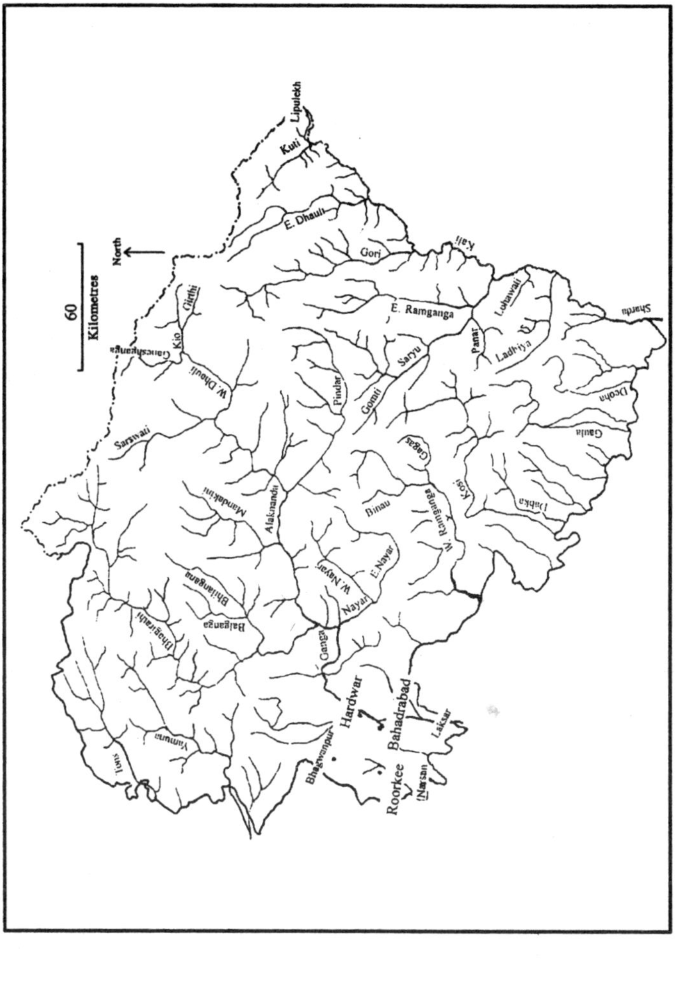

FIG. 3.4 : Uttarakhand Drainage

Minor rivers like Song, Khoh, Rispana, Dhela, Dabka, Baur, Bhakhara, Gaula, Nandhaur and Deoha; drain the outer belt of the Lesser Himalayan domain. Due to the porous nature of Bhabar areas these rivulets become dry and reappear in the Tarai region where these are checked in the form of artificial reservoirs for multipurpose.

Climate

The Tarai-Bhabar and low-lying valleys below 800 m of elevation have hot and humid climate. Between 800-1200 m elevations, it is subtropical, temperate from 1200 to 2000 m, cool temperate between 2000 to 2400 m, cold temperate between 2400 to 3000 m elevations. Above 3000 m elevation, the area experiences alpine climate.

The mean temperate in the January is about 12°C in the sub-mountain belt of Tarai, Bhabar and Duns while 8°C in the inner valleys. June register highest temperatures-around 40°C in Tarai-Bhabar and Dun belts, 24°C in the Lesser Himalayan domain and 15-29°C at higher places. About 80% of the total rainfall occurs in the monsoon months alone. The average annual rainfall is 150 cm in the Tarai-Bhabar and Dun belts, while the Nainital hills receives the highest i.e. 250 cm, then decreasing north-wards in the inner Lesser Himalaya where the average annual rainfall is only 90 cm. The Trans-Himalaya region falls in the rain shadow zone, because the southeast monsoon clouds cannot cross the Great Himalaya.

Vegetation—Forests, Bugyals, National Parks and Sanctuaries

Forests

Diversity in vegetation leads the diversities in the spatial environment. Vegetation of any area depends on the several atmospheric, edaphic, and biotic phenomena (latitude, elevation, temperature, rainfall, terrain, soil, human and animal interference). These constraints not only determine the growth but also the variety of vegetation. About 54000 km^2 area of Uttarakhand exhibits a great deal of variation in altitude ranging from 250 m in the Tarai to more than 7000 m (up to tree line) in the Great Himalaya.

The tree line touches at an altitude about 4200 m above mean sea level. On the basis of agro-climatic and altitudinal zone, the forests of Uttarakhand have been broadly classified into six types.

1. ***Dry Deciduous Forests:*** This scattered forest zone occurs in Bhabar and southern part of Siwalik Hills mainly Haridwar and U.S. Nagar districts. The main species occurring in this zone include. Haldu (*Adina Cordifolia*), Semal (*Bombax ceiba*), Bel (*Aeglemarmelos*), Tendu (*Diospyrosmelanoxylon*), etc.

2. ***Moist Deciduous Forest:*** These forests are generally found in the districts of Nainital, U.S. Nagar, Hardwar, Southern part of Pauri district and Narendranagar forest division. This zone is popularly known as Sal forest because the main vegetation of this zone is Sal (*Sorea robusta*). Due to the low elevation from sea level, this region is also characterized by a hot and humid climate and high rainfall. A number of wild animals are found in this tract. Therefore two main wild life sanctuaries of Uttarakhand (Corbet Tiger Reserve and Rajaji National Park) are located within this zone. The principal species occurring in this zone include Haldu (*Adina Cordifolia*), Dhauri (*Anogeissus Itifolia*), Sal (*Sorea robusta*), Harar-Bahera (*Terminalia spp.*), Amaltas (*Cassia fistula*), Amla (*Amblica officinalis*), Sadan (*Ougeinia spp.*), Karipatta (*Murraya Koenigii*), Maljhan (*Bauhiia vahlii*), Bamboo (*Dendrocalmus Strictus*), Eucalyptus, Khair, Shisam etc.

3. ***Himalayan Subtropical Pine Forest:*** These forests are generally found between 800 m to 2000 m altitude in Uttarakhand. This zone is characterized by its transitional nature between the lower and higher zones. This zone reflects the presence the Sal as well as Chir Pine. Although Chir may be found mixed with Sal but at its upper limits it is seen with Burash (*Rhododendron arboretan*) and Banj-Oak (*Quercus incana Syn.*). The principal species occurring these forests include Chir pine (*Pinus roxburghii*), Kaphal (*Myrica nagi*), Tun (*Toon ciliate*), Hararh (*Terminalia Cherbula*), Bahera (*Terminalia belerica*), Amla (*Amblica officinalis*) etc.

4. ***Himalayan Moist Temperate Forest:*** These forests occur between 1800-3000 m above mean sea level. These forests are found along lower slopes of the Greater Himalaya and around

lower valleys in the region. These forests include conifers and broad leaves species found in the Himalayan zone. The species found in this zone are economically very significant. The main vegetation of this zone is Badam (*Carpinus viminea*), Banj-Oak (Quercus *incana Syn Q. Leucotrichophora*) Moru (*Quercus dilatata*), Burash (*Rhododendron arboretan*), Thuner (*Taxus baccata*), Kingoda (*Berberis arisatata*), Akhrot (*Juglans regia*), Pangar (*Asculus nepalensis*), Ringal (*Arundinaria spp.*), Sprus (*Abies pindrow*), Deodar (*Cedras deodara*), Fir (*Picea smithiana*), Birch (*Betula utilizes*) etc.

5. ***Moist Alpine Forest:*** These types are generally found from 2500 m elevation in the region. In this region vegetation is mainly found in form of bushes. The main dwarfed species of vegetation include Cyprus (*Cuperessu torulosa*), Oak-Banj (*Quercus incana Syn. Q. Leucotrichophora*), Moru (*Quercus dilatata*), Kharsu (*Quercus semicarpifolia*), Bhojpatra (*Betula utilis*), etc. are generally found in the bank of rivers.

6. ***Dry Alpine Scrub:*** This zone extends the northern part of Uttarkashi, Tehri, Rudraprayag, Chamoli, Bageshwar and Pithoragarh districts. This zone characterized by the occurrence of a large variety of plants including herbs, medicinal and aromatic plants, flowers and various types of scrubs. Many of these species have a great economic, medicinal and aromatic value. Therefore a number of people economically depend on these in this zone. A major portion of this zone is covered by the alpine pastures (meadows), locally known as Bugyals—abundant growth of Buggi grass (*Trachydium roylei lindle*) which is a very nutritious fodder for the cattle. The characteristic vegetation of this zone consists of dwarfed variety of Junipers (*Juniprus communis spp., Juniprus macropoda, Juniprus wallichiam*), Bhojpatra (*Betula utilis*), White Burash (*Rhododendron, Campanulatum*) Malijhan (*Salix spp.*). These alpine meadows are found up to 4200 m and some times may be seen in small patches even above a few square meters up to a hectare. Auli, Bedani, Dyara, Kedarkanthà, Shambhu, Khalia, Manatoili, Chiplakot, are important Bugyals in Uttarakhand.

Bugyals

Kedakantha, Maneg, Dyara, Auli, Bedani, Shambhu, Baggi

Bugyal, Tangukharak, Madri, Manatoli, Mangthil, Khaliya Bugiyal, Sheesakhani and Chhiplakot.

National Park and Sanctuaries

Corbet National Park, Rajaji National Park, Nandadevi Biosphere, Valley of Flower, Gangotri National Park, Govind Ballabh Pant National Park, Kedarnath Wild Life Sanctuary, Govind Ballabh Pant Wild Life Sanctuary, Askot Wild Life Sanctuary, Sona Nadi Wild Life Sanctuary, Binsar Wild Life Sanctuary and Dharmdhar Wild Life Sanctuary.

Soil

A complete soil survey of the Uttarakhand has not been carried out so far. Based on the available data, it becomes difficult to determine the remarkable characteristics of the soil. The foothill soil near Dehradun show that the soils are loam to clay-loam in texture and acidic in nature. In Ranikhet area four broad soil groups have been identified—red loam, brown forest soil, podzolic soil and meadow soil (Ghildyal, 1981). On the basis of altitude, lithology, landscape, slope aspect, gradient, vegetation, drainage and field work the soil of Kotadun, south western part of Kumaun Himalaya is classified into seven group-loamous soil, conglomeratic sandy soil, stony hilly soil, crushed slaty soil, hill sandy soil, podzolic soil and rocky thin regolithic soil (Pant, 1994 and Jalal *et al.* 2001).

Summary

The Himalayan lying in Indian sub-continent constitute one of the greatest and youngest folded mountain systems in the world rising from about 300 m to more than 800 m above the mean sea level. It acts as a protector, regulator and creator of natural resources, climate and soil respectively. Uttarakhand Himalaya is considered as densely forested area and in an abode of God and Goddesses and natural home for wild animals. It is also meeting place for various cultural groups which have come down from Central Asia in the North and Indo-Ganga-Brahmaputra plain in the south. From the Indo-Gangetic Plain in the south to a comparatively less elevated rain shadow zone of Tethys (Trans) Himalaya in the north; the Uttarakhand comprises all the four latitudinal physiographic-geological zones: the Outer Himalaya including the Tarai-Bhabar, the Siwaliks with duns, the Lesser Himalaya, the Great Himalaya and the Trans Himalaya. These Geo-tectonic divisions are respectively separated from one another by Main Boundary Thrust (MBT), Main Central Thrust (MCT) and Trans Himadri Thrust (THT). These faults thrusts zones are geologically very sensitive and ecologically very fragile. In the Higher Himalayan area there are number of known and unknown important lofty peaks, tough passes and magnificent glaciers. Uttarakhand is mainly drained by the Ganga and Kali rivers. These two rivers include all main tributaries such as Yamuna, Bhagirathi, Bhilangana, Alaknanda, Pindar, Nayar, Saryu, Gomti, W. Ramganga, Bino, Gagas, Kosi, E. Ramganga, Gori, Kuti, Western and Eastern Dhauli, Gaula, Dabka, etc. Uttarakhand is world wide known region for fresh water high and low altitude lakes and hot water springs. Diversified topography of the region has offered different climatic features. The Indian Meteorological Department has divided the year into four seasons—viz. cold weather season-December to February, hot weather season—March to mid June, rainy season-mid June to September, and the season of Retreating Monsoon-October to November. Although in recent years the duration and cycle of the seasons is very uncertain. Similarly the intensity to temperature and spatial distribution of rainfall is very abnormal. On the basis of agro-climatic and altitudinal zone, the forests of Uttarakhand have been broadly classified not six types—dry deciduous forest, moist deciduous forest, Himalayan subtropical pine forest, Himalayan moist temperature forest, moist alpine forest. Auli Bedani, Dyara, Kedarkantha, Shyambhu, Khalia, Manatoili, Chiplakot, are important Bugyals in Uttarakhand. There are number of national parks and sanctuaries in Uttarakhand. On the basis of physical blatures the soils of Uttarakhand have been broadly divided in to seven types—leanous, sandy, padzalic, conglomentic sandy, stony hilly, crushed slaty and rocky then rigolithic soils.

4

Tribal Setting of Uttarakhand

Distribution

The tribal population of Uttarakhand is concentrated in the remote/forest areas of Tarai and Bhabar and higher reaches of Pithoragarh, Chamoli, Uttarkashi districts and Jaunsar-Bhabar area of Dehradun district. As per 2001 census it comes to 2,56,129 people constitute about 3% to the total population of the state. Uttarakhand state contributes only 0.83% to total population and 0.3% to the tribal population of India. Among the 13 districts of the state, Udham Singh Nagar with a tribal population of 1,10,220 (43.03%) is at the top followed by Dehradun (99,329 person or 38.78%), Pithoragarh (19,279 person or 7.53%) and Chamoli (4.09%). In fact four districts of Uttarakhand contribute about 93% of total tribal population. The districts with lowest tribal population in the state are Rudraprayag, Tehri, Champawat, Almora, Pauri, Bageshwar, Uttarkashi, Hardwar and Nainital contributing 0.07, 0.27, 0.29, 0.34, 0.62, 0.76, 1.05, 1.22 and 1.94 per cent to the total tribal population of the state respectively. But their largest proportion to total population among all the districts is found in U.S. Nagar (8.9%) followed by Dehradun (7.7%), Pithoragarh (4.2%) and Chamoli (2.8%). Proportion of the tribal population to the total population of the remaining districts is found less than 1% (Table 4.1).

The concentration of state's tribal population has been grouped into four categories -below 1% population, 1.01-2.0, 2.01-5.0 and more than 5.01% population respectively termed as very low, low, moderate and high concentrated zones (Table 4.2). Out of total thirteen districts in the state 46.1% have less than 1% population. These districts are Rudraprayag, Tehri, Pauri,

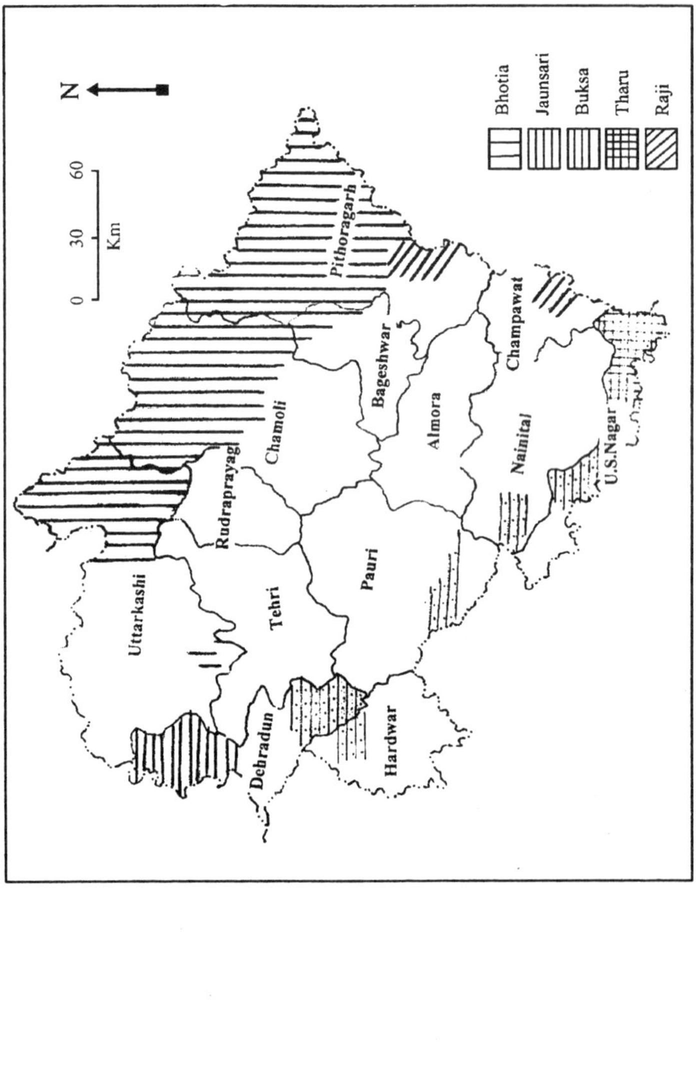

Fig. 4.1 : Uttarakhand : Main Habitats Scheduled Tribes

TABLE 4.1

Distribution of Total and Scheduled Tribe Population, 2001

Sl. No.	Districts	Area	Total Population Numbers	Total Population % of State Population	Total Population H.H. Size	Scheduled Tribes Population Numbers	Scheduled Tribes Population %of State Population	Scheduled Tribes Population % of District Population	Scheduled Tribes Population H.H. Size
1.	Uttarkashi	Total	2,95,013	3.47	5.3	2,685	1.05	0.9	4.4
		Rural	272,095	4.31	5.4	2,449	1.02	0.9	4.4
		Urban	22,918	1.05	4.5	236	1.48	1.0	4.3
2.	Chamoli	Total	370,359	4.36	4.9	10,484	4.09	2.8	3.9
		Rural	3,19,656	5.07	5.0	7,730	3.22	2.4	3.8
		Urban	50,703	2.33	4.3	2,754	17.30	5.4	4.1
3.	Rudraprayag	Total	227,439	2.68	4.8	186	0.07	0.1	3.8
		Rural	224707	3.56	4.8	157	0.07	0.1	3.7
		Urban	2732	0.13	4.0	29	0.18	1.1	4.1
4.	Tehri	Total	604747	7.12	5.1	691	0.27	0.1	5.1
		Rural	544901	8.63	5.2	273	0.11	0.1	3.6
		Urban	59846	2.75	4.6	418	2.63	0.7	7.1
5.	Dehradun	Total	1282143	15.1	5.3	99329	38.78	7.7	7.2
		Rural	603401	9.56	5.7	94910	39.51	15.7	7.5
		Urban	678742	31.15	5.0	4419	27.76	0.7	4.3
6.	Pauri	Total	697.078	8.21	4.6	1594	0.62	0.2	4.3
		Rural	607203	9.62	4.6	1348	0.56	0.2	4.6
		Urban	89875	4.12	4.9	246	1.54	0.3	3.3
7.	Pithoragarh	Total	462289	5.45	4.7	19279	7.53	4.2	4.0
		Rural	402456	6.38	4.7	14934	6.22	3.7	3.9
		Urban	59833	2.75	4.4	4345	27.29	7.3	4.1
8.	Bageshwar	Total	249462	2.94	4.8	1943	0.76	0.8	4.0

Table Contd...

Table Contd....

Sl. No.	Districts	Area	Total Population			Scheduled Tribes Population			
			Numbers	% of State Population	H.H. Size	Numbers	%of State Population	% of District Population	H.H. Size
		Rural	241659	3.83	4.8	1619	0.67	0.7	3.9
		Urban	7803	0.36	4.6	324	2.04	4.2	4.5
9.	Almora	Total	630567	7.43	4.8	878	0.34	0.1	3.8
		Rural	576062	9.13	4.8	488	0.20	0.1	3.8
		Urban	54505	2.5	4.8	390	2.45	0.7	3.9
10.	Champawat	Total	224542	2.64	5.1	740	0.29	0.3	4.4
		Rural	190764	3.02	5.2	573	0.24	0.3	4.7
		Urban	33778	1.55	4.9	167	1.05	0.5	3.7
11.	Nainital	Total	762909	8.99	5.4	4961	1.94	0.7	4.6
		Rural	493859	7.84	5.4	3962	1.65	0.8	4.9
		Urban	269050	12.36	5.3	999	6.28	0.4	3.8
12.	U. S. Nagar	Total	1235614	14.55	5.9	110220	43.03	8.9	6.6
		Rural	832600	13.19	6.0	108808	45.3	13.1	6.6
		Urban	403014	18.5	5.8	1412	8.87	0.4	5.7
13.	Hardwar	Total	1447187	17.06	6.0	3139	1.22	0.2	5.2
		Rural	1000912	15.86	6.2	2958	1.23	0.3	5.3
		Urban	446275	20.49	5.6	181	1.14	0.0	3.9
	Uttarakhand	**Total**	**8489349**	**100.0**	**5.3**	**256129**	**0.3**	**3.0**	**6.1**
		Rural	**6310275**	**100.0**	**5.3**	**240209**	**3.10**	**3.8**	**6.3**
		Urban	**2179074**	**100.0**	**5.2**	**15920**	**0.23**	**0.7**	**4.3**
	India	**Total**	**1028610328**	**100**	**5.3**	**84326240**	**100**	**8.2**	**5.1**
		Rural	**742490639**	**100**	**5.4**	**7733597**	**100**	**10.4**	**5.2**
		Urban	**286119689**	**100**	**5.1**	**6987643**	**100**	**2.4**	**4.8**

Source : Census of India 2001 b.

TABLE 4.2

Distribution of Districts by Ranges of Percentage Share of Total Population in Uttarakhand

Level	*Ranges (%)*	*Total Population*		*S.T. Population*		*Districts Name (% in Brackets)*
		(No)	*(%)*	*(No)*	*(%)*	
Very Low	Below 1.00	Nil	Nil	6	46.1	Rudraprayag (0.07), Tehri (0.27), Pauri (0.62), Bageshwar (0.76), Almora (0.34) & Champawat (0.29).
Low	1.01 - 2.00	Nil	Nil	3	23.1	Uttarkashi (1.01), Nainital (1.94) & Hardwar (1.22).
Moderate	2.01 - 5.00	5	38.46	1	7.7	Chamoli (4.09).
High	Above 5.01	8	61.54	3	23.1	Dehradun (38.78), Pithoragarh (7.53) & Udham Singh Nagar (43.03).
Total		**13**	**100.00**	**13**	**100.00**	

Source: Anon. 2001 b.

TABLE 4.3

Tribe-wise Distribution of Scheduled Tribe Population,1991-2001

Sl. No.	District	Tribes: Bhotia	Buksa	Jaunsari	Tharu	Raji	Unclassifed	All Tribes 1991	All Tribes 2001
1.	Uttarkashi	1768 {5.28} {76.9}	26{0.8} {1.1}	505{0.70} {22.0}	1 {0.0}	0{0.00} {0.0}	0 {0.0}	2300{1.08} {100.0}	2685 {1.05} {0.9}
2.	Chamoli	9549{28.52} {93.0}	543 {1.65} {5.3}	12{0.02} {0.1}	9 {0.1}	152{11.88} {1.5}	8{0.70} {0.1}	10273{4.85} {100.0}	10484 {4.09} {2.8}
3.	Rudraprayag	— Did not exit as a separate district —							186{0.07} {0.01}
4.	Tehri	283 {0.85} {46.0}	18 {0.05} {2.9}	292{0.40} {47.5}	18{0.03} {2.9}	0{0.00} 0{0.00}	4{0.35} {0.7}	615{0.29} {100.0}	691{0.27} {0.1}
5.	Dehradun	462{1.38} {0.5}	10359 {31.50} {12.3}	71660{98.79} {85.2}	1506{2.14} {1.8}	42{3.28} {0.0}	47{4.09} {0.1}	84076{39.68} {100.0}	99329{38.78} {7.7}
6.	Pauri	204{0.61} {13.6}	1071{3.56} {71.3}	1{0.0} {0.1}	203{0.28} {13.5}	23{1.80} {1.5}	1{0.09} {0.1}	1503{0.71} {100.0}	1594{0.62} {0.2}
7.	Pithoragarh	17657{52.74} {96.4}	12{0.04} {0.1}	6{0.01} {0.0}	18{0.03} {0.1}	620{48.48} {3.4}	0{0.0} {0.0}	18313{8.64} {100.0}	19279{7.53} {4.2}
8.	Bageshwar	— Did not exit as a separate district —							1943{0.76} {0.08}
9.	Almora	2335{6.98} {85.3}	10{0.03} {0.4}	1{0.00} {0.0}	8{0.01} {0.3}	382{29.87} {13.9}	3{0.26} {0.1}	2739{1.29} {100.0}	878{0.34} {0.01}

10.	Champawat	Did not exit as a separate district							740{0.29} {0.3}
11.	Nainital	1220{3.64} {1.4}	20180{64.4} {22.4}	56{0.08} {0.1}	67422{95.59} {74.9}	59{4.61} {0.1}	1083{94.34} {1.2}	90020{42.48} {100.0}	4961{1.94} {0.7}
12.	U.S.Nagar	Did not exit as a separate district							110220{43.03} {8.9}
13.	Hardwar	0{0.0} {0.0}	671{2.04} {33.1}	3{0.00} {0.1}	1349{1.92} {66.6}	1{0.08} {0.0}	2{0.17} {0.1}	2026{0.95} {100.0}	3139{1.23} {0.2}
	Uttarakhand	**33478 {15.80}**	**32890 {15.52}**	**72536 {34.24}**	**70534 {33.30}**	**1279 {0.6}**	**1148 {0.54}**	**211865 {100.0}**	**256129{100.0} {3.0}**
	Uttar Pradesh	**38584 {13.4}**	**34621 {12.0}**	**74263 {25.8}**	**136929 {47.6}**	**1728 {0.6}**	**1785 {0.6}**	**287910 {100.0}**	**107963 {100.0}**

Source: Census of India 1991 and 2001 b.

Note: Figures in parentheses refer to the percentage of the total.

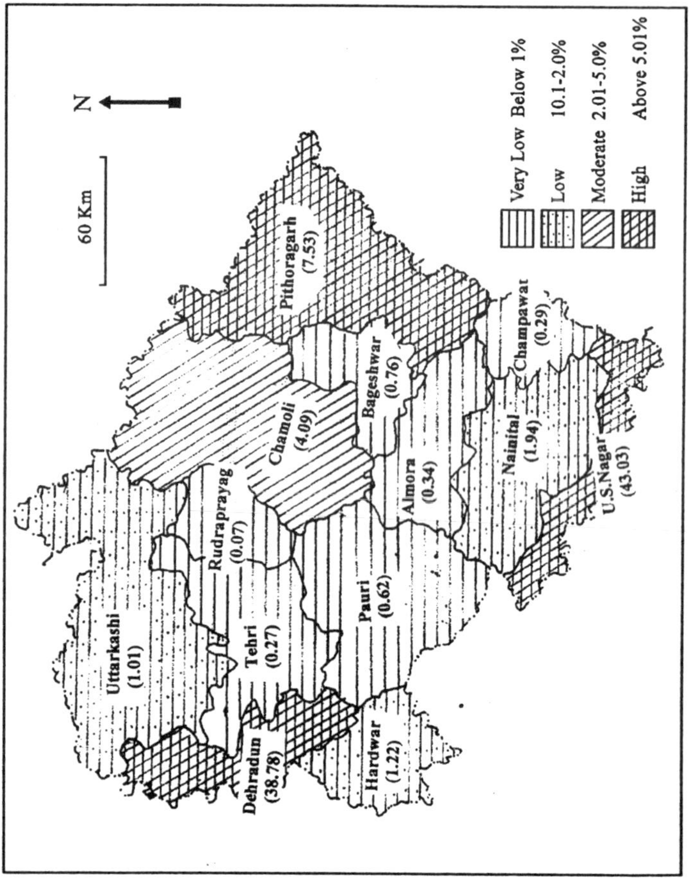

Fig. 4.2 : Uttarakhand : Distribution of Scheduled Tribes Population (% of ST Population)

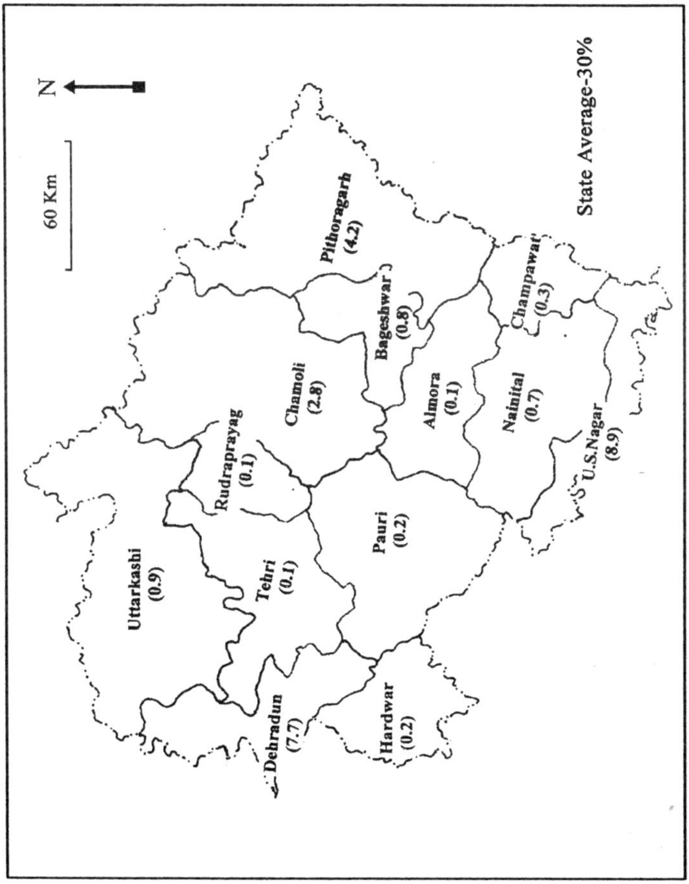

Fig. 4.3 : Uttarakhand: Distribution of Scheduled Tribes Population (% of Total population)

TABLE 4.4

Distribution of Districts by Ranges of Household Size (P/H.H.) of S.T. Population in Uttarakhand

Level	*Ranges (%)*	*Total Population*		*S.T. Population*		*Districts Name (% in Brackets)*
		(No)	*(%)*	*(No)*	*(%)*	
Very Low	Below 4.00	Nil	Nil	5	38.4	Chamoli (3.9), Rudraprayag (3.8), Pithoragarh (4.00), Bageshwar (4.0) & Almora (3.8).
Low	4.1 - 5.00	6	46.2	4	30.8	Uttarkashi (4.4), Nainital (4.6), Pauri (4.3) & Champawat (4.4).
Moderate	5.1 - 6.00	7	53.8	2	15.4	Hardwar (5.2) & Tehri (5.1).
High	Above 6.1	Nil	Nil	2	15.4	Dehradun (7.2) & Udham Singh Nagar (6.6).
Total		**13**	**100**	**13**	**100**	

Source: Anon. 2001 b.

Bageshwar, Almora, and Champawat. Only three districts (23.1%) have more than 5% state's tribal population. These are U.S. Nagar, Dehradun and Pithoragarh districts. The high concentration of tribal population in these districts is because there is relatively more inhospitable conditions such as undulating terrain, extreme hot, cold and moist climate, dense forest and proneness to malaria.

It is worth to mention that tribe-wise population for the 2001 census is yet not available but as per 1991 census Jaunsari (34.24%) and Tharu (33.3%) contribute more than two third tribal population of the state. Bhotia and Buksa both the tribes have respectively about 15.8 and 15.52% and only 0.6% tribal population belongs to Raji while 0.54% population is enumerated as unclassified (Table 4.3).

The average household size of the tribal population in the state is found 6.1 people per family, which is higher than that of the all castes population (5.3) of the state and country (5.1) while the size of family in urban area (4.31) is less than the all castes population (5.2). The household size varies from minimum of 3.8 people in Almora and Rudraprayag to maximum of 6.6 people per household in the U.S. Nagar. In 2001 census, 15.4% districts are registered above and remaining districts are below the state's average (6.1). Table 4.4 shows that the maximum (38.4%) districts are falling in the group of below 4 persons per household. The same table reveals that 84.6% and 69.2% districts have lower household size from the state (6.1) and country (5.1) averages respectively. Only 6.2% tribal population to the total tribal population of the state resides in urban centres (cities). The household size of the urban tribal population in the Uttarakhand is 4.3 persons per household which is lower than country average (4.8) because the urbanization process in the tribal society is slow than that of non tribal population as a results the family size of the urban areas is less than the total tribal or total population (3.1).

Density

Arithmetic density means the number of persons residing in a square kilometre area. For the states as a whole it works out to 159 p/km^2 as against to 132 in 1991 census while the tribal density is 4.79 person in 2001 as against to 3.46 person per km^2 in 1991, which is lower than that of the country average. This means that the total and tribal pressure in the states has increased. Maximum tribal density about 40 people per km^2 is registered in the U.S. Nagar followed by the Dehradun with 32 people per km^2. Out of total 13 districts of the Uttarakhand, 6 districts have less than one person per km^2 tribal density. As a whole the highest density of population has been observed is Hardwar district (612) followed by U.S. Nagar (424) and Dehradun (414) which is higher than the country (324) and state (159) averages.

TABLE 4.5

Population Density, 1991 and 2001

S.No.	*District*	*Total Population*		*S.T. Population*	
		1991	*2001*	*1991*	*2001*
1.	Uttarkashi	30	37	0.29	0.33
2.	Chamoli	43	48	1.08	1.38
3.	Rudraprayag	106	120	*	0.1
4.	Tehri	128	148	0.15	0.17
5.	Dehradun	332	414	27.22	32.17
6.	Pauri	124	129	0.28	0.30
7.	Pithoragarh	59	65	2.06	2.72
8.	Bageshwar	99	108	*	0.84
9.	Almora	198	205	0.51	0.28
10.	Champawat	107	126	*	0.42
11.	Nainital	149	198	13.30	1.20
12.	U.S. Nagar	432	442	*	37.9
13.	Hardwar	485	612	0.86	1.33
	Uttarakhand	**132**	**159**	**3.96**	**4.79**
	India	**267**	**324**	**20.64**	**25.69**

Source : Census of India 1991 and 2001 b.

*Did not exist as a separate district.

TABLE 4.6

Distribution of Districts by Ranges of Density (P/Sq. Km.) of S.T. Population in Uttarakhand

Level	*Ranges (%)*	*Total Population*		*S.T. Population*		*Districts Name (% in Brackets)*
		(No)	*(%)*	*(No)*	*(%)*	
Very Low	Below 1.00	Nil	Nil	7	53.8	Uttarkashi (0.33), Bageshwar (0.84), Almora (0.28), Rudraprayag (0.1), Tehri (0.17), Pauri (0.3) & Champawat (0.42).
Low	1.01 - 2.00	Nil	Nil	3	23.1	Nainital (1.2), Hardwar (1.33) & Chamoli (1.38).
Moderate	2.01 - 3.00	Nil	Nil	1	7.7	Pithoragarh (2.72).
High	Above 3.01	13	100	2	15.4	Dehradun (32.17) & Udham Singh Nagar (37.9).
Total		**13**	**100**	**13**	**100**	

Source: Anon. 2001 b.

It is observed that the district lying in the plain area of the states have higher density as compared to those lying in the hill area. More than 93% of the total tribal population of the state is residing in the four districts—U.S. Nagar, Dehradun, Pithoragarh and Chamoli. Therefore these districts have more tribal density in comparison to the other districts (Table 4.6).

Table 4.6 shows that 53.8% districts have below 1 person/ km^2 density. These are Uttarkashi, Rudraprayag, Tehri, Pauri, Bageshwar, Almora and Champawat. Only 15.4% districts (Dehradun and U.S. Nagar) have more than 3.01 persons/km^2 density. The study reflects that only Dehradun and U.S. Nagar have more tribal density than the state (4.79) and country (25.69) averages.

Growth

The total growth of tribal population of Uttarakhand during 1991-2001 was 20.89% which is higher than the growth of all castes population (Table 4.7). The decadal growth rate of tribal population of India and Uttarakhand has increased while the growth rate of all castes population for both the state and country has decreased during 1981-1991 to 1991-2001. Barring Hardwar, Pithoragarh Dehradun and Nainital, decadal growth (1991-2001) of tribal population has declined in all the districts of the state. About 15.38% districts—Chamoli (3.85%) and Almora (3%) have the decadal growth rate less than 5%. Similarly Pauri and Pithoragarh districts are laying between the growth rate 5 to 10% range. Tehri district lies in the growth rate of 10-15%. Among the remaining districts, Uttarkashi and Dehradun are in the range of 15-20% while Hardwar and Nainital fall in the range exceeding 25% (Table 2.7). The main reason behind this higher growth rate in Nainital, Dehradun and Hardwar is immigration from the mountainous districts of the state. Consequently, the hill districts have lower growth than the state and country averages.

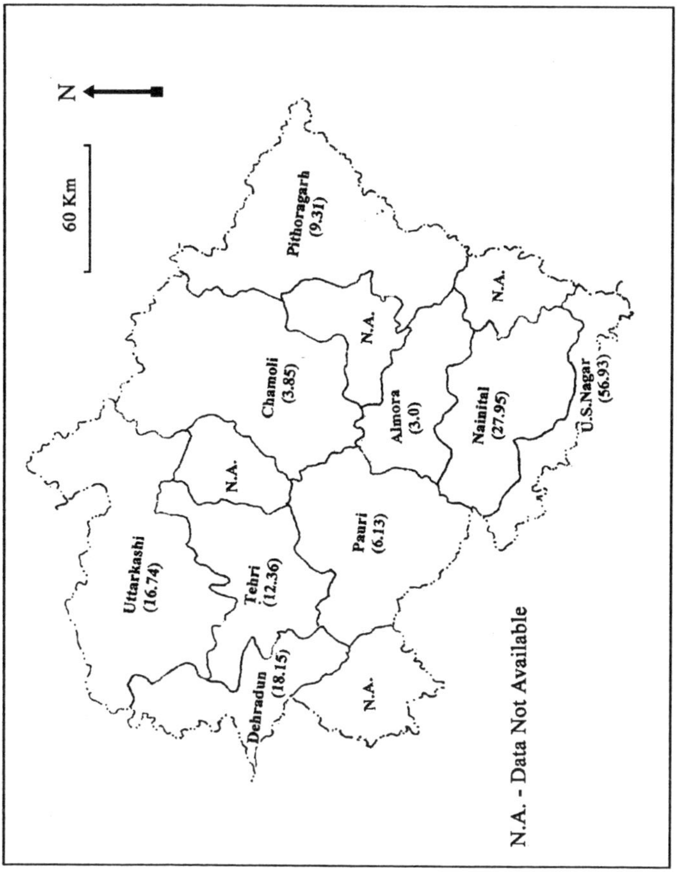

Fig. 4.4 : Uttarakhand Growth (%) of Scheduled Tribes Population (1991-2001)

TABLE 4.7

Growth of Population (%)

S.No.	*District*	*Total Population*			*Scheduled Tribe Population*		
		1971-1981	*1981-1991*	*1991-2001*	*1971-1981*	*1981-1991*	*1991-2001*
1.	Uttarkashi	29.19	25.54	22.72	544.33	26.58	16.74
2.	Chamoli	24.53	21.97	13.51	12.37	12.1	3.85
3.	Rudraprayag	24.68	17.4	13.44	N.A.	N.A.	N.A.
4.	Tehri	25.25	16.59	16.15	84.37	804.4	12.36
5.	Dehradun	31.93	34.66	24.71	23.37	10.5	18.14
6.	Pauri	15.34	9.05	3.87	168.22	36.92	6.13
7.	Pithoragarh	17.85	14.11	10.92	12.88	5.63	9.31
8.	Bageshwar	18.98	15.5	9.21	N.A.	N.A.	N.A.
9.	Almora	16.77	9.43	3.14	15.2	27.69	3.00
10.	Champawat	25.34	26.38	17.56	N.A.	N.A.	N.A.
11.	Nainital	43.85	29.87	32.88	40.79	21.65	27.95
12.	U.S. Nagar	48.16	44.35	27.79	N.A.	N.A.	N.A.
13.	Hardwar	32.72	28.44	26.3	N.A.	N.A.	56.93
	Uttarakhand	**27.45**	**24.23**	**19.2**	**N.A.**	**15.48**	**20.89**
	India	**24.66**	**23.86**	**21.53**	**N.A.**	**N.A.**	**24.45**

Source : Census of India 1981, 1991 and 2001 b.

Sex Ratio

The number of females per thousand males is termed as sex ratio. It reveals the numerical relationship between women and men. A ratio of one thousand indicates equal balance of males and females in the population, less than one thousand indicates numerical deficit of women (low sex ratio) and above one thousand indicates numerical surplus of women (high sex ratio) in the population. Average sex ratio of the tribal total population is 950, which is less than the sex ratio of the all castes population (962) while the sex ratio in below six years aged population is numerically higher (955) than that of the total population (908). The sex ratio has usually been quite high in the hill districts as compared to districts in plains of Uttarakhand. Out of 13 districts, 61.53 and 23.1% have sex ratio favourable i.e. more females than males of the all castes and tribal population respectively. These districts which have favourable sex ratio in all castes population are Chamoli (1016), Rudraprayag (1115), Almora (1146) Tehri (1049), Pauri (1106), and Pithoragarh (1031), Bageshwar (1105) and Champawat (1021) while the sex ratio in the tribal population is favourable in Chamoli (1063), Pithoragarh (1046) and Bageshwar (1161). The lowest sex ratio in the total population has however been registered in Hardwar (865) preceded by Dehradun (887) while in the tribal population the lowest sex ratio has been notice in Tehri (337) preceded by Rudraprayag (755) (Table 2.8). It is worth the mention that the main cause of favourable sex ratio in the hilly rural based districts is out migration of male population in search of employment and better education. As a result, the urban centres have low sex ratio.

TABLE 4.8

Sex Ratio of Total and Scheduled Tribes Population, 2001

S.No.	*Districts*	*Area*	*Total Population*		*S.T. Population*	
			Total	*0-6 Years*	*Total*	*0-6 Years*
1.	Uttarkashi	Total	941	942	899	818
		Rural	961	952	907	855
		Urban	726	783	815	545
2.	Chamoli	Total	1,016	935	1063	877
		Rural	1,073	944	1,096	900
		Urban	716	858	974	809
3.	Rudraprayag	Total	1,115	953	755	1000
		Rural	1,127	954	805	882
		Urban	444	865	526	0
4.	Tehri	Total	1049	927	337	846
		Rural	1109	932	615	655
		Urban	628	866	201	1400
5.	Dehradun	Total	887	894	913	958
		Rural	914	919	920	965
		Urban	863	866	777	769

Table Contd....

6. Pauri	Total	1106	930	795	897
	Rural	1155	941	812	898
	Urban	821	844	708	882
7. Pithoragarh	Total	1031	902	1046	956
	Rural	1066	912	1034	1010
	Urban	824	825	1088	773
8. Bageshwar	Total	1105	930	1161	1110
	Rural	1116	932	1170	1083
	Urban	810	838	1118	1214
9. Almora	Total	1146	933	905	647
	Rural	1189	936	914	561
	Urban	774	881	893	778
10. Champawat	Total	1021	934	922	1333
	Rural	1055	946	936	1382
	Urban	849	857	876	1143
11. Nainital	Total	906	910	932	1018
	Rural	922	920	929	1048
	Urban	878	891	944	855
12. Udham Singh Nagar	Total	902	913	970	955
	Rural	916	923	975	958
	Urban	876	891	642	755
13. Hardwar	Total	865	862	817	997
	Rural	874	862	817	987
	Urban	844	865	810	1188
Uttarakhand	**Total**	**962**	**908**	**950**	**955**
	Rural	**1007**	**918**	**956**	**964**
	Urban	**845**	**872**	**867**	**806**
India	**Total**	**933**	**927**	**978**	**973**
	Rural	**946**	**934**	**981**	**974**
	Urban	**900**	**906**	**944**	**951**

Source: Census of India 2001 b.

The sex ratio below the age of 6 years tribal population in Uttarakhand is registered 955 which is higher from the same segment of all castes population. The average sex ratio of tribal population in the state is lower than the country averages (973). The sex ratio of this segment varies from minimum of 647 in Almora district to maximum of 1333 in Champawat (Table 4.9). About 38.4% districts have registered sex ratio below from the state average. These are Uttarkashi, Chamoli, Tehri and Pauri districts. About 23.1% districts are in the range of 951 to 975

TABLE 4.9

Distribution of Districts by Ranges of Total Sex Ratio of S.T.Population in Uttarakhand

Level	*Ranges (%) (F/1000M)*	*Total Population*		*S.T. Population*		*Districts Name (% in Brackets)*
		(No)	*(%)*	*(No)*	*(%)*	
Very Low	Below 900	2	15.4	5	38.4	Uttarkashi (899), Hardwar (817), Tehri (337), Rudraprayag (755) & Pauri (795).
Low	901 - 950	3	23.0	4	30.8	Dehradun (913), Champawat (922) Almora (905) & Nainital (932).
Moderate	951-1000	Nil	Nil	1	7.7	Udham Singh Nagar (970).
High	1001-1050	4	30.8	1	7.7	Pithoragarh (1046).
Very high	Above 1051	4	30.8	2	15.4	Chamoli (1063) & Bageshwar (1151).
Total		**13**	**100.0**	**13**	**100.0**	

Source: Ancn. 2001 b.

TABLE 4.10

Distribution of Districts by Ranges of Total Sex Ratio of > 6 Years Age S.T.Population in Uttarakhand

Level	*Ranges (%) (F/1000M)*	*Total Population*		*S.T. Population*		*Districts Name (% in Brackets)*
		(No)	*(%)*	*(No)*	*(%)*	
Very Low	Below 900	2	15.4	5	38.4	Uttarkashi (818), Pauri (897), Tehri (846), Almora (647) and Chamoli (877).
Low	901 - 950	10	76.9	Nil	Nil	Nil.
Moderate	951-1000	1	7.7	5	38.4	Rudraprayag (1000), Dehradun (958), Hardwar (997), Pithoragarh (956) & Udham Singh Nagar (955).
High	Above 1001	Nil	Nil	3	23.2	Bageshwar (1110), Nainital (1018) and Champawat (1333).
Total		**13**	**100.0**	**13**	**100.0**	

Source: Anon. 2001 b.

females per thousand males. These are Dehradun, Pithoragarh and U.S. Nagar. These districts have 93% of total tribal population. The study of sex ratio reflects that there is no much differentiation in regard to born and brought up between the male and female child in tribal population. About 23.1% districts have more females than males. These are Bageshwar, Champawat and Nainital districts.

Literacy

Literacy is one of the important social aspects on which information is obtained on every individual in census. For the purpose of census 2001 a person aged seven and above who can both read and write with understanding any language is treated as literate. It denotes the most basic and essential criterion for human development. It is a qualitative indicator of social awakening and cultural advancement of the inhabitants in a geographical region; whereas a change in literacy reflects the socioeconomic and cultural transformation of the society. Keeping in view the significance of literacy, the United Nations Development Programme (UNDP) has included in the criteria to determine the Human Development Index (HDI). Lack of literacy can certainly be an impediment in the development progress. Table 4.11 shows the literacy rates and gender gap in literacy of all castes and tribal population for the year 2001. The total literacy in the Uttarakhand (71.6%) is higher than the national average (64.8%). Similarly in case of tribal literacy Uttarakhand with 63.2% literates is quite ahead of average literacy registered for the country (47.1%). The level of male and female literacy among the tribal community of Uttarakhand is higher than that of the country average. The tribal literacy varies from minimum 46.3% in Hardwar districts to maximum 93.3% in Almora district while the literacy rates for all castes population is higher than that of tribal population in the state (Table 4.11). Table 4.12 gives the spatial distribution of districts by different ranges and categories of all castes and tribal literacy for Uttarakhand as a whole. About 15.4% districts of the state where total literacy rates are still below 60% can be recognized as a region with very low level of literacy. These are Dehradun (57.01%) and Hardwar (46.3%). The low level of tribal literacy region covers 38.4% districts.

TABLE 4.11

Literacy Rates By Sex (%),2001

S.No.	Districts	Area	Total Population			Scheduled Tribes Population			Gender Gap in Literacy	
			Persons	Male	Female	Persons	Male	Female	Total	S.T.
1	Uttarkashi	Total	65.7	83.6	46.7	78.1	90.2	64.8	36.9	25.4
		Rural	63.8	82.6	44.3	77.4	89.7	64.0	38.3	25.6
		Urban	86.6	93.2	77.5	85.1	95.4	73.4	15.7	22.0
2	Chamoli	Total	75.4	89.7	61.6	79.3	92.4	67.2	28.0	25.2
		Rural	73.4	89.1	59.1	76.5	91.3	63.3	30.0	28
		Urban	87.6	92.3	80.9	87.1	95.4	78.8	11.4	16.6
3	Rudraprayag	Total	73.6	89.8	59.6	75.7	84.3	63.5	30.2	20.8
		Rural	73.5	89.9	59.4	76.0	87.1	61.8	30.5	25.3
		Urban	82.4	82.9	81.0	74.1	73.7	75	2.0	-1.3
4	Tehri	Total	66.7	85.3	49.4	68.7	66.5	75.9	35.9	-9.4
		Rural	64.5	84.6	47.0	82.2	87.9	72.9	37.5	14.9
		Urban	86.1	90.3	79.0	60.9	57.7	80.4	11.3	-22.7
5	Dehradun	Total	79.0	85.9	71.2	57.0	69.9	42.8	14.7	27.1
		Rural	70.5	79.8	60.4	55.7	68.9	41.2	19.4	27.6
		Urban	86.2	90.9	80.7	84.3	89.8	77.1	10.2	12.7
6	Pauri	Total	77.5	90.9	65.7	66.3	79.0	49.8	25.2	29.2
		Rural	75.9	90.6	63.6	60.6	75.2	42.3	27.0	32.8
		Urban	87.8	92.4	82.2	95.3	97.6	92	10.1	5.7
7	Pithoragarh	Total	75.9	90.1	62.6	77.4	89.1	66.4	27.5	22.7
		Rural	73.7	89.1	59.7	74.3	87.3	61.7	29.4	25.6
		Urban	90.2	95.3	83.9	87.9	95.3	81.4	11.4	13.9

8	Bageshwar	Total	71.3	87.7	57.0	80.3	92.0	70.3	30.7	21.7
		Rural	70.8	87.5	56.3	78.9	92.0	67.9	31.2	24.1
		Urban	86.7	90.8	81.6	87.8	92.0	83.9	9.2	8.1
9	Almora	Total	73.6	89.2	60.6	93.3	97.2	89.3	28.6	7.9
		Rural	71.8	88.5	58.4	92.7	96.7	88.6	30.1	8.2
		Urban	91.7	94.5	88.0	94.2	97.8	90.2	6.5	7.6
10	Champawat	Total	70.4	87.3	54.2	64.6	76.3	50.6	33.1	25.7
		Rural	68.6	87.4	51.2	61.1	73.4	46.3	36.2	27.2
		Urban	80.1	86.5	72.5	75.9	85.3	64.5	14.0	20.8
11	Nainital	Total	78.4	86.3	69.6	63.1	73.2	52	16.8	21.[illegible]
		Rural	76.3	86.1	65.6	55.2	67.5	41.6	20.5	25.9
		Urban	82.1	86.8	76.8	92.2	94.7	89.6	10.0	5.1
12	U.S.Nagar	Total	64.9	75.2	53.4	63.9	78.5	49	21.9	29.5
		Rural	61.8	73.4	49.2	63.7	78.3	48.8	24.2	29.5
		Urban	71.0	78.9	62.0	83.6	92.9	68.8	16.9	24.1
13	Hardwar	Total	63.7	73.8	51.1	46.3	59.2	29.7	21.7	29.5
		Rural	57.2	69	43.6	44.2	57.5	27.1	25.4	30.3
		Urban	77.4	83.6	70.0	80.8	86.9	72.6	13.5	14.3
	Uttarakhand	**Total**	**71.6**	**83.3**	**59.6**	**63.2**	**76.4**	**49.4**	**23.6**	**27.0**
		Rural	**68.1**	**81.8**	**54.7**	**61.7**	**75.3**	**47.4**	**27.1**	**27.9**
		Urban	**81.4**	**87.1**	**74.8**	**85.9**	**91.5**	**79.5**	**12.3**	**12.1**
	India	**Total**	**64.8**	**75.3**	**53.7**	**47.1**	**59.2**	**34.8**	**21.6**	**24.4**
		Rural	**58.7**	**70.7**	**46.1**	**45.0**	**57.4**	**32.4**	**24.6**	**24.9**
		Urban	**79.9**	**86.3**	**72.9**	**69.1**	**77.8**	**59.9**	**13.4**	**17.9**

Source: Census of India 2001b.

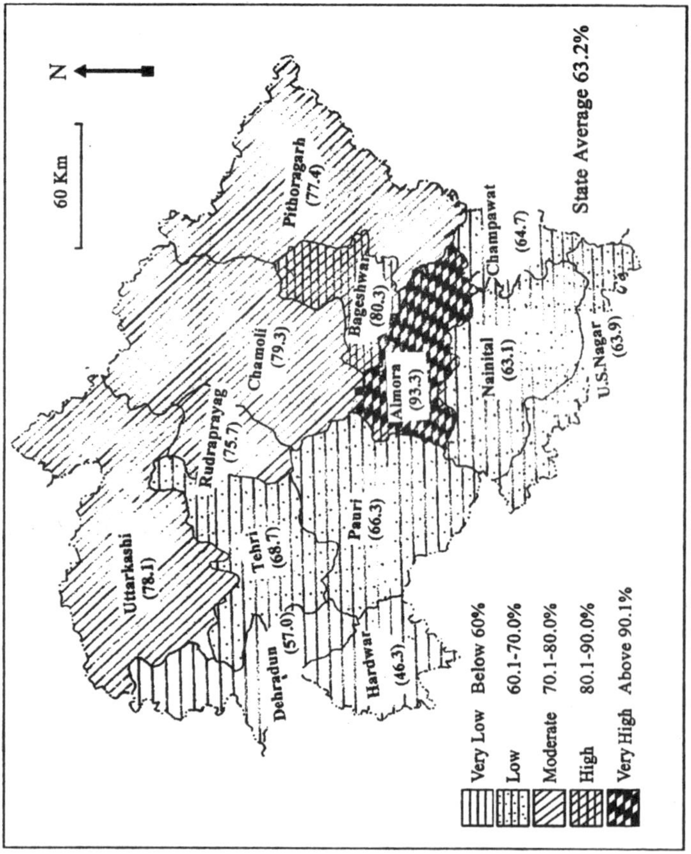

Fig. 4.5 : Uttarakhand: Total Literacy Among Scheduled Tribes population (2001)

These are Tehri (68.7%), Pauri (66.3%), Champawat (64.6%), Nainital (63.1%) and U.S. Nagar (63.95). There are 30.8% districts (Uttarkashi, Chamoli, Rudraprayag and Pithoragarh) of the state with total tribal literacy rates between 70 to 80% can be termed as moderate level of literacy zone. Bageshwar and Almora districts have reported respectively high (80-90%) and very high (above 90%) level of total tribal literacy rates.

Highest proportion of the male literates in the tribal population has been registered in Almora district (97.2%) while the Hardwar district has the lowest proportion (59.2%) of the male literates in the state which is also lower than that of state average (76.4%). Distribution of districts by different ranges of male literacy is presented in Table 4.13. There is only one district (Hardwar) in the state with male literacy below 60% termed as very low literacy region while 15.4% districts (Tehri and Dehradun) are found in the region of low literacy region i.e. range between 60.1 to 70.0%. The moderate literacy region covers 30.8% districts of the state. These are Pauri, Champawat, Nainital and U.S. Nagar. There are 15.4% districts of the state have registered high level of male tribal literacy. Four districts (30.8%) —Uttarkashi, Chamoli, Bageshwar and Almora of the state have recorded more than 90% male literacy termed as very high level of literacy region.

In respect of female literacy of tribal population Almora district stands at the top (89.3%) followed by Tehri (75.9%). Lowest proportion of female literacy in the tribal population has been observed in Hardwar district (29.7%), which is lower than that of the state and country averages (Table 4.11). Table 4.14 gives spatial distribution of districts by the different ranges and groups of female literacy for Uttarakhand. It shows that 7.7% district—Hardwar only—of the state where the tribal female literacy is still below 40% can be termed as a very low level literacy region There are 23.1% districts of the state with female literacy rates between 40-50% can be called as a low literacy region. These districts are Dehradun, Pauri and U.S. Nagar. Out of total thirteen districts, 15.4% (Champawat and Nainital) are in the group of moderate region while 30.7% districts—Uttarkashi, Chamoli,

TABLE 4.12

Distribution of Districts by Ranges of Total Literacy of S.T.Population in Uttarakhand

Level	*Ranges (%)*	*Total Population*		*S.T. Population*		*Districts Name (% in Brackets)*
		(No)	*(%)*	*(No)*	*(%)*	
Very Low	Below 60.0	Nil	Nil	2	15.4	Hardwar (46.3) & Dehradun (57.0).
Low	60.1 - 70.0	4	30.8	5	38.4	Tehri (68.7), Pauri (66.3), Champawat (64.6). Nainital (63.1) & Udham Singh Nagar (63.9).
Moderate	70.1 - 80.0	9	69.2	4	30.8	Uttarkashi (78.1), Chamoli (79.3), Rudraprayag (75.7) & Pithoragarh (77.4).
High	80.1- 90.0	Nil	Nil	1	7.7	Bageshwar (80.3).
Very high	Above 90.1	Nil	Nil	1	7.7	Almora (93.3).
Total		**13**	**100**	**13**	**100**	

Source: Anon. 2001.

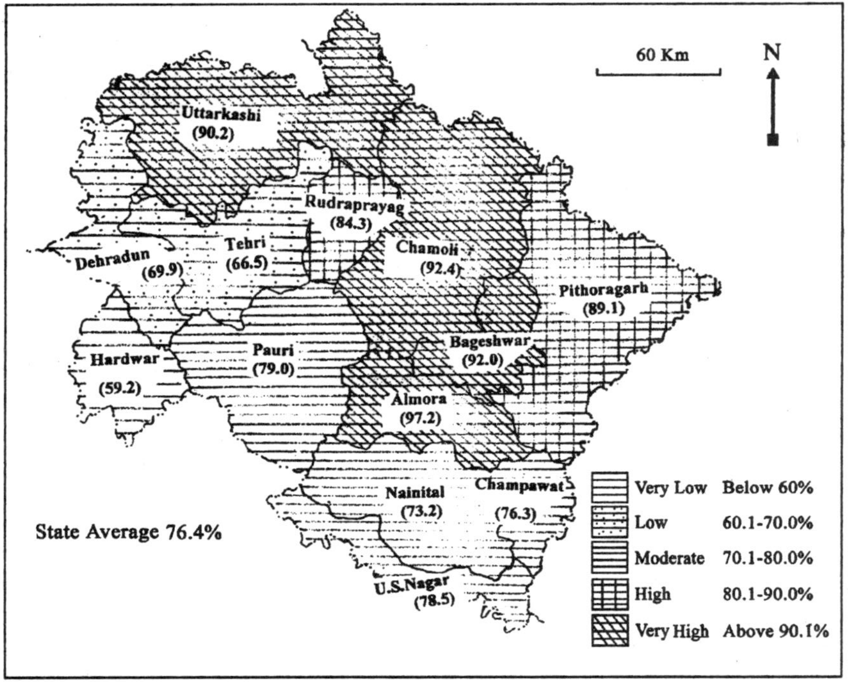

Fig. 4.6 : Uttarakhand: Male Literacy Among Scheduled Tribes Population (2001)

Rudraprayag and Pithoragarh—are in the region of high level of female literacy. About 23.1% districts (Tehri, Bageshwar and Almora) have registered more than 70% tribal female literacy. It is very interesting to note that the tribal female literacy is higher than that of their male counterpart in Tehri district where male literacy is 66.5% and female literacy is 75.9%.

It is observed that there are some particular regions of the state and districts where the tribal literacy rates are relatively low. The region situated comparatively more rugged topography and adverse climatic conditions have recorded low literacy rates while the region having high literacy associated with comparatively high level of urbanization and high proportion of population in tertiary and secondary jobs. The low level of total, male and female literacy of the districts particularly Hardwar and Dehradun is associated with tribal traditions in which proper emphasis was not placed on education in one hand and economically backward on the other.

Gender Gap in Literacy

Table 4.10 depicts that the districts having higher literacy reflects less gap between male and female literacy. On an average 27% points gap between male and female literacy of the total tribal population in the state has been registered in 2001 census which is higher than the state's all castes (23.6%) and country total (21.6%) and tribal (24.4%) population. The gap between male and female literacy rate varies from minimum even minus 9.4% in Tehri to maximum of 29.9% in U.S. Nagar and Hardwar districts. Out of total thirteen districts only 46.2% districts have fewer gaps in male female literacy rate than state (27.0%) and national (24.4%) averages. Table 2.15 gives the distribution of districts by the ranges of gap in male female literacy rates. There are 53.8% districts of the state have more than 25% male female literacy gap. These are Uttarkashi, Chamoli, Dehradun, Pauri, Champawat, U.S. Nagar and Hardwar. Only 30.8% districts are found between 20 to 25% gap in male female tribal literacy. These are Rudraprayag, Pithoragarh, Bageshwar and Nainital. The gender gap in literacy study shows that the gap is fewer in urban dominated areas in comparison to rural based areas.

TABLE 4.13

Distribution of Districts by Ranges of Male Literacy of S.T. Population in Uttarakhand

Level	*Ranges (%)*	*Total Population*		*S.T. Population*		*Districts Name (% in Brackets)*
		(No)	*(%)*	*(No)*	*(%)*	
Very Low	Below 60.0	Nil	Nil	1	7.6	Hardwar (59.2).
Low	60.1 - 70.0	Nil	Nil	2	15.4	Tehri (66.5) & Dehradun (69.9)
Moderate	70.1 - 80.0	2	15.4	4	30.8	Pauri (79.0), Champawat (76.3), Nainital (73.2) & Udham Singh Nagar (78.5).
High	80.1- 90.0	9	69	2	15.4	Rudraprayag (84.3) & Pithoragarh (89.1).
Very high	Above 90.1	2	15.4	4	30.8	Uttarkashi (90.2), Chamoli (92.4), Bageshwar (92.0) & Almora (97.2).
Total		**13**	**100.0**	**13**	**100.0**	

Source: As Table 5.1.

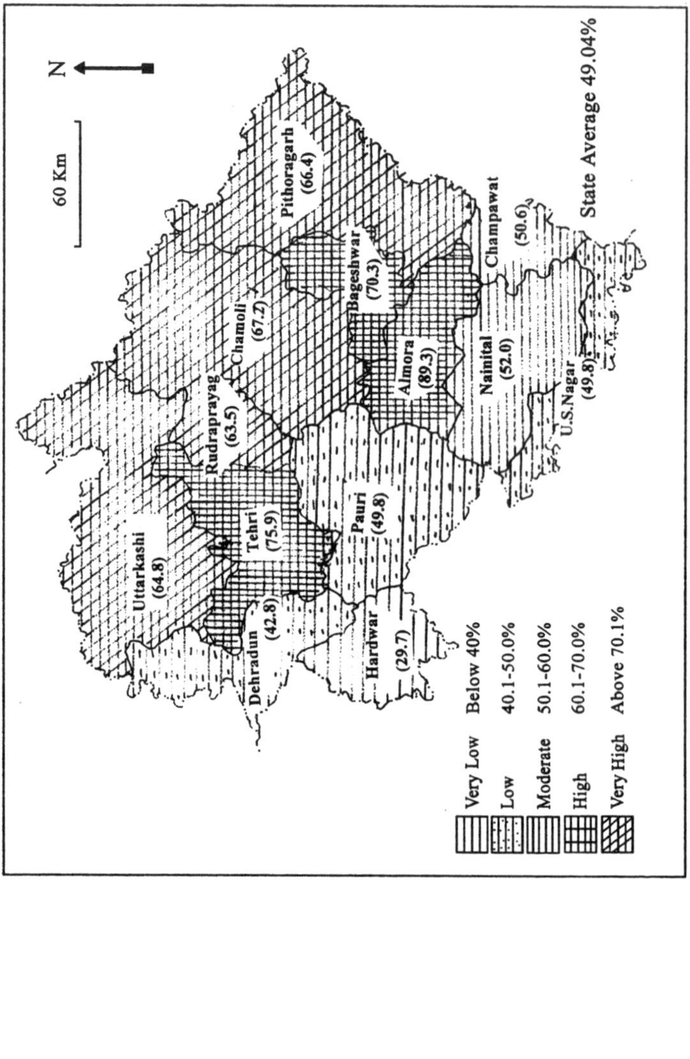

Fig. 4.7 : Uttarakhand: Female Literacy Among Scheduled Tribes Population (2001)

TABLE 4.14

Distribution of Districts by Ranges of Female Literacy of S.T.Population in Uttarakhand

Level	*Ranges (%)*	*Total Population*		*S.T. Population*		*Districts Name (% in Brackets)*
		(No)	*(%)*	*(No)*	*(%)*	
Very Low	Below 40.0	Nil	Nil	1	7.7	Hardwar (29.7).
Low	40.1 - 50.0	2	15.4	3	23.1	Dehradun (42.8), Pauri (49.8) and U.S. Nagar (49.0).
Moderate	50.1 - 60.0	5	38.4	2	15.4	Champawat (50.6) & Nainital (52.0).
High	60.1- 70.0	5	38.4	4	30.7	Uttarkashi (64.8), Chamoli (67.2), Rudraprayag (63.5) & Pithoragarh (66.4).
Very high	Above 70.1	1	7.8	3	23.1	Bageshwar (70.3), Tehri (75.9) & Almora (89.3).
Total		**13**	**100.0**	**13**	**100.0**	

Source: Anon. 2001b.

TABLE 4.15

Distribution of Districts by Ranges of Gender Gap in Total Literacy Rates of S.T. Population in Uttarakhand

Level	*Ranges (%)*	*Total Population*		*S.T. Population*		*Districts Name (% in Brackets)*
		(No)	*(%)*	*(No)*	*(%)*	
Very Low	Below 15.0	1	7.7	2	15.4	Tehri (-9.4) , & Almora (7.9)
Low	15.1-20.0	1	7.7	Nil	Nil	Nil.
Moderate	20.1 - 25.0	2	15.4	4	30.8	Rudraprayag (20.8), Pithoragarh (22.7) Bageshwar (21.7) & Nainital (21.1).
High	25.1- 30.0	4	30.8	7	53.8	Chamoli (25.2), Pauri (29.2), Uttarkashi (25.4), Dehradun (27.1), Champawat (25.7), Hardwar (29.5) & U.S. Nagar (29.5).
Very high	Above30.1	5	38.40	Nil	Nil	Nil.
Total		**13**	**100.0**	**13**	**100.0**	

Source: Anon. 2001.

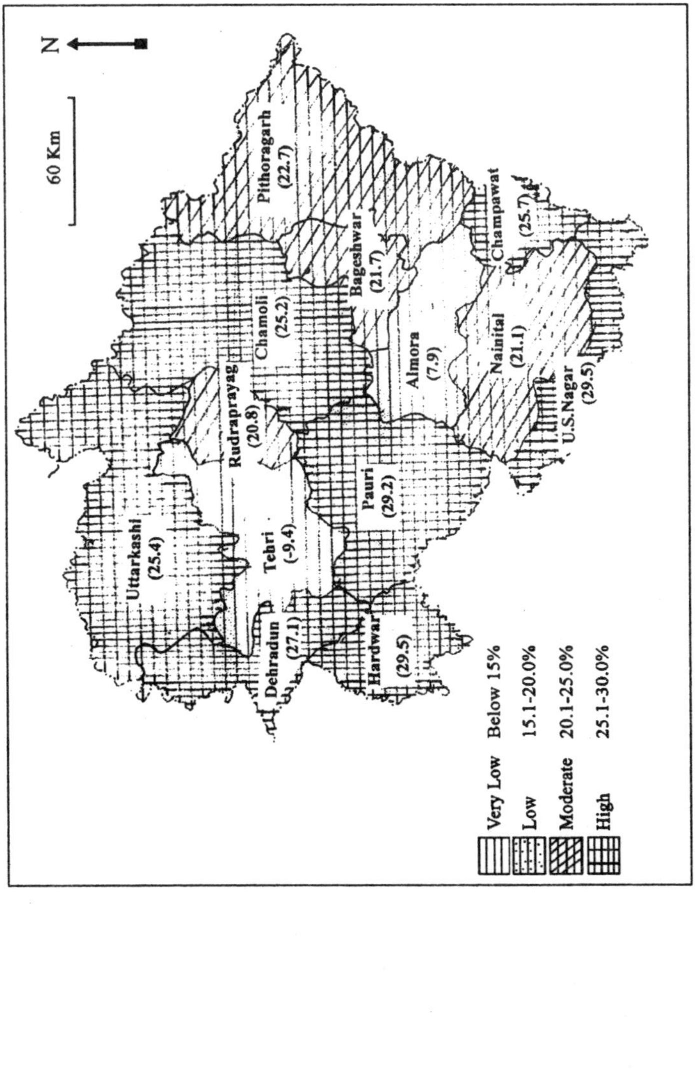

Fig. 4.8 : Uttarakhand: Gap in Male-Female Literacy Among Scheduled Tribes population (2001)

Work Participation Rates

District-wise work participation rates for total and tribal population is depicted in Table 4.16. The percentage of total workers in tribal population is registered higher 41.1% in comparison to the all castes population 36.9% in state as a whole which figures are respectively lower than the national averages. The percentage of total worker in the tribal population varies minimum 32.6% in Hardwar to the maximum of 59.5% in Tehri district. About 49.9% tribal males of the state are found as workers in 2001 which is higher than the all castes workers (46.1%). The work participation rate of male tribal population varies minimum 42.3% in Almora districts to maximum of 76% in Tehri district. Out of total tribal female population in the state only 31.9% are considered as workers which are also higher than the females of all castes population (27.3%). Although the percentage of female workers in the Uttarakhand is lower than the average of the nation (44.8%). The work participation rates of females vary from minimum of 10.3% in Tehri to the maximum of 51.3% in Bageshwar districts. It is noteworthy that the percentage of tribal workers in any geographical area is always higher in comparison to all castes population.

Tables 4.17-4.19 give the spatial distribution of districts by the ranges and groups of participation rates of total workers for persons, males and females for all castes and tribal population of the state as a whole. There are 23.1% districts where the participation rates are falling between 30 to 35%. These districts are Almora, Champawat and Hardwar. The participation rate of Uttarkashi district is in the range of 35-40%. About 53.8% districts of the state have 40-45% workers. These are Chamoli, Rudraprayag, Dehradun, Pauri, Pithoragarh, Nainital and U.S. Nagar. Only Bageshwar and Tehri districts have more than 50% workers. (Table 4.17).

The work participation rate of male tribal is higher than that the total tribal population in the state. Table 4.18 shows that 38.5% districts have more than 50% tribal male workers. These are Tehri, Pauri, Nainital, Dehradun and U.S. Nagar. Only 23% districts have 40-45% tribal male workers while 38.5% districts have 45-50% male tribal workers.

TABLE 4.16

Work Participation Rates by Sex, 2001

S.No.	Districts	Area	Total Population									Scheduled Tribes Population								
			Total Workers			Main Workers			Marginal Workers			Total Workers			Main Workers			Marginal Workers		
			P	M	F	P	M	F	P	M	F	P	M	F	P	M	F	P	M	F
1.	Uttarkashi	Total	46.1	48.3	43.7	38.9	42.3	35.3	7.1	6.0	8.4	38.7	44.1	32.7	34.8	41.9	27.0	3.8	2.2	5.7
		Rural	47.1	48.5	45.7	39.5	42.2	36.8	7.6	6.3	8.9	39.7	44.3	34.6	35.6	42.1	28.5	4.0	2.2	6.1
		Urban	33.8	46.3	16.5	31.6	44.1	14.3	2.2	2.2	2.2	28.0	41.5	11.3	26.3	39.2	10.4	1.7	2.3	0.9
2.	Chamoli	Total	44.5	44.9	44.1	26.2	29.8	22.6	18.3	15.1	21.5	44.7	44.1	45.3	30.4	33.8	27.1	14.3	10.3	18.2
		Rural	45.6	43.8	47.3	25.2	26.9	23.6	20.4	16.9	23.7	47.2	45.1	49.1	29.9	32.6	27.4	17.3	12.5	21.7
		Urban	37.2	50.7	18.4	32.3	44.8	14.7	5.0	5.9	3.7	37.7	41.4	33.8	31.7	37.0	26.2	6.0	4.4	7.7
3.	Rudraprayag	Total	44.9	42.3	47.1	33.4	33.5	33.4	11.4	8.8	13.8	43.5	49.1	36.3	32.8	40.6	22.5	10.8	8.5	13.8
		Rural	44.8	41.8	47.4	33.3	32.9	33.6	11.5	8.9	13.9	41.4	42.5	40.0	28.7	32.2	24.3	12.7	10.3	15.7
		Urban	51.7	71.1	8.0	48.6	66.9	7.6	3.1	4.3	0.4	55.2	78.9	10.0	55.2	78.9	10.0	0.0	0.0	0.0
4.	Tehri	Total	43.8	45.1	42.5	30.0	35.8	24.4	13.8	9.2	18.2	59.5	76.0	10.3	51.8	67.1	6.3	7.7	8.9	4.0
		Rural	44.4	43.4	45.4	29.3	33.3	25.8	15.1	10.1	19.6	32.2	43.8	13.5	27.5	40.2	6.7	4.8	3.6	6.7
		Urban	37.8	56.8	7.6	35.6	53.7	6.9	2.2	3.1	0.7	77.3	91.7	5.7	67.7	80.2	5.7	9.6	11.5	0.0
5.	Dehradun	Total	31.2	47.8	12.6	26.2	41.8	8.7	5.0	6.0	3.9	41.2	50.3	31.1	33.1	44.0	21.2	8.0	6.4	9.9
		Rural	33.2	47.4	17.7	25.5	39.0	10.7	7.7	8.4	7.0	41.9	50.9	32.1	33.6	44.4	21.9	8.3	6.5	10.3
		Urban	29.5	48.1	7.9	26.9	44.3	6.8	2.6	3.8	1.1	24.8	38.8	6.7	22.8	35.8	6.1	2.0	3.0	0.7
6.	Pauri	Total	38.7	40.8	36.8	24.6	29.4	20.3	14.1	11.4	16.5	41.7	55.1	24.9	24.1	35.0	10.3	17.6	20.0	14.6
		Rural	40.3	40.1	40.4	24.4	27.3	22	15.8	12.8	18.5	43.0	55.8	27.2	22.5	32.5	10.1	20.5	23.3	17.1
		Urban	28.2	44.9	7.9	25.9	41.5	6.9	2.2	3.3	0.9	35.0	51.4	11.8	32.9	47.9	11.8	2.0	3.5	0.0
7.	Pithoragarh	Total	43.0	43.4	42.6	26.8	31.1	22.7	16.1	12.3	19.8	44.0	45.3	42.8	28.6	34.1	23.4	15.4	11.2	19.3
		Rural	44.9	43.3	46.5	27.0	29.5	24.6	17.9	13.8	21.8	47.6	47.7	47.5	30.9	35.6	26.3	16.8	12.2	21.2
		Urban	29.9	44.2	12.5	25.8	40.4	8.2	4.1	3.8	4.4	31.5	36.5	26.9	21.0	28.7	13.8	10.5	7.8	13.1

Table Contd....

Table Contd....

S.No.	Districts	Area	Total Population									Scheduled Tribes Population								
			Total Workers			Main Workers			Marginal Workers			Total Workers			Main Workers			Marginal Workers		
			P	M	F	P	M	F	P	M	F	P	M	F	P	M	F	P	M	F
8.	Bageshwar	Total	47.6	45.1	49.9	34.3	34.0	34.6	13.3	11.2	15.3	50.1	48.7	51.3	41.4	39.3	43.3	8.7	9.5	8.0
		Rural	48.2	45.1	50.9	34.5	33.6	35.3	13.7	11.5	15.6	53.5	50.3	56.2	44.6	41.6	47.2	8.9	8.7	9.0
		Urban	31.6	47.5	12	28.8	43.9	10.1	2.8	3.6	1.9	33.3	41.2	26.3	25.6	28.1	23.4	7.7	13.1	2.9
9.	Almora	Total	46.3	44.5	47.9	32.5	33.5	31.6	13.9	11.1	16.3	32.9	42.3	22.5	30.5	40.6	19.4	2.4	1.7	3.1
		Rural	47.7	43.9	50.9	32.7	31.9	33.3	15.0	12.0	17.5	34.8	40.8	28.3	30.9	38.4	22.7	3.9	2.4	5.6
		Urban	32.2	49.5	9.9	30.3	46.6	9.2	1.9	2.9	0.7	30.5	44.2	15.2	30.0	43.2	15.2	0.5	1.0	0.0
10.	Champawat	Total	40.2	43.5	36.9	25	32.6	17.5	15.2	10.8	19.4	33.2	47.0	18.3	22.7	35.1	9.3	10.5	11.9	9.0
		Rural	42.1	42.7	41.5	24.9	30.7	19.3	17.2	12.0	22.1	32.6	46.3	18.1	20.4	31.4	8.7	12.2	14.9	9.4
		Urban	29.5	47.6	8.1	25.8	42.5	6.2	3.6	5.0	2.0	35.3	49.4	19.2	30.5	47.2	11.5	4.8	2.2	7.7
11.	Nainital	Total	36.6	48.1	23.9	29.0	41.1	15.6	7.6	7.0	8.3	45.0	53.9	35.4	26.3	40.8	10.7	18.7	13.1	24.7
		Rural	41.4	49.2	32.9	30.9	40.2	20.8	10.5	9.0	12.1	48.9	56.7	40.5	26.2	41.5	9.8	22.6	15.2	30.7
		Urban	27.7	45.9	6.8	25.4	42.6	5.8	2.3	3.4	1.0	29.4	42.8	15.3	26.4	37.9	14.2	3.0	4.9	1.0
12.	U.S. Nagar	Total	31.7	48	13.7	24.3	40.6	6.2	7.4	7.4	7.5	40.2	50.5	29.5	27.4	43.0	11.4	12.7	7.5	18.1
		Rural	33.8	49	17.3	24.3	40.1	7.1	9.5	8.9	10.2	40.3	50.7	29.5	27.5	43.2	11.5	12.7	7.6	18.0
		Urban	27.4	46.1	6.1	24.3	41.7	4.3	3.2	4.4	1.8	35.0	38.0	30.3	21.5	31.6	5.6	13.5	6.4	24.6
13.	Hardwar	Total	29.4	47.2	8.8	24.4	41.6	4.6	5.0	5.6	4.2	32.6	49.0	12.5	26.6	45.1	3.9	6.0	3.9	8.6
		Rural	29.9	47.3	9.9	23.8	40.7	4.4	6.1	6.7	5.4	33.0	49.3	12.9	26.7	45.3	3.8	6.3	4.0	9.1
		Urban	28.3	46.9	6.3	25.9	43.7	4.9	2.4	3.2	1.5	26.5	43.0	6.2	24.9	41.0	4.9	1.7	2.0	1.2
	Uttarakhand	**Total**	**36.9**	**46.1**	**27.3**	**27.4**	**37.9**	**16.4**	**9.6**	**8.3**	**10.9**	**41.1**	**49.9**	**31.9**	**30.0**	**42.3**	**17.1**	**11.1**	**7.5**	**14.8**
		Rural	**39.6**	**45.7**	**33.6**	**27.7**	**35.7**	**19.6**	**11.9**	**9.9**	**13.9**	**41.7**	**50.4**	**32.9**	**30.3**	**42.7**	**17.3**	**11.4**	**7.7**	**15.2**
		Urban	**29.1**	**47.4**	**7.6**	**26.5**	**43.6**	**6.2**	**2.7**	**3.7**	**1.4**	**32.1**	**41.7**	**21.1**	**25.7**	**36.4**	**13.5**	**6.4**	**5.3**	**7.7**
	India	**Total**	**39.1**	**51.7**	**25.6**	**30.4**	**45.1**	**14.7**	**8.7**	**6.6**	**11.0**	**49.1**	**53.2**	**44.8**	**33.8**	**43.5**	**23.9**	**15.2**	**9.7**	**20.9**
		Rural	**41.7**	**52.1**	**30.8**	**30.9**	**44.3**	**16.6**	**10.9**	**7.8**	**14.1**	**50.4**	**53.8**	**46.9**	**34.3**	**43.7**	**24.6**	**16.1**	**10.0**	**22.3**
		Urban	**32.3**	**50.6**	**x11.9**	**29.3**	**47.2**	**9.4**	**3.0**	**3.4**	**2.5**	**34.7**	**46.8**	**21.6**	**28.7**	**41.3**	**15.5**	**5.8**	**5.5**	**6.1**

Source : Census of India 2001 b.

TABLE 4.17

Distribution of Districts by Ranges of Total Workers (Main & Marginal) of S.T. Population in Uttarakhand

Level	*Ranges (%)*	*Total Population*		*S.T. Population*		*Districts Name (% in Brackets)*
		(No)	*(%)*	*(No)*	*(%)*	
Very Low	Below 30.0	1	7.7	Nil	Nil	Nil.
Low	30.1 - 35.0	2	15.4	3	23.1	Champawat (33.2), Hardwar (32.5), Almora (32.9).
Moderate	35.1 - 40.0	2	15.4	1	7.7	Uttarkashi (38.7).
High	40.1- 45.0	5	38.4	7	53.8	Chamoli (44.7), Pauri (41.7), Dehradun (41.2), Rudraprayag (43.5), Pithoragarh (44.0). Nainital (45.0) & Udham Singh Nagar (40.2).
Very high	Above 45.1	3	23.10	2	15.4	Tehri (59.5) & Bageshwar (50.1).
Total		**13**	**100.0**	**13**	**100.0**	

Source: Anon. 2001 b.

TABLE 4.18

Distribution of Districts by Ranges of Male Workers (Main & Marginal) of S.T.Population in Uttarakhand

Level	*Ranges (%)*	*Total Population*		*S.T. Population*		*Districts Name (% in Brackets)*
		(No)	*(%)*	*(No)*	*(%)*	
Very Low	< 35.0	Nil	Nil	Nil	Nil	Nil.
Low	35.1 - 40.0	Nil	Nil	Nil	Nil	Nil.
Moderate	40.1 -45.0	6	46.2	3	23.0	Uttarkashi (44.1), Chamoli (44.1) & Almora (42.3).
High	45.1- 50.0	7	54	5	38.5	Rudraprayag (49.1), Pithoragarh (45.3), Hardwar (49.0), Bageshwar (48.7) & Champawat (47.0).
Very high	Above 50.1	Nil	Nil	5	38.5	Tehri (76.0), Pauri (55.1), Dehradun (50.3), Nainital (53.9) & Udham Singh Nagar (50.5).
Total		**13**	**100.0**	**13**	**100.0**	

Source: Anon. 2001 b.

TABLE 4.19

Distribution of Districts by Ranges of Female Workers (Main & Marginal) of S.T.Population in Uttarakhand

Level	*Ranges (%)*	*Total Population*		*S.T. Population*		*Districts Name (% in Brackets)*
		(No)	*(%)*	*(No)*	*(%)*	
Very Low	Below 20.0	3	23.1	3	23.1	Tehri (10.3), Hardwar (12.5) & Champawat (18.3).
Low	20.1 - 25.0	1	7.7	2	15.4	Almora (22.5) & Pauri (24.9).
Moderate	25.1 - 30.0	Nil	Nil	1	7.7	Udham Singh Nagar (29.5).
High	30.1- 35.0	Nil	Nil	2	15.4	Uttarkashi (32.7) & Dehradun (31.1).
Very high	Above 35.1	9	69.2	5	38.4	Chamoli (45.3), Bageshwar (51.3), Nainital (35.4), Rudraprayag (36.3) & Pithoragarh (42.8),
Total		**13**	**100.0**	**13**	**100.0**	

Source: Anon. 2001 b.

Out of total, 23.1% districts (Tehri, Champawat and Hardwar) have less than 20% female tribal workers while 38.4% districts (Chamoli, Rudraprayag, Bageshwar, Pithoragarh and Nainital) have more than 35% female tribal workers. About 15.4% districts are respectively in the range of 20-25 and 30-35% female workers. Out of total, 53.8% and 84.6% districts have less female tribal workers than the state and national averages respectively (Table 4.19).

Work Participation Rates by Occupational Category

About 63% of the total tribal workers of the state are registered as cultivators which are 10% and 18% points more than the all castes and tribal cultivators of the state and country respectively. The percentage of tribal cultivators in the state varies from 2.2% in Tehri to 71% in Dehradun district followed by 70% in U.S. Nagar. Out of total male and female tribal workers in the state, 61.7% males and 65.3% females are registered as cultivators. The percentage of male tribal cultivators varies from minimum 1.3% in Tehri district to maximum of 70.5% in U.S. Nagar. About 85% districts of the state have less male cultivators than the state average (61.7%). The maximum 80.8% female cultivators are found in Dehradun district while Almora district has minimum 18.1% cultivators (Table 4.21). The study shows that on an average in the state there are more females in the cultivation activities than males in both the segments. Contrary this the nation has more male tribal than female tribal cultivators.

Tables 4.22-4.24 give the distribution of districts of the state by the ranges of total, male and female tribal and all castes cultivators. Out of total 13 districts, 30.8% districts—Almora, Champawat, Uttarkashi and Tehri have less than 20% tribal cultivators while 15.4% districts (Dehradun and U.S. Nagar) have more than 50% cultivators. Maximum 38.4% districts have 30.1 to 40.0% cultivators. These are Bageshwar, Chamoli, Pithoragarh, Nainital and Hardwar districts. About 46.1% districts of the region have less than 20% male cultivators. These are Uttarkashi, Rudraprayag, Tehri, Pauri, Almora and Champawat. Only 15.4% districts have more than 50.1% male tribal cultivators in the state. These are Dehradun and U.S. Nagar. About 31%

TABLE 4.20

Total Population : Distribution of Total Worker By Category in Percentage, 2001

Sl. No.	Districts	Area	Cultivators			Agri.labourers			H.H Industries			Other Workers		
			P	M	F	P	M	F	P	M	F	P	M	F
1.	Uttarkashi	Total	74.8	61.7	90.1	2.0	2.0	2.0	1.5	1.6	1.5	21.7	34.7	6.4
		Rural	78.8	67.0	91.7	2.1	2.1	2.1	1.6	1.6	1.5	17.6	29.2	4.7
		Urban	8.6	4.00	26.2	0.2	0.2	0.4	1.1	0.9	2.0	90.1	94.9	71.4
2.	Chamoli	Total	69.6	48.7	90.5	0.8	0.9	0.8	2.6	2.4	2.7	27.0	48.1	5.9
		Rural	76.8	58.4	92.6	0.8	0.8	0.8	2.5	2.7	2.4	19.8	38.0	4.2
		Urban	13.7	4.6	48.4	1.1	0.9	1.5	2.7	1.2	8.3	82.6	93.2	41.8
3.	Rudraprayag	Total	75.9	52.2	95.0	0.6	0.7	0.6	1.1	1.8	0.5	22.4	45.3	4.0
		Rural	76.9	53.7	95.1	0.6	0.7	0.6	1.1	1.8	0.5	21.4	43.7	3.9
		Urban	0.1	0.1	0.0	0.0	0.0	0.0	0.9	0.9	1.5	98.9	99.0	98.5
4.	Tehri	Total	7.0	47.7	92.5	1.3	1.4	1.2	0.9	1.3	0.4	27.8	49.5	5.9
		Rural	76.5	56.6	93.7	1.4	1.6	1.2	0.9	1.5	0.4	21.20	40.3	4.7
		Urban	0.6	0.3	3.6	0.2	0.2	0.6	0.7	0.5	2.6	98.6	99.0	93.2
5.	Dehradun	Total	18.8	14.1	38.8	7.0	6.1	1.6	2.5	2.2	4.1	71.7	77.6	46.4
		Rural	36.9	30.0	57.0	13.0	12.3	14.9	2.9	2.4	4.2	47.3	55.3	23.9
		Urban	0.7	0.6	1.5	0.9	0.8	1.8	2.2	2.0	4.1	96.1	96.6	92.6
6.	Pauri	Total	66.5	43.5	89.5	1.7	1.8	1.5	1.3	2.0	0.6	30.6	52.7	8.4
		Rural	73.2	51.9	91.4	1.8	2.1	1.6	1.2	2.1	0.5	23.8	43.9	6.5
		Urban	1.8	0.8	9.4	0.4	0.4	0.4	1.7	1.6	2.5	96.1	97.3	87.8
7.	Pithoragarh	Total	67.6	47.7	87.2	1.3	1.2	1.3	4.0	3.6	4.4	27.1	47.4	7.1
		Rural	73.8	55.6	89.7	1.4	1.4	1.3	3.8	3.9	3.8	21.0	39.1	5.2
		Urban	4.9	1.9	17.4	0.3	0.2	0.7	5.7	1.9	22.0	89.2	96.0	59.8
8.	Bageshwar	Total	74.5	54.7	90.8	3.0	3.0	3.1	2.1	2.8	1.5	20.3	39.5	4.7
		Rural	76.1	56.9	91.3	3.1	3.1	3.1	2.1	2.9	1.5	18.8	37.1	4.2
		Urban	2.4	0.6	11.5	0.4	0.1	2.1	2.6	1.3	8.8	94.5	98.0	77.6

Table Contd....

Table Contd....

Sl. No.	Districts	Area	Cultivators			Agri.labourers			H.H Industries			Other Workers		
			P	M	F	P	M	F	P	M	F	P	M	F
9.	Almora	Total	74.7	53.2	92.1	1.6	1.5	1.6	1.3	2.2	0.6	22.4	43.0	5.7
		Rural	79.4	60.2	93.4	1.6	1.6	1.7	1.3	2.4	0.5	17.6	35.8	4.4
		Urban	1.3	0.3	7.4	0.3	0.3	0.3	1.3	1.4	0.9	97.1	98.0	91.4
10.	Champawat	Total	69.7	51.9	90.1	2.0	2.2	1.8	1.7	2.2	1.2	26.6	43.8	6.8
		Rural	77.5	62.7	91.9	2.1	2.4	1.8	1.7	2.2	1.2	18.7	32.7	5.1
		Urban	6.4	2.6	32.4	1.3	1.2	2.1	2.1	2.0	2.7	90.2	94.2	62.8
11.	Nainital	Total	41.8	31.2	65.5	8.7	7.5	11.5	2.1	1.7	2.9	47.4	59.7	20.1
		Rural	56.8	47.1	72.5	11.7	11.1	12.6	2.2	1.9	2.8	29.2	39.9	12.0
		Urban	0.7	0.6	1.5	0.5	0.4	1.4	1.6	1.3	3.7	97.2	97.7	93.4
12.	U.S.Nagar	Total	30.3	28.5	37	25.9	24.1	32.8	2.5	1.7	5.5	41.4	45.7	24.7
		Rural	40.5	39.9	42.5	32.7	31.7	36.0	2.5	1.6	5.1	24.3	26.8	16.4
		Urban	4.1	4.2	3.5	8.4	7.8	13.6	2.5	1.9	8.0	85.0	86.1	74.9
13.	Hardwar	Total	22.8	23.7	17.3	19.0	18.7	20.9	4.2	2.9	12.1	54.0	54.6	49.8
		Rural	31.9	33.7	21.8	26.0	26.0	25.9	4.5	3.1	11.8	37.6	37.1	40.5
		Urban	1.4	1.4	1.3	2.4	2.4	3.0	3.5	2.4	13.0	92.7	93.8	82.8
	Uttarakhand	**Total**	**50.1**	**34.3**	**77.8**	8.3	9.5	6.1	2.3	2.2	2.5	39.3	54.0	13.6
		Rural	**62.3**	**47.0**	**82.9**	9.8	12.4	6.3	2.3	2.3	2.2	25.7	38.3	8.6
		Urban	**2.2**	**1.6**	**6.5**	2.4	2.2	3.5	2.5	1.8	6.9	93.0	94.3	83.0
	India	**Total**	**31.7**	**31.1**	**32.9**	26.5	20.8	38.9	4.2	3.2	6.5	37.6	44.9	21.7
		Rural	**40.2**	**42.0**	**37.1**	33.0	27.5	43	3.9	3.0	5.5	22.8	27.5	14.4
		Urban	**2.8**	**2.5**	**4.1**	4.7	3.4	10.7	5.2	3.6	12.8	87.3	90.4	72.5

Source: Census of India 2001 b.

TABLE 4.21

Scheduled Tribes Population : Distribution of Total Worker By Category in Percentage, 2001

S. No.	Districts	Area	Cultivators			Agri.labourers			H.H Industries			Other Workers		
			P	M	F	P	M	F	P	M	F	P	M	F
1.	Uttarkashi	Total	16.3	13.6	20.2	0.3	0.3	0.2	35.5	13.63	68.2	48.0	72.4	11.3
		Rural	17.4	14.9	20.8	0.1	0.2	0.0	37.9	14.9	70.2	44.7	69.9	8.9
		Urban	0.0	0.0	0.0	3.0	1.9	8.3	0.0	0.0	0.0	97.0	98.1	91.7
2.	Chamoli	Total	30.9	28.2	33.5	0.5	0.6	0.5	37.9	16.4	57.6	30.6	54.8	8.4
		Rural	33.7	32.9	34.5	0.5	0.7	0.4	40.4	18.8	58.5	25.3	47.6	6.6
		Urban	21.1	14.7	29.1	0.5	0.2	0.9	29.1	9.5	53.7	49.3	75.6	16.3
3.	Rudraprayag	Total	29.6	11.5	62.1	0.0	0.0	0.0	13.6	7.7	24.1	56.8	80.8	13.8
		Rural	36.9	16.2	64.3	0.0	0.0	0.0	16.9	10.8	25.0	46.2	73.0	10.7
		Urban	0.0	0.0	0.0	0.0	0.0	0.0	0.0	0.0	0.0	100.0	100.0	100.0
4.	Tehri	Total	2.2	1.3	22.2	0.0	0.0	0.0	0.2	0.3	0.0	97.6	98.5	77.8
		Rural	10.2	6.8	28.6	0.0	0.0	0.0	1.1	1.4	0.0	88.6	91.9	71.4
		Urban	0.0	0.0	0.0	0.0	0.0	0.0	0.0	0.0	0.0	100.0	100.0	100.0
5.	Dehradun	Total	71.0	65.6	80.8	8.7	9.9	6.7	2.0	1.5	2.7	18.2	22.9	9.8
		Rural	73.0	68.0	81.5	8.9	10.2	6.7	2.0	1.5	2.7	16.1	20.2	9.1
		Urban	3.1	2.8	5.4	1.8	1.7	3.1	1.9	1.6	4.6	93.2	94.0	86.9
6.	Pauri	Total	26.6	9.0	47.7	29.2	27.8	33.0	0.8	0.6	1.1	43.5	52.6	18.2
		Rural	30.6	22.4	51.2	33.5	32.8	35.4	0.5	0.7	0.0	35.4	44.1	13.4
		Urban	0.0	0.0	0.0	0.0	0.0	0.0	2.3	0.0	16.7	97.7	100.0	83.3
7.	Pithoragarh	Total	34.0	36.0	32.0	1.2	1.3	1.2	33.8	12.9	55.0	30.9	49.8	11.8
		Rural	40.2	43.3	37.2	1.4	1.5	1.4	33.7	13.7	53.0	24.7	41.5	8.4
		Urban	1.9	2.6	1.0	0.3	0.3	0.3	34.7	8.9	66.8	63.1	88.2	31.9

Table Contd....

Table Contd....

S. No.	Districts	Area	Cultivators			Agri.labourers			H.H Industries			Other Workers		
			P	M	F	P	M	F	P	M	F	P	M	F
8.	Bageshwar	Total	35.8	29.9	40.7	0.3	0.5	0.2	35.0	21.5	46.1	28.9	48.2	13.1
		Rural	40.3	34.9	44.4	0.3	0.5	0.2	38.2	24.5	48.7	21.1	40.0	6.7
		Urban	0.0	0.0	0.0	0.0	0.0	0.0	9.3	3.2	17.8	90.7	96.8	82.2
9.	Almora	Total	12.8	10.3	18.1	1.7	0.0	5.3	2.4	0.0	7.4	83.0	89.7	69.1
		Rural	21.8	19.2	25.8	2.9	0.0	7.6	4.1	0.0	1.6	71.2	80.8	56.1
		Urban	0.0	0.0	0.0	0.0	0.0	0.0	0.0	0.0	0.0	100.0	100.0	100
10.	Champawat	Total	17.5	14.4	26.2	38.6	37.0	43.1	7.3	4.4	15.4	36.6	44.2	15.4
		Rural	23.0	19.0	34	42.2	42.3	42.0	8.6	5.1	18.0	26.2	33.6	6.0
		Urban	0.0	0.0	0.0	27.1	20.5	46.7	3.4	2.3	6.7	69.5	77.3	46.7
11.	Nainital	Total	36.4	35.5	37.8	32.0	24.8	43.9	0.4	0.2	0.8	31.2	39.5	17.5
		Rural	41.8	42.1	41.5	36.7	29.3	47.8	0.5	0.3	0.8	21.1	28.4	10.0
		Urban	0.3	0.5	0.0	1.7	1.4	2.7	0.3	0.0	1.4	97.6	98.2	95.9
12.	U.S.Nagar	Total	70.0	70.5	69.1	19.5	17.5	22.9	0.8	0.7	0.8	9.8	11.2	7.2
		Rural	70.2	70.9	69.0	19.7	17.7	23.1	0.8	0.7	0.8	9.4	10.6	7.1
		Urban	54.3	39.8	82.6	2.0	1.5	3.0	0.2	0.0	0.6	43.5	58.7	13.8
13.	Hardwar	Total	33.0	33.6	30.5	51.6	50.6	56.5	1.6	1.7	1.1	13.8	14.2	11.9
		Rural	34.7	35.4	31.4	53.7	53.1	57.0	1.6	1.7	1.2	9.9	9.8	10.5
		Urban	0.0	0.0	0.0	8.3	4.7	40.0	0.0	0.0	0.0	91.7	95.7	60.0
	Uttarakhand	**Total**	**63.0**	**61.7**	**65.3**	13.2	13.1	13.3	6.2	**2.6**	**12.1**	**17.6**	**22.6**	**9.3**
		Rural	**65.7**	**64.8**	**67.2**	13.8	13.8	13.7	5.7	**2.6**	**10.9**	**14.8**	**18.8**	**8.2**
		Urban	**10.7**	**7.4**	**18.2**	1.3	1.1	1.7	15.9	**4.0**	**43.1**	**72.1**	**87.5**	**36.9**
	India	**Total**	**44.7**	**47.6**	41.2	36.9	30.3	**44.8**	2.1	**1.5**	**2.9**	**16.3**	**20.6**	**11.1**
		Rural	**47.1**	**51.0**	42.5	38.4	32	45.9	2.1	**1.4**	**2.8**	**12.5**	**15.6**	**8.8**
		Urban	**6.5**	**5.6**	8.7	12.4	9.2	19.8	2.9	1.9	**5.2**	**78.2**	**93.4**	**66.3**

Source : Census of India 2001 b.

TABLE 4.22

Distribution of Districts by Ranges of Total Cultivators (Main & Marginal) of S.T. Population in Uttarakhand

Level	*Ranges (%)*	*Total Population*		*S.T. Population*		*Districts Name (% in Brackets)*
		(No)	*(%)*	*(No)*	*(%)*	
Very Low	Below 20.0	2	15.4	4	30.8	Almora (12.8), Champawat (17.5), Uttarkashi (16.3), & Tehri (2.2).
Low	20.1 - 30.0	1	7.7	2	15.4	Rudraprayag (78.9) & Pauri (51.4).
Moderate	30.1 -40.0	1	7.7	5	38.4	Chamoli (30.9), Bageshwar (35.8), Nainital (36.4), Pithoragarh (34.0) & Hardwar (33.0).
High	40.1- 50.0	1	7.7	Nil	Nil	Nil.
Very high	Above 50.1	8	61.5	2	15.4	Dehradun (71.0) & Udham Singh Nagar (70.0).
Total		**13**	**100.0**	**13**	**100.0**	

Source: Anon. 2001 b.

TABLE 4.23

Distribution of Districts by Ranges of Male Cultivators (Main & Marginal) of S.T.Population in Uttarakhand

Level	*Ranges (%)*	*Total Population*		*S.T. Population*		*Districts Name (% in Brackets)*
		(No)	*(%)*	*(No)*	*(%)*	
Very Low	Below 20.0	1	7.7	6	46.1	Almora (10.3), Champawat (14.4), Uttarkashi (13.6), Rudraprayag (11.5), Pauri (9.0) & Tehri (1.3).
Low	20.1 – 30.0	2	15.4	2	15.4	Chamoli (28.2) & Bageshwar (29.9).
Moderate	30.1 -40.0	1	7.7	3	23.1	Pithoragarh (36.0) Nainital (35.5) & Hardwar (33.6).
High	40.1- 50.0	4	30.8	Nil	Nil	Nil.
Very high	Above 50.1	5	38.4	2	15.4	Dehradun (65.6) & Udham Singh Nagar (70.5).
Total		**13**	**100.0**	**13**	**100.0**	

Source: Anon. 2001 b.

TABLE 4.24

Distribution of Districts by Ranges of Female Cultivators (Main & Marginal) of S.T.Population in Uttarakhand

Level	*Ranges (%)*	*Total Population*		*S.T. Population*		*Districts Name (% in Brackets)*
		(No)	*(%)*	*(No)*	*(%)*	
Very Low	Below 30.0	1	7.7	4	30.8	Almora (18.1), Champawat (26.2), Uttarkashi (20.2), & Tehri (22.2).
Low	30.1 - 40.0	2	15.4	4	30.8	Pithoragarh (32.0), Nainital (37.8), Hardwar (30.5) & Chamoli (33.5).
Moderate	40.1 - 50.0	Nil	Nil	2	15.4	Pauri (47.7) & Bageshwar (40.7).
High	50.1 - 60.0	Nil	Nil	Nil	Nil	Nil.
Very high	Above 60.1	10	76.9	3	23.0	Rudraprayag (11.5), Dehradun (65.6), U.S. Nagar (69.1)
Total		**13**	**100.0**	**13**	**100.0**	

Source: Anon. 2001 b.

TABLE 4.25

Distribution of Districts by Ranges of Total Agricultural Labors (Main & Marginal) of S.T.Population in Uttarakhand

Level	*Ranges (%)*	*Total Population*		*S.T. Population*		*Districts Name (% in Brackets)*
		(No)	*(%)*	*(No)*	*(%)*	
Very Low	Below 5.0	9	69.2	7	53.8	Uttarkashi (0.3), Rudraprayag (0.0), Tehri (0.0), Chamoli (0.5), Bageshwar (0.3), Pithoragarh (1.2), & Almora (1.7).
Low	5.1 - 10.0	2	15.4	1	7.7	Dehradun (8.7).
Moderate	0.1 -15.0	Nil	Nil	Nil	Nil	Nil.
High	15.1- 20.0	1	7.7	1	7.7	Udham Singh Nagar (19.5).
Very high	Above 20.1	1	7.7	4	30.8	Pauri (29.2), Nainital (32.0), Hardwar (51.6) & Champawat (38.6).
Total		**13**	**100.0**	**13**	**100.0**	

Source: Anon. 2001 b.

TABLE 4.26

Distribution of Districts by Ranges of Male Agricultural Labours (Main & Marginal) of S.T. Population in Uttarakhand

Level	*Ranges (%)*	*Total Population*		*S.T. Population*		*Districts Name (% in Brackets)*
		(No)	*(%)*	*(No)*	*(%)*	
Very Low	Below 5.0	9	69.2	7	53.8	Uttarkashi (0.3), Rudraprayag (0.0), Tehri (0.0), Chamoli (0.6), Bageshwar (0.5), Pithoragarh (1.3) & Almora (0.0).
Low	5.1 - 10.0	2	15.4	1	7.7	Dehradun (9.9).
Moderate	10.1 -15.0	Nil	Nil	Nil	Nil	Nil.
High	15.1- 20.0	1	7.7	1	7.7	Udham Singh Nagar (17.5).
Very high	Above 20.1	1	7.7	4	30.8	Pauri (27.8), Nainital (24.8), Hardwar (50.6) & Champawat (37.0).
Total		**13**	**100.0**	**13**	**100.0**	

Source: Anon. 2001 b.

TABLE 4.27

Distribution of Districts by Ranges of Female Agricultural Labors (Main & Marginal) of S.T. Population in Uttarakhand

Level	*Ranges (%)*	*Total Population*		*S.T. Population*		*Districts Name (% in Brackets)*
		(No)	*(%)*	*(No)*	*(%)*	
Very Low	Below 5.0	10	76.9	6	46.1	Uttarkashi (0.2), Rudraprayag (0.0), Tehri (0.0), Chamoli (0.5), Bageshwar (0.2), Pithoragarh (1.2)
Low	5.1 - 10.0	Nil	Nil	2	15.4	Dehradun (6.7) & Almora (5.3).
Moderate	10.1 -15.0	1	7.7	Nil	Nil	Nil.
High	15.1- 20.0	Nil	Nil	Nil	Nil	Nil.
Very high	Above 20.1	2	15.4	5	38.5	Pauri (33.0), Nainital (43.9), Hardwar (56.5) & Champawat (43.1) & Udham Singh Nagar(22.9)
Total		**13**	**100.0**	**13**	**100.0**	

Source: Anon. 2001 b.

districts have less than 30% while 23% districts of the state have more than 60% female tribal cultivators.

Out of total tribal workers in the state, 13.2, 13.1 and 13.3% persons, males and females are respectively registered as agricultural labourers (Table 4.21). It is higher than the percentage of all castes agricultural labourers in the state but these figures are much lower than the country averages. Table 4.21 shows that plain and semi plain districts of the state have more than 15% tribal agricultural labourers. The agricultural labourer varies from minimum of zero in Tehri and Rudraprayag to maximum of 51.6% in Hardwar district. Tables 4.25-4.26 give the distribution of districts of the state by the ranges of total, male and female agricultural labourers. More than 50% districts (Uttarkashi, Chamoli, Rudraprayag, Tehri, Pithoragarh, Bageshwar and Almora) have less than 5% tribal agricultural labourers while 30.8% districts (Pauri, Champawat, Nainital and Hardwar) have more than 20% agricultural labourers. Similar trend is found in male and female tribal agricultural labourers.

About 6.2% tribal workers are found in household industries while 2.6% males and 12.1% female workers are found in household industries. Table 4.21 reflects that more females than males are registered in household works. Maximum household female workers are engaged in woollen industries. Minimum household industries workers are registered in Tehri (0.2%) while maximum of 37.9% in Chamoli district. About 38.5% districts have less than 1% workers in household industries while 38.4% districts have more than 8.01% (Tables 4.28-4.30). Workers in household industries in the state are higher than the national average.

Out of total tribal workers 17.6% persons are registered as other workers i.e. persons engaged in white colour jobs which is higher than the other workers of all castes population (16.3%). The percentage of other workers of tribal total workers varies minimum of 9.8% in U.S. Nagar to maximum of 97.6% in Tehri district. Out of total male tribal workers, 22.6% males are considered as other workers which are less than the half of all castes other workers. Similarly about 9.3% female workers are

TABLE 4.28

Distribution of Districts by Ranges of Total Workers in H.H.Industries (Main & Marginal) of S.T. Population in Uttarakhand

Level	*Ranges (%)*	*Total Population*		*S.T. Population*		*Districts Name (% in Brackets)*
		(No)	*(%)*	*(No)*	*(%)*	
Very Low	Below 1.0	1	7.7	5	38.5	Tehri (0.2), Udham Singh Nagar (0.8), Pauri (0.8), Nainital (0.4), Hardwar (1.6).
Low	1.1 - 3.0	10	76.9	2	15.4	Dehradun (2.0) & Almora (2.4).
Moderate	3.1 -5.0	2	15.4	Nil	Nil	Nil.
High	5.1- 8.0	Nil	Nil	1	7.7	Champawat (7.3).
Very high	Above 8.1	Nil	Nil	5	38.4	Uttarkashi (35.5), Rudraprayag (13.6), Chamoli (37.9), Bageshwar (35.0), Pithoragarh (33.8).
Total		**13**	**100.0**	**13**	**100.0**	

Source: Anon. 2001 b.

TABLE 4.29

Distribution of Districts by Ranges of Male Workers in H.H. Industries (Main & Marginal) of S.T. Population in Uttarakhand

Level	*Ranges (%)*	*Total Population*		*S.T. Population*		*Districts Name (% in Brackets)*
		(No)	*(%)*	*(No)*	*(%)*	
Very Low	Below 1.0	Nil	Nil	5	38.5	Almora (0.0), Tehri (0.3), Pauri (0.6), Nainital (0.2) & Udham Singh Nagar (0.7).
Low	1.1 - 2.0	6	46.1	2	15.4	Dehradun (1.5) & Hardwar (1.7).
Moderate	2.1 -3.0	6	46.1	Nil	Nil	Nil
High	3.1- 4.0	1	7.8	Nil	Nil	Nil
Very high	Above 4.1	Nil	Nil	6	46.1	Chamoli (16.4), Bageshwar (21.5), Pithoragarh (12.9), Uttarkashi (13.5), Rudraprayag (7.7), & Champawat (4.4).
Total		**13**	**100.0**	**13**	**100.0**	

Source: Anon. 2001 b.

TABLE 4.30

Distribution of Districts by Ranges of Female Workers in H.H. Industries (Main & Marginal) of S.T. Population in Uttarakhand

Level	*Ranges (%)*	*Total Population*		*S.T. Population*		*Districts Name (% in Brackets)*
		(No)	*(%)*	*(No)*	*(%)*	
Very Low	Below 3.0	12	92.3	6	46.1	Tehri (0.0), Pauri (1.1), Dehradun (2.7), Hardwar (1.1), Nainital (0.8) & Udham Singh Nagar(0.8).
Low	3.1 - 5.0	1	7.7	Nil	Nil	Nil.
Moderate	5.1 - 8.0	Nil	Nil	1	7.8	Almora (7.4)
High	8.1- 11.0	Nil	Nil	Nil	Nil	Nil.
Very high	Above 11.1	Nil	Nil	6	46.1	Chamoli (57.6), Bageshwar (46.1), Pithoragarh (55.0), Uttarkashi (68.2), Rudraprayag (24.1), & Champawat (15.4).
Total		**13**	**100.0**	**13**	**100.0**	

Source: Anon. 2001b.

TABLE 4.31

Distribution of Districts by Ranges of Total Other Workers (Main & Marginal) of S.T. Population in Uttarakhand

Level	*Ranges (%)*	*Total Population*		*S.T. Population*		*Districts Name (% in Brackets)*
		(No)	*(%)*	*(No)*	*(%)*	
Very Low	Below 35.0	9	69.2	7	53.8	Chamoli (30.6), Bageshwar (28.9), Pithoragarh (30.9), Nainital (31.2), Udham Singh Nagar (9.8). Dehradun (18.2) & Hardwar (13.8).
Low	35.1 - 40.0	Nil	Nil	1	7.7	Champawat (36.6).
Moderate	40.1 -45.0	1	7.7	1	7.7	Pauri (43.5).
High	45.1- 50.0	1	7.7	1	7.7	Uttarkashi (48.0).
Very high	Above 50.1	2	15.4	3	23.1	Rudraprayag (56.8), Almora (83.0) & Tehri (97.6).
Total		**13**	**100.0**	**13**	**100.0**	

Source: Anon. 2001b.

TABLE 4.32

Distribution of Districts by Ranges of Male Other Workers (Main & Marginal) of S.T. Population in Uttarakhand

Level	*Ranges (%)*	*Total Population*		*S.T. Population*		*Districts Name (% in Brackets)*
		(No)	*(%)*	*(No)*	*(%)*	
Very Low	Below 20.0	Nil	Nil	2	15.4	Hardwar (14.2) & Udham Singh Nagar (11.2).
Low	21.1 - 30.0	Nil	Nil	1	7.7	Dehradun (22.9).
Moderate	30.1 - 40.0	2	15.4	1	7.7	Nainıtal (39.5).
High	40.1 - 50.0	7	53.8	3	23.1	Bageshwar (48.2), Pithoragarh (49.8) and Champawat (44.2).
Very high	Above 4.1	4	30.8	6	46.1	Rudraprayag (80.8), Almora (89.7), Tehri (98.5). Uttarkashi (72.4), Chamoli (54.8) & Pauri (52.6).
Total		**13**	**100.0**	**13**	**100.0**	

Source: Anon. 2001b.

TABLE 4.33

Distribution of Districts by Ranges of Female Other Workers (Main & Marginal) of S.T. Population in Uttarakhand

Level	Ranges (%)	Total Population		S.T. Population		Districts Name (% in Brackets)
		(No)	(%)	(No)	(%)	
Very Low	< 5.0	1	7.7	Nil	Nil	Nil.
Low	5.1 - 10.0	8	61.5	3	23.1	Dehradun (9.8), Chamoli (8.4) & U.S. Nagar (7.2).
Moderate	10.1 - 15.0	Nil	Nil	5	38.4	Uttarkashi (11.3), Rudraprayag (13.8), Hardwar (11.9), Bageshwar (13.1) & Pithoragarh (11.8),
High	15.1- 20.0	Nil	Nil	3	23.1	Pauri (18.2), Nainital (17.5) & Champawat (15.4).
Very high	> 20.1	4	30.8	2	15.4	Almora (69.1) & Tehri (77.8).
Total		**13**	**100.0**	**13**	**100.0**	

Source: Anon. 2001b.

found in this category. It reflects that the percentage of female workers in both tribal and non tribal categories is still very low. Tables 4.31-4.33 give the distribution of districts by the ranges of total, male and female tribal and all castes other workers. It shows that about 61% districts have less than 40% total other workers.

About 41% districts have more than 50.1% male tribal other workers while 85% districts have less than 2% female other workers.

Urbanization

The state of socio-economic development of any society is often viewed by the degree of urbanization attained by the particular society in a specified space of time. About 6.2% of the total tribal population is registered as urban population, which is lower than the total population (25.66%) of the state. It reveals that still maximum tribal population resides in their ancestral remote villages. The economic and educational status of the urban tribal population is much higher than the rural tribal population.

Summary

The tribal population of Uttarakhand is concentrated in the remote/forest areas of Tarai and Bhabar and higher reaches of Pithoragarh, Chamoli, Uttarkashi districts and Jaunsar-Bhabar area of Dehradun district. As per 2001 census it comes to 2,56,129 people constitute about 3% to the total population of the states. Uttarakhand state contributes only 0.83% to total population and 0.3% to the tribal population of India. Among the 13 districts of the states, Udham Singh Nagar with a tribal population of 1,10,220 (43.03%), is at the top followed by Dehradun (99,329 person or 38.78%) Pithoragarh (19,279 person or 7.53%) and Chamoli (4.09%). In fact four districts of Uttarakhand contribute about 93% of total tribal population. But their largest proportion to total population among all the districts is found in U.S. Nagar (8.9%) followed by Dehradun (7.7%), Pithoragarh (4.2%) and Chamoli (2.8%). Proportion of the tribal population to the total population of the remaining districts is found less than 1%.

The average household size of the tribal population in the state is found 6.1 people per family, which is higher than that of the all castes population (5.3) of the state and country (5.1) while the size of family in urban area (4.31) is less than the all castes population (5.2). Arithmetic density of the states as a whole works out to 159 p/km^2 in 2001 as against to 132 in 1991 census while the tribal density is 4.79 person in 2001 as against to 3.46 person per km^2 in 1991, which is lower than that of the national average. This means that the total and tribal pressure in the states has increased. The total growth of tribal population of Uttarakhand during 1991-2001 was 20.89% which is higher than the growth of all castes population. The decadal growth rate of tribal population of India and Uttarakhand has increased while the growth rate of all castes population for both the state and country has decreased during 1981-1991 to 1991-2001.

Average sex ratio of the tribal total population is 950, which is less than the sex ratio of the all castes population (962) while the sex ratio in below the six years population is numerical higher (955) than that of the total population (908). The sex ratio has usually been quite high in the hill districts as compared to districts in plains of Uttarakhand. The total literacy of the Uttarakhand is 71.6% which is higher than the country average (64.8%). Similarly in case of tribal literacy Uttarakhand with 63.2% literates is quite ahead of average literacy registered for the country (47.1%). The Level of male and female literacy among the tribal community of Uttarakhand is higher than that of the national average. The tribal literacy varies from minimum 46.3% in Hardwar districts to maximum 93.3% in Almora district while the literacy rates for all castes population is higher than that of tribal population in the state. It is observed that there are some particular regions of the state and districts where the tribal literacy rates are relatively low. The region having comparatively more rugged topography and adverse climatic conditions have recorded low literacy rates while the region having high literacy associated with comparatively high level of urbanization and high proportion of population in tertiary and secondary jobs. The low level of total, male and female literacy of the districts particularly Hardwar and Dehradun is associated with tribal traditions where proper emphasis was not placed on education on the one hand and economically backward on the other.

On an average 27% points gap between male and female literacy of the total tribal population in the state has been registered in 2001 census which is higher than the state's all castes (23.6%) and country total (21.6%) and tribal (24.4%) population. The gap between male and female literacy rate varies from minimum even minus 9.4% in Tehri to maximum of 29.9% in U.S. Nagar and Hardwar districts. Out of total thirteen districts only 46.2% districts have fewer gaps in male-female literacy rate than state (27.0%) and national (24.4%) averages.

The percentage of total workers in tribal population is registered higher (41.1%) in comparison to the all castes population (36.9%) in state as a whole which figures are respectively lower than the country averages. The percentage of total workers in the tribal population varies from minimum 32.6% in Hardwar to the maximum of 59.5% in Tehri district. About 49.9% tribal males of the state are found as workers in 2001 which is higher than the all castes workers (46.1%). The work participation rate of male tribal population varies from minimum 42.3% in Almora districts to maximum of 76% in Tehri district. Out of total tribal female population in the state only 31.9% are considered as workers which are also higher than the females of all castes population (27.3%). Although the percentage of female workers in the Uttarakhand is lower than the average of the nation (44.8%). The work participation rates of females vary from minimum 10.3% in Tehri to the maximum 51.3% in Bageshwar districts.

About 63% of the total tribal workers of the state are registered as cultivators which are 10% and 18% points more than the all castes and tribal cultivators of the state and country respectively. The percentage of tribal cultivators in the state varies from 2.2% in Tehri to 71% in Dehradun district followed by 70% in U.S. Nagar. Out of total male and female tribal workers in the state, 61.7% males and 65.3% females are registered as cultivators. Out of total tribal workers in the state, 13.2, 13.1 and 13.3% persons, males and females are respectively registered as agricultural labourers. About 6.2% tribal workers are found in household industries consisting of 2.6% males and 12.1% female workers.

Out of total tribal workers 17.6% persons are registered as other workers i.e. persons engaged in white colour jobs which is higher than the other workers of all castes population (16.3%). The percentage out of other workers of tribal total workers varies minimum of 9.8% in U.S. Nagar to maximum of 97.6% in Tehri district. Out of total male tribal workers, 22.6% males are considered as other workers which are less than the half of all castes other workers. Similarly about 9.3% female workers are found in this category. It reflects that the percentage of female workers in both tribal and non-tribal categories is still very low.

About 6.2% of the total tribal population is registered as urban population, which is lower than the total population (25.66%) of the state. It reveals that still maximum tribal population resides in their ancestral remote villages. Remarkably, economic and educational status of the urban tribal population is relatively higher than the rural tribal population.

5

Tharu Tribe

Geographical Background of Tharu Habitat

The main habitat of Tharus is Sitarganj and Khatima tehsils of U.S. Nagar district in Uttarakhand state. It stretches from the Sharda River on the east to the Kichha tehsils of the same district on the west and lies between 28°44' to 29°0'30" North latitude and 79°28'to 80° East longitude. It is bounded by the Nainital district on the north, districts Bareilly and Pilibhit on the south, Kichha tehsil on the west and Nepal on the east. It comprises a narrow strip of the country running for 40 km long and 25 km wide along the foot of the Himalaya with reporting area of 68206 km^2 and supports 358498 total and 82385 Tharu populations as per census 2001 (Fig. 5.1).

Tarai region physiographically is a vast alluvial land lying at the southernmost part of the Outer Himalaya. It separates from the Bhabar by the spring line in the north and densely populated Gangetic plain in the south. It is characterized by a deposit a fine sediments carried by the rivers flowing down from the Bhabar region. Tarai is a zone of super abundance of water because the underground water of the Bhabar zone reappears on the surface on the junction of Bhabar and Tarai called to as the spring line belt. The Tarai belt is the lowest part of Uttarakhand with an altitude of ***200 m or less. There is a general decrease of elevation towards south. The surface of the area is formed of the fine alluvial material of sand and clay. Presently due to the construction of artificial water reservoirs and other land reclamation plans, once swampy Tarai mainly known for its malarial climate and luxuriant growth of broad leaved vegetation cover has now turned in to a zone of fertile agriculture.

The soil of Tarai is almost alluvial deposit. It is mainly loam, clay and clay-sand but the clay is predominates. The soil is rich in humus content because the accumulated deposit of centuries of grass and foliage. As a result, the out put of the soil is satisfactory, and not required much labour and manures.

The drainage system of the study region consists of the streams and rivers which flow directly from the Himalaya. The Sharda River is the main river flowing in the extreme east of the study region. From east to west there are Saniha, Chauka, Khakra, Lohia, Jagbura, Kamin, Deoha, Kailash, Bahgul and Dhaura streams in the study region. The drainage of the region as a whole ultimately leads to water logging resulting into breeding of mosquitoes and finally into unhealthy climate, as most of these streams are subject to heavy floods during the rains. There is one main reservoir Nanaksagar which is useful for irrigation and fishing. Khatima hydropower project is constructed in Sharda River on east of the region. From the earliest time, the Tharu inhabitants of the region were using the streams and rivers for irrigation and fishing purposes. The most common method employed by them was to construct earthen dams wherever required across the small streams and rivers. This had caused a ruinous effect both to land and climate.

In general, the study region experiences extreme climate, summer being severely hot and winter very foggy cold. It receives most of its rain in June, July, August and September; winter has only few showers. The direct and reflected sun's heat makes it close, hot and muggy. The average annual rainfall of this region is 150 to 200 cm. During the rainy season when the forest under growth grows up, the climate is extremely unhealthy. During rest of the year the climate though enervating is not so unhealthy. Because of unhealthy climate Atkinson characterized the habitat of the Tharus as a region of 'Mar' the land of death (Atkinson, 1886).

The Savanah type of forests is found within an altitudinal range of 150 to 350 m. The forests of this region are generally of poor value and mostly contain scrubs jungles. There are mixed broad leaved species occurring below 350 m. The vegetation mainly consists of tall grasses and mixed tree species such as Amla, Bahera, Bamboo, Dhank, Gutel, Haldu, Jamun, Jhingan, Kachnar, etc. together with newly introduced, Eucalyptus, Poplar and Teak which are either found along the road sides or as a plantations inside forest areas. The forest areas have encroached by the in-migrated population for expansion of cultivation and habitation.

The study area abounds in carnivorous animals. Wild beast including tigers, panthers, elephants, bears, blue bulls and many species of deer have played lively part in the continual deterioration and destruction of the tract. About a century back wild animals were numerous in this area but owing to the extension and growth of cultivation in recent years and greater use of arms and effective weapons they are definitely on decrease.

This tract is a happy hunting ground for the ornithologists as hundreds of species of game birds, namely jungle fowls, quails, partridges, peacocks, and snips are found in large number in the Tarai forests. There is a frequent visit of migratory birds from the Central Asia in the water bodies such as Nanaksagar, Dhaura, and Sharda Sagar. In addition to this fishes of all kinds and description abound the streams and artificial water bodies.

The habitat of the Tharus is a land of numerous sluggish stream and water locked morasses, full of forests and swamp with scattered patches of cultivation. The region is suitable for grazing purposes, though of late there has been a marked extension of cultivation from the south to north. Owing to fertility of the soil the cultivation has made a rapid progress in the study area. The average area brought under cultivation is about 40% of the total rural area, though there still remains a considerable waste land. It is known as rice producing area. The principal crops grown in this area, are rice, sugarcane, wheat, sunflower, gram, peas, mustard, lentil and red pepper.

The means of communication in the study area are so poor that it is not at all economical to transport field produce to distant market. The only track of railway in this region is that of N.E. Railway which connects the main habitat of the Tharus.

The nearest railway stations are Kichha (25 km.) and Khatima (30 km). In this study region the metalled roads are rare except Haldwani to Khatima—Tanakpur via Kichha, and via Chorgalia, though unmetalled roads are numerous. The low-lying parts of the region are not easily accessible during the rainy season. Hence the habitat of the Tharus is most inadequately connected by means of transport and communication which their easy and direct contact with people of other parts of the country.

The Udham Singh Nagar district has been carved out from Nainital district in 1994. It is generally spread over the Tarai region of the state. The U.S. Nagar district is administratively divided into seven tehsils, same are development blocks, namely, Jaspur, Kashipur, Bajpur, Gadarpur, Rudrapur (Kichha), Sitarganj, and Khatima of these seven tehsils last two, that is Sitarganj and Khatima are inhabited by the Tharus whose socioeconomic and nutritional status is the main subject of the study. Although they are concentrated in these two tehsils of U.S. Nagar, but they have also their settlements in the districts of Gonda, Gorakhpur, Bahraich, Lakhimpur, Kheri and Pilibhit of U.P. and Nepal. According to various census figures the U.S. Nagar colder Nainital Tarai) Tharus have shown an increase from 15397 in 1891 to 82385 in 2001 i.e. 435% in a steady manner except in the decade between 1911-1921 when influenza was responsible for their considerable mortality and 1941 when epidemic of Cholera was responsible for the decrease of Tharu population.

Thus the Tharus, on the whole, may not have shown a steady phenomenal increase in their population in every decade but it certainly shows that they have adapted to and successfully survived the unhealthy climate of the region.

Historical Background of Tharu Habitat

There are number anthropologists, sociologists, anthropogeographers and historians who have traced the origin of Tharu tribes in the Tarai region hold conflicting views on the matter. They trace various etymological sources, i.e. to *'tahre'* which means 'they halted' after their alleged fight into the Tarai forests; or to *'tarhuwa'* which means 'became wet' or *'thatharana'* signifying 'trembling' or 'quaking' during their flight from Hastinapur to the Tarai after a fierce battle between the Rajputs and the Muslims. S. Knowles traces the origin of the Tharus to the word *tharua* (Knowles, quoted by Srivastava, 1958) of hill dialect, meaning a 'paddler'. *Tharu* word denotes a wine bibber (Crooke, 1896). Dr. Buchnan introduces another idea when he makes a reference to the expulsion of the Gurkhas from Magadh by a people called Tharu. These are said to have descended from the hills and spread over every part of the north of the Ganga River. But, this again is a controversial point, because the Tharus themselves claim Chittor as their original home and to have descended from Jaimal, Fateh Singh and Tarran Singh of Sisodiya clan of Rajputs (1303 AD). They say that they were driven out apparently in the third siege of Chittor by Akbar in 1567 AD and they were originally Rajputs who lost caste by using intoxicating liquor and rearing fowls. They never claim Gurkha and hill origin (Srivastava, 1958).

According to H.R. Nevill (1904), the Tharus are an aboriginal race who claims royal descent on the female side. He gives a story that 'once upon a time in the remote past when the king of these parts was defeated by the forces of an invader, the women of the royal palace rather than fall in to the hands of foe fled in to the jungles with the Saises and Chamars belonging to the palace. From these sprang the two indigenous races of the Tharus and Buksas, the former is said to have descended from the Chamars and the later from the Saises. This tradition is further explained by the dominance of women among the Tharus. Some are of opinion that the Tharus a Mongoloid tribe and they could not be placed in any other constellation of tribes and castes of the Province, Indo-Aryan or Australoid. In features they possess, more or less, oblique eyes, mostly brown or yellow-brown complexion, very scanty and straight hair on the body and the face, thin nose of medium size; while in other features they resemble Nepalese more than any of the Australoid or pre-Dravidian castes and tribes. Furthermore, Majumdar (1942) has contested the supposed Rajput origin of the Tharus on the basis of the blood group tests carried by him in connection with the Census Operations of the United Provinces, 1941. On the basis of the studies done by the various people, we can conclude that the

Tharus are a Mongoloid people, or predominantly so, who have successfully assimilated non-Mongoloid physical features as well.

Cultural Setup of Tharu Habitat

The scheduled tribe population particularly Tharus are very bold and strenuous. They have done a lot of struggle for their existence in the study region. As a result they are more or less successful in their efforts to exploit the natural resources to meet their primary requirements like food, shelter and clothing. But at the present time their mode of living is changed because of their increasing contact with the people of other castes and cultures. The Tharu villages are generally scattered and often located at a distance of three to four kilometres from one another. They settled in isolated locations in their village. They are always in search of a good location for founding their villages. A good location means it must be the land on high level with proximity to a river or some water supply yet to safe from water logging and inundation during the rainy season. It must have a fertile soil and safety from the constant attacks of wild animals. The practice of deserting the villages and shifting the field cultivation off and on has brought to the Tharus additional responsibilities and labour, also insecurity and instability of life. But today they have permanent settlement which has materially benefited to lead a more settled and regulated life. The Tharus have a separate mandir (temple) for their village deity—Bhumsen.

In Tharu village agricultural fields separates one house to another. A Tharu house is generally surrounded by vegetable garden (*bari)* and small fields. He grows seasonal vegetables in his bari and maize, mustard, tobacco, potatoes and onion in his fields for his personal consumption. A narrow and recently metalled lane runs through the village. On either side of the lane the houses are arranged in a lane on a higher level. It is noticed that there is a neat and clean arrangement of the houses in the Tharus hemlets (Villages). A Tharu village represents a closely-knit society.

A Tharu house occupies more area with its fields and vegetable garden. They construct their houses in the month of April and May before the rainy season. The house must face to east to bring the prosperity. The size of the house depends upon the size of the family. Every house must consist of at least two partitions. The roof is thatched with *bharai* or *kans* grass which grow in abundance in the region. The plastering of walls on both side and decorations on them are done by women. The home made plaster for walls is made of clay, cow dung, water and chaff of wheat (*Tatar*). Economically well off Tharu families have made a pucca houses with iron, cement, khaprail and bricks. They have a separate cattle sheds.

Social Setup

The Tharu tribe can be divided into two groups, higher and lower. The higher group comprised the Batha, Birlja, Badvait, Dahait, Mathum and Ranathakur, and the lower group, the Buksa, Khunka, Rajia, Sansa, Jugia and Dangra. The former was hypergamous to the latter but in course of time the higher group stopped taking brides from lower one. Gotra (kuri) is generic name which is given after ancestors or preferably a sage or a holy person. One of the main functions of this name is that it serves as very important distinguishing category between the higher and lower castes. Thus, they prefer to marry the members of the same gotra. In the sample villages, Rana Thakur forms the bulk of Tharu population while other groups constitute a negligible proportion of the total population. It is also noticed that Tharu of lower castes do not want to be known as lower groups. Though all these sections restrict themselves in inter-marriage and inter-dining, Tharus as a whole may be said to have a common culture.

The nucleus of social organization in the Tharu society is the family. Both the joint and single family system is found among the Tharus. At present there is a tendency towards breaking of the joint family. The structure of joint family varies in form and size from village to village and from family to family.

Village community is a compact social unit which consists of a number of different families living in a common settlement and performing certain functions together which the family alone cannot adequately and satisfactorily perform. It is also responsible for maintaining law and order in Tharu society. The Panchayat is only powerful tribunal for settling numerous disputes of their community. Tribal Panchayat is recognized as the custodian of law and morals.

Women of the Tharu tribe enjoy a very dominant position in their community. They have considerable freedom and wield great influence in the domestic sphere. The majority of the women do all the marketing while their counterpart only assists them in bringing the article home purchased by their wives. The significant role of Tharu women in economic and social spheres of their life can never be estimated. Tharu women help men in manifold economic activities like, plastering the house, cleaning the cattle sheds, sowing and harvesting, winnowing, storing, pounding and grinding the grain, selling and purchasing the articles of their daily use. In addition to this tribal customs and conventions also provide for their right of ownerships of property and possessions of the family. It is noticed that all women in the family have not equal status. Their status is determined by the positions they hold in their own family.

The religion of the Tharus is based on a belief in ghosts, demons and the spirits of the dead whom they fear. They are worshipping Mahadeva and possessing same idea of a Supreme, being known as Narayana who give them sunshine, rain and harvest. The contact with the Hindus has enabled the Tharus to include the worship of Satyanarayana and few other Hindu god and goddesses in their religion (Majumdar, 1942).

The Tharu tribe celebrates a number of religious festivals, such as Holi, Tij, Janmasthami, Anthai, Diwali etc. The fundamental idea underlying all religious rites, rituals, and ceremonies is to ensure the well-being of an individual family, its cattle and the crop, the village and finally of the whole community and to protect them from unforeseen dangers and hardships. Though there is an absence of the idea of a definite pantheon of the Tharus as such, it is clear that there is a tendency growing among them to absorb the deities of Hindu religion on large scale and to respect the saints and pirs of other religions. It is observed the educated and progressive Tharus have given up their faith in these gods due to the influence of other religion particularly Arya Samaji. As a result they are weakening their faith in their old religions and spirits to some extent.

Economic Setup

In present time agriculture is the main occupation of the Tharu. But in older time the economic life of the Tharus consisted of hunting, fishing, collecting forests fruits and roots, stock raising and a crude form of agriculture. The Tharus are more industrious in their farming than people of the plains. Along with agriculture they have allotted sufficient time in their calendar to the supplementary pursuits of fishing, hunting, gathering of fuel and fruits from the forests and making net, mat and rope. The cycle of economic activities chalk out for the Tharus a definite scheme of work for the whole year and also regulates their daily routine work. During their sowing and harvesting seasons they are busy with their fields all the day. In those months when the field labour relaxes they employ their time in repairing and constructing house or engage themselves in the supplementary occupations. The Tharus have division of labour according to sex, age and class. Children and aged people are mostly employed in various vocations requiring less physical strain. Certain occupations are exclusively assigned to particular sex, for example, ploughing, levelling of the agricultural fields, hunting, building and repairing the houses etc. are done by man, while cooking meals, cleaning utensils, fetching water, plastering walls, collection of fuels and fodder, making mat, rearing livestock etc. are some of the duties allotted to women. There are number of works like sowing of seeds, harvesting, gardening, poultry farming and fishing which are jointly done by them to help each other. It is observed that the number of old occupations are left by the Tharus and presently they are mainly engaged themselves in agriculture, government and semi-government services, business, animal husbandry, work contract etc. The awareness and education level of the tribal people has tremendously increased. It is noticed that tribal people sold or gave their agricultural land on rent (*rehan*) and became landless. As a result few families are categorized as labourer.

Geographical Background of the Sample Villages

In order to study the socio-economic and nutritional status of the Tharu tribe in Uttarakhand, ten Tharu dominated sample villages have been selected from Sitarganj and Khatima tehsils of U.S. Nagar district which is the only habitat of the Tharus in the state. General information of the sample villages is given in Tables 5.1 and 5.2 (Figure 5.1).

I. **Bidaura**—Village Bidaura (28°56' N and 79°46'30" E) is situated at 160 m above sea level which is 49 km and 3 km away from district headquarter Rudrapur and block headquarter Sitarganj, respectively. It encompasses an area of 361 ha and supports 2031 population of 310 households. Out of the total population 43.1% belongs to Tharu tribe. It is bounded by Purangarh village on the east, Khairana in the west, Dohra in the north and Bidauri village is demarcated its southern boundary. The village is situated along the Khatima-Sitarganj highway. The climate is hot and humid. The average temperature in summer is 40°C and in winter is about 10°C. The village receives 150 cm average annual rainfall. The main vegetation in the village : Jamun, Shisham, Neem, Bamboo, Sal, Eucalyptus, Poplar, Lukat, etc. The soil of the village is sandy loam with fine grains. There are mainly four types of families, namely, Tharus (S.T.), Sikhs (Punjabi), people of eastern Uttar Pradesh (Purbiye) and Scheduled Castes (Harijan). For detailed and deep study of Tharu tribe, out of total 101 Tharu households 50 (49.5%) are selected from each economic strata (Tables 5.1 and 5.2). It represents the situation of the nearest village from block headquarter.

II. **Baruwabagh**—The Baruwabagh village lies in 200 m asl at 29°45′ N latitude and 79°40′ E longitude in the Sitarganj tehsil of district U.S. Nagar. It is 9 and 55 km away from block (Sitarganj) and district (Rudrapur) headquarters. It encompasses an area of 321 ha with a population of 1098 in 167 households. Out of total population, 26.6% belongs to tharu population in the sample village. The village is surrounded by village Sisonia on the east,

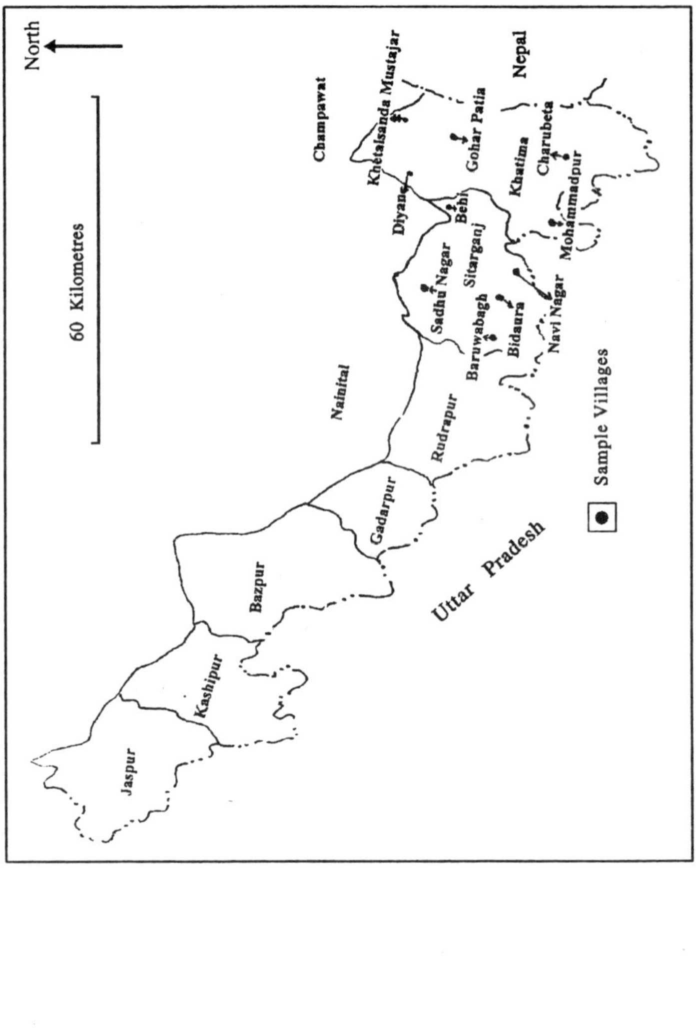

FIG. 5.1 : Location of Sample Villages in Sitaganj Khatima Tehsil of U.S. Nagar District

TABLE 5.1

Sample Villages: At a Glance

S. No.	Name of Sample Villages	Total Area (ha)	Total Population (No.)	Total House-hold (No.)	S.C. Population (%)	S.T.Popu-lation (%)	Latitude North	Longitude East	Height MSL (m.)	Distance From Block Hq.(km.)	Distance From Dist Hq. (km.)
1.	Bidaura	361	2031	310	4.5	43.1	28° 56'	79° 46'30"	160	3	49
2.	Baruwabagh	321	1098	167	25.3	26.6	29° 0'45"	79° 40'	200	9	55
3.	Sadhu Nagar	600	1709	250	21.9	63.2	29° 0'48"	79°43'4"	240	16	58
4.	Navi Nagar	85	346	46	Nil	100	28° 54'45"	79° 47'45"	160	19	63
5.	Behi	106	578	87	Nil	52.1	29° 0'24"	79° 51'25"	210	24	69
6.	Charubeta	821	2450	434	18.4	27.9	29° 0' 30"	79° 55'20"	150	4	78
7.	Gohar Patia	730	1810	316	5.9	41.9	28° 57'	79° 59'	200	10	84
8.	Khetalsanda Mustajar	925	2703	463	16.4	29.4	28° 1'	79° 59'30"	205	15	90
9.	Mohammadpur	722	1783	236	36.4	53.6	29° 0' 25"	79°50'40"	180	20	94
10.	Diyan	690	1911	252	47.8	36.9	29° 1'15"	79° 55'44"	210	26	100
	Grand Total	**5361**	**16419**	**2561**	**20.1**	**41.4**	**N.A.**	**N.A.**	**N.A.**	**N.A.**	**N.A.**

Source: Anon. 2001b., S.O.I. Toposheets and Personal Observations.

TABLE 5.2

Distribution of Tharu Households in the Sample Villages

S. No.	Name of Sample Villages	Economic Groupwise Households																	
		Very Low Income			*Low Income*			*Moderate Income*			*High Income*			*Very High Income*			*Average*		
		Total	*Sample*		*Total*	*Sample*		*Total*	*Sample*		*Total*	*Sample*		*Total*	*Sample*		*Total*	*Sample*	
		No.	*No.*	%	*No.*	*No.*	%	*No.*	*No.*	%	*No.*	*No.*	%	*No.*	*No.*	%	*No.*	*No.*	%
1.	Bidaura	23	12	52.2	26	12	46.1	17	9	52.9	7	3	42.8	28	14	50.0	101	50	49.5
2.	Baruwabagh	32	16	50.0	10	4	40.0	2	1	50.0	1	1	100.0	1	1	100.0	46	23	50.0
3.	Sadhu Nagar	20	10	50.0	41	21	51.2	32	16	50.0	15	8	53.3	31	15	48.4	139	70	50.0
4.	Navi Nagar	13	7	53.8	18	9	50.0	6	3	50.0	6	3	50.0	4	2	50.0	47	24	51.1
5.	Behi	21	10	47.6	18	8	44.4	1	1	100.0	1	1	100.0	2	1	50.0	43	21	48.8
6.	Charubeta	13	8	61.5	20	9	45.0	18	9	50.0	8	4	50.0	20	10	50.0	79	40	50.6
7.	Gohar Patia	30	15	50.0	41	20	48.8	23	11	47.8	11	6	54.5	16	8	50.0	121	60	49.6
8.	Khetalsanda Mustajar	26	13	50.0	22	12	54.5	12	6	50.0	9	5	55.5	4	2	50.0	73	38	52.1
9.	Mohammadpur	33	16	48.5	51	25	49.0	29	14	48.3	8	4	50.0	33	17	51.5	154	76	49.3
10.	Diyan	18	9	50.0	23	12	52.2	16	8	50.0	15	7	46.7	15	7	46.7	87	43	49.4
	Grand Total	**229**	**116**	**50.6**	**270**	**132**	**48.9**	**156**	**78**	**50.0**	**81**	**42**	**51.8**	**154**	**77**	**50.0**	**890**	**445**	**50.0**

Source: Field Survey, 2005-2006.

Rajnagar on the west, Nirmalnagar on the north and Arbindnagar village located on the south. The other environmental conditions (relief, climate, vegetation and soils) are same as Bidaura village. The village name is after the name of a kind of grass (*Baruwa*) and *bagh* means garden i.e. 'garden of Bruwagrass'. It lies along the Shaktifarm to Sitarganj road. There was no routine transport service. Out of total 46 Tharu families 50% have been selected for detailed survey ((Tables 5.1 and 5.2).

III. **Sadunagar**—It (29°48' N and 79°43'4" E) is situated at an 240 m asl which is 16 and 58 km respectively away from block (Sitarganj) and district (Rudrapur) headquarters. It encompasses an area of 600 ha with a support of 1098 population of in 250 households. Out of total population, 63.2% belongs to Tharu population in the sample village. The village boundary is demarcated Pahsaini village from the east, Kalyanpur on the west, Naleei on the north and village Lamakhera demarcated its southern boundary. Village name Sadhunagar is after a Sadhu (Saint) who came and settled first. The soil of the village is loamy with coarse grains. Remaining geographical conditions are same as previous villages. Out of total 139 Tharu households 50% (70) have been selected for detailed study (Tables 5.1 and 5.2).

IV. **Navi Nagar**—Navi Nagar (28°54' 45"N and 79°47' 45"E) is situated at about 19 and 63 km away from block headquarter Sitarganj and district headquarter Rudrapur respectively. It encompasses an area of 85 ha and supports 346 only tribal people in 46 households. The total population belongs to Tharu tribe. Village Vedaiya makes the eastern boundary of the sample village while Deen Nagar situated on the west. Its northern boundary is demarcated by Sundarpur and Goriya village makes it southern boundary. The village name is after a Muslim man Navi. The other geographical conditions are same as previous villages. Out of total 47 Tharu households 51.1% have been selected for detailed study (Tables 5.1 and 5.2).

V. **Behi**—Fifth and last village of Sitarganj tehsil, village Behi (29°0'24" N and 79°51'25") is situated at 195 m asl which is 24 and 69 km away from block headquarter Sitarganj and district headquarter Rudrapur respectively. It encompasses an area of 106 ha and supports 578 people in 87 households. Out of total population 52.1% belongs to Tharu tribe. It is bounded by village Diyan in the east, Ainchata in the south, while western and northern boundaries are demarcated by reserve forests. The other geographical conditions are same as Bidaura village. Out of total 43 Tharu households 48.8% have been selected for detailed study. It is remotest village of Sitarganj tehsil (Tables 5.1 and 5.2).

VI. **Charubeta**—Village Charubeta (29°0'30" N and 79°55'20") is situated at 150 m asl which is 4 and 78 km away from tehsil headquarter Khatima and district headquarter Rudrapur respectively. It is nearest sample village from block headquarter of Khatima. It encompasses an area of 821 ha with 2450 souls in 434 households. Out of total population 27.9% belong to Tharu tribe. Its eastern boundary is demarcated by Mundeli village while Naugaon Thaggu village lies on the west. Village Khetalsanda Khas is situated its north and village Chanda in the south. The other geographical conditions are same as previous villages. Out of total 79 Tharu households 50.6% have been selected for detailed study (Tables 5.1 and 5.2).

VII. **Gohar Patia**—Lying between 28°57′ N latitudes and 79°59′E longitudes at 200 m asl, village Gohar Patia encompasses an area of 730 ha and a population of 1810 persons in 316 households. Out of total population 41.9% belongs to Tharu tribe. It is 10 and 84 km away from block headquarter Khatima and district headquarters Rudrapur, respectively. Kutari village is situated in the east while Bigrabagh in the west and Naugaonnath and Pachacuria villages make its northern and southern boundaries, respectively. Other environmental conditions are same as described in previous villages. Gohar Patia village is situated near to Bhabar belt. Out of total 121

Tharu families 49.6% families have been selected for detailed study (Tables 5.1 and 5.2).

VIII. **Khetalsanda Mustajar**—Village Khetalsanda Mustajar (28°1' N and 79°59' 30" E) is situated at an elevation of 185 m asl. It is 15 and 90 km away from block and district headquarters Khatima and Rudrapur, respectively. It encompasses an area of 925 ha and supports 1810 persons in 463 households. Out of total population 29.4% belong to Tharu tribe. It is bounded by Naugaonnath village on the west and Bichhpuri on the south while eastern and northern boundaries are demarcated by the reserve forests. The village was settled by a Muslim man whose name was Mustajar. The environmental conditions are same as already described in previous villages. Out of total 73 Tharu families 52.1% have been selected for detailed study (Tables 5.1 and 5.2).

IX. **Mohammadpur**—Village Mohammadpur lies in 180 m asl at 29°0′25" N and 79°50′ 40" E in Khatima tehsil of U.S. Nagar district. It is 20 and 94 km away from block and district headquarters Khatima and Rudrapur, respectively. It encompasses an area of 722 ha and supports 1783 persons in 236 households. More than fifty percent (53.6%) population belongs to Tharu tribe. Village Bhuriadesi makes its northern boundary and Gangapur village lies on the south. The eastern and western boundaries are demarcated by Nausar and Khamariya villages. The environmental conditions are same as already described in previous villages respectively. Out of total 154 Tharu families 49.3% have been selected for detailed survey (Tables 5.1 and 5.2).

X. **Diyan**—It (2901′ 15" N and 790 55′ 44" E) is situated at an 210 m above sea level which is 26 and 100 km away from block and district headquarters Khatima and Rudrapur, respectively. It encompasses an area of 690 ha and supports 1911 persons in 252 households. Out of total 36.9% population belong to Tharu tribe. The village is situated in the north-west direction of the study area. The village boundary is demarcated by village Biriya (east) and Chandpur (south); while western and northern boundaries are demarcated by the Nanaksagar reservoir. The environmental conditions are same as already described in previous villages. Out of total 87 Tharu families 49.4% families have been selected for detailed survey. It is remotest village of Khatima tehsil (Tables 5.1 and 5.2).

Demographic and Socio-Economic Structure of the Sample Villages

Demographic study of any segment of the population is very important aspect for understanding the socio-economic and nutritional profile of any society or geographical unit. Total 450 Tharu households in ten sample villages have been selected for detailed study. A total 2528 Tharu persons of 450 households have been surveyed during the entire period. Out of total surveyed population 1228 (48.6%) belong to females. General characteristics of the sample villages, study region, district, state and country as a whole are depicted in Table 5.3.

TABLE 5.3

Demographic Characteristics of Sample Villages, Study Region, U.S. Nagar, Uttarakhand and India

S. No.	*Particulars*	*Sample Villages (Nos. 10)*	*Study Region (2 Tehsils)*	*U.S. Nagar (District)*	*Uttar-akhand (State)*	*India (Nation)*
1.	Total Population	16419	358498	1235614	8489349	1028610328
2.	Male Population	8392	184897	649484	4325924	532156772
3.	Female Population	8027	173601	586130	4163425	496453556
4.	No of Villages	10	209	671	15761	640000
5.	Urban Population (%)	Nil	2.4	32.6	25.7	27.8
6.	Scheduled Castes Population (%)	20.1	9.8	13.2	17.9	16.2
7.	Scheduled Tribe Population (%	41.4	23.0	8.9	3.0	8.2
8.	Below 6 Years age Total Population	2716	61974	219291	1360032	163819614
9.	Below 6 Years age Male Population	1402	31967	114607	712949	84999203
10.	Below 6 Years age Female Population	1314	30007	104684	647083	78820411
11.	Growth of Population (%)1991-2001	N.A.	N.A.	27.79	19.2	21.53
12.	No. of Households	2561	58466	208076	1603242	193579954
13.	Household Size (Persons/Household)	5.7	6.1	5.9	5.3	5.3
14.	Sex Ratio (Total)	945	939	902	962	933

Table Contd....

Table Contd....

15. Sex Ratio (< 6 years age population)	937	938	913	908	927
16. Literacy Rate Total (%)	71.4	64.9	64.9	71.6	64.8
17. Literacy Rate Male (%)	83.5	76.7	75.2	83.3	75.3
18. Literacy Rate Female (%)	57.2	52.3	53.4	59.6	53.7
19. Gap in Male-Female Literacy Rate (%)	26.3	24.4	21.9	23.6	21.6
20. Work Participation Rate Total (% of total)	39.7	37.2	31.7	36.9	39.1
21. Work Participation Rate Male (% of total)	49.0	48.8	48.0	46.5	51.7
22. Work Participation Rate Female (% of total)	29.7	24.7	13.7	27.3	25.6
23. Main Workers Total (% of total workers)	24.5	24.7	24.3	27.4	30.4
24. Main Workers Male (% of total workers)	39.0	39.3	40.6	37.9	45.1
25. Main Workers Female (% of total workers)	9.2	9.1	6.2	16.4	14.7
26. Marginal Workers Total (% of total workers)	15.2	12.5	7.4	9.6	8.7
27. Marginal Workers Male (% of total workers)	10.0	9.6	7.4	8.3	6.6
28. Marginal Workers Female (% of total workers)	20.5	15.6	7.5	10.9	11.0
29. Cultivators Total (% of workers)	55.6	48	30.3	50.1	31.7
30. Cultivators Male (% of workers)	60.9	45.9	28.5	34.3	31.1
31. Cultivators Female (% of workers)	43.2	50.8	37	77.8	32.9
32. Agricultural Labourers Total (% of workers)	25.6	21.5	25.9	8.3	26.5
33. Agricultural Labourers Male (% of workers)	21.1	19.6	24.1	9.5	20.8
34. Agricultural Labourers Female (% of workers)	37.2	25.8	32.8	6.1	38.9
35. Workers in H.H. Industries Total (% of workers)	0.7	3.6	2.5	2.3	4.2
36. Workers in H.H. Industries Male (% of workers)	0.6	1.9	1.7	2.2	3.2
37. Workers in H.H. Industries Female (% of workers)	2.4	7.8	5.5	2.5	6.5
38. Other Workers Total (% of workers)	18.1	26.8	4.4	39.3	37
39. Other Workers Male (% of workers)	17.3	32.6	45.7	54	44.9
40. Other Workers Female (% of workers)	18.4	15.5	24.7	13.6	21.7

Source: Anon. 2001a, 2001b & Field Survey, 2005-2006.

The analysis of sex ratio reveals the numerical relationship between women and men, which can be expressed as number of females with 1000 males. A ratio of 1000 indicates equal balance of males and females in the population, less than 1000 denotes deficit of women (low sex ratio), and more than 1000 indicates numerical surplus of women (high sex ratio) in the population. On an average sex ratio of the sample villages is 945 females/

1000 males which is higher than that of study area (935) district U.S. Nagar (902) and country (933) and lower than state average (962) (Table 5.3). The sex ratio varies from minimum 808 in village Navi Nagar to maximum 1145 females/1000 males in Baruwabagh. Only Baruwabagh and Mohammadpur villages have sex ratio more than 1000 (Table 5.4). Economic level-wise the sex ratio varies from minimum 864 in high income group to maximum 981 in very high income groups. Overall low sex ratio is found in all the economic groups. There is no impact of economic level on the sex ratio in the sample villages.

TABLE 5.4

Distribution of Tharu Population in the Sample Village

Sample Villages	*Population*			*Household Size (P/HH)*	*Sex Ratio (F/1000 M)*
	Persons	*Males*	*Females*		
01-Bidaura	291	149	142	5.8	953
02-Baruwabagh	133	62	71	5.8	1145
03-Sadhu Nagar	377	198	179	5.4	904
04-Navi Nagar	132	73	59	5.5	808
05-Behi	96	53	43	4.6	811
06-Charubeta	192	100	92	4.8	920
07-Gohar Patia	356	183	173	5.9	945
08-Khetalsanda Mustajar	238	122	116	6.3	950
09-Mohammadpur	462	230	232	6.1	1009
10-Diyan	251	130	121	5.8	931
Grand Total	**2528**	**1300**	**1228**	**5.7**	**945**

Source: Field Survey, 2005-2006.

The age group-wise sex ratio in the sample villages varies from minimum 822 females/1000 males in the age group of 41-50 to maximum 1531 in above. The study reveal that except between the age of 41-50 the sex ratio shows increasing trend from the below 10 year population (898) to above 61 (1531). It reveals that the sex ratio is very low in juvenile age groups.

Due to the influence of other Hindu society the prominent factor for low sex ratio in the Tharu society are—son preference,

TABLE 5.5

Distribution of Tharu Population by Age Group in the Sample Villages (% of Total)

Sample Villages	*Total*	*Age Groups (in years)*													
		Below 10		*11 to 20*		*21 to 30*		*31 to 40*		*41 to 50*		*51 to 60*		*Above 61*	
	No.	*No.*	*%*	*No.*	*%*	*No.*	*%*	*No.*	*%*	*No.*	*%*	*No.*	*%*	*No.*	*%*
01- Bidaura	291	51	17.5	86	29.6	55	18.9	44	15.1	33	11.3	10	3.4	12	4.1
02- Baruwabagh	133	29	21.8	43	32.3	14	10.5	20	15.0	17	12.8	5	3.8	5	3.8
03- Sadhu Nagar	377	96	25.5	98	26.0	55	14.6	63	16.7	41	10.9	15	4.0	9	2.4
04- Navi Nagar	132	57	43.2	16	12.1	33	25.0	14	10.6	8	6.1	4	3.0	0	0.0
05- Behi	96	27	28.1	20	20.8	23	24.0	16	16.7	5	5.2	4	4.2	1	1.0
06- Charubeta	192	32	16.7	53	27.6	31	16.1	32	16.7	23	12.0	13	6.8	8	4.2
07-Gohar Patia	356	69	19.4	98	27.5	66	18.5	56	15.7	34	9.6	16	4.5	17	4.8
08 -Khetalsanda Mustajar	238	56	23.5	73	30.7	45	18.9	24	10.1	26	10.9	10	4.2	4	1.7
09- Mohammadpur	462	103	22.3	131	28.4	82	17.7	66	14.3	38	8.2	26	5.6	16	3.5
10- Diyan	251	57	22.7	78	31.1	28	11.2	43	17.1	21	8.4	15	6.0	9	3.6
Grand Total	**2528**	**577**	**22.8**	**696**	**27.5**	**432**	**17.1**	**378**	**15.0**	**246**	**9.7**	**118**	**4.7**	**81**	**3.2**

Source: Field Survey, 2005-2006.

unequal treatment given to boys and girls, female infanticide, neglect of female infants, early marriage, death during pregnancy and hard work. On contrary this average sex ratio in the hill districts of the state is high because of out migration of male population from the villages for employment and better education.

The average household size of the sample villages is 5.7 persons. It varies from 4.6 in village Behi to 6.3 in the village Khetalsanda Mustajar (Table 5.4). The household size of 60% villages is more than average (5.7) of the sample villages which is lower than the study region (6.1) and district U.S. Nagar (5.9) and higher than the state (5.3) and country average (5.3).

The household size of very low income, low, moderate, high and very high income group is respectively 6.0, 5.6, 5.2 and 5.1 persons. It shows that number of persons are more in the household of lower income groups because tribals are not such aware about the consequences of more births in one hand and lack of entertainment means on the other.

Total surveyed population of the sample villages has been categorized into seven age groups—below 10 years, 11 to 20, 21 to 30, 31 to 40, 41 to 50, 51 to 60 and above 61 years. About 22.8% of the total population belongs to the age group below 10 years at the base of the population pyramid and 3.2% of the people are above 61 years in age. Maximum 27.5 people lie between the ages of 11 to 20 years while 46.5% of the surveyed population belongs to the age 21 to 60 years (Table 5.5). It is clear that about one third of the total population is considered as dependant. However, all members of the tribal family except (infants), ill and old persons who do not perform work properly are engaged in household and other agricultural activities.

Data on anthropometric measurements of tribal people was very scanty. It is during last fifteen years that some information has become available through studies done by National Nutrition Monitoring Bureau and National Family Health Survey. The mean height and weight of the sample people have been worked out. The mean height of the total surveyed people is 152.7 cms while mean height of male and female is 154.4 cms and 150.2

TABLE 5.6

Average Height of the Tharu Population by Income Group in the Sample Villages (in cms.)

Sample Villages	VLI			LI			MI			HI			VHI			Average		
	M	F	P	M	F	P	M	F	P	M	F	P	M	F	P	M	F	P
01- Bidaura	159.0	158.7	158.6	155.8	157.3	156.4	159.7	156.7	159.3	156.7	155.9	154.3	158.8	155.5	156.7	159.5	157.3	158.3
02- Baruwabagh	152.1	147.3	149.9	145.6	142.6	147.0	144.0	123.7	123.7	163.7	162.0	161.7	155.0	147.0	150.2	149.9	145.0	146.2
03- Sadhu Nagar	160.1	154.5	198.9	157.4	155.6	156.5	160.8	152.1	155.9	148.0	151.1	149.2	159.9	152.2	156.8	157.9	153.8	155.7
04- Navi Nagar	157.2	150.9	155.9	152.3	151.5	152.5	149.9	135.1	150.3	143.3	131.3	142.6	165.5	162.0	163.1	155.0	151.5	154.0
05- Behi	152.1	150.1	151.4	154.2	150.3	153.2	155.0	161.0	156.4	163.0	150.0	158.2	124.0	158.0	135.3	154.3	150.0	154.1
06- Charubeta	153.5	145.9	149.4	155.8	146.7	151.1	158.7	154.1	156.4	154.3	134.4	141.1	157.9	141.1	150.8	157.0	144.6	150.9
07-Gohar Patia	152.8	144.5	148.7	157.3	146.4	151.8	148.8	151.1	150.9	151.5	145.6	149.7	159.0	150.4	154.7	153.9	147.6	151.2
08-Khetalsanda	153.6	151.0	154.0	150.1	151.3	151.6	156.1	152.2	154.6	148.6	151.1	153.3	150.4	147.2	151.4	151.7	150.6	153.0
09- Mohammadpur	154.3	147.5	150.8	155.5	148.1	151.8	153.8	150.8	152.8	142.0	147.9	147.5	155.5	153.7	154.7	152.2	149.6	151.5
10- Diyan	153.7	151.2	153.0	151.3	152.6	152.5	153.7	150.9	149.7	149.3	154.3	152.6	152.9	149.8	151.3	152.2	151.8	151.8
Grand Total	**154.8**	**150.2**	**157.3**	**153.5**	**150.2**	**152.4**	**154.1**	**148.8**	**151.0**	**152.2**	**148.4**	**151.0**	**153.9**	**151.7**	**152.5**	**154.4**	**150.2**	**152.7**

Source: Field Survey, 2005-2006.

TABLE 5.7

Average Weight of the Tharu Population by Income Group in the Sample Villages(in kgs.)

Sample Villages	VLI			LI			MI			HI			VHI			Average		
	M	F	P	M	F	P	M	F	P	M	F	P	M	F	P	M	F	P
01- Bidaura	40.9	42.9	45.0	41.1	36.7	39.0	44.4	46.3	48.0	38.6	31.0	37.2	51.1	43.0	46.4	49.4	43.8	45.3
02- Baruwabagh	46.0	41.0	43.3	45.3	38.1	42.4	46.0	39.1	44.1	55.3	53.0	51.9	48.5	42.0	45.6	47.8	42.6	45.5
03- Sadhu Nagar	49.2	42.6	46.4	48.6	45.2	46.8	45.9	42.0	44.2	47.1	43.0	45.4	48.8	43.2	46.4	47.9	43.2	45.8
04- Navi Nagar	33.9	44.1	48.6	47.9	44.6	46.4	47.3	38.3	46.2	42.8	33.0	43.0	62.5	55.5	57.6	46.9	43.1	47.9
05- Behi	51.0	45.3	47.6	54.6	46.2	49.8	48.6	48.0	48.0	56.7	43.5	51.9	37.5	52.0	42.3	49.7	47.0	47.9
06- Charubeta	47.3	42.5	44.1	48.7	43.1	46.1	45.7	39.8	42.8	46.1	46.7	45.6	52.5	44.9	48.6	48.1	43.4	45.4
07-Gohar Patia	47.6	39.2	43.4	49.8	41.6	45.7	44.4	41.7	44.0	45.1	41.1	43.1	51.2	41.8	44.9	47.6	41.1	44.2
08- Khetalsanda Mustajar	46.9	41.9	45.1	47.0	40.0	42.1	48.3	45.4	46.9	44.6	40.9	43.5	47.1	46.8	41.9	46.8	43.0	43.9
09- Mohammadpur	47.8	41.7	44.6	47.5	41.2	44.3	47.9	42.8	45.5	42.8	39.7	42.1	49.1	42.8	45.9	47.0	41.6	44.5
10- Diyan	48.0	46.1	47.5	49.7	45.7	46.8	50.4	46.2	48.3	47.7	46.2	47.0	50.2	45.1	47.6	49.2	45.9	47.4
Grand Total	**46.5**	**42.1**	**45.6**	**48.7**	**42.8**	**45.3**	**47.6**	**42.9**	**45.8**	**47.3**	**43.1**	**45.7**	**49.8**	**45.7**	**46.7**	**48.0**	**44.2**	**45.8**

*Source:*Field Survey, 2005-2006.

Table 5.8

Average Body Mass Index (BMI) of the Tharu Population by Age Group in the Sample Villages

Sample Villages	*VLI*			*LI*			*MI*			*HI*			*VHI*			*Average*		
	M	*F*	*P*	*M*	*F*	*P*	*M*	*F*	*P*	*M*	*F*	*P*	*M*	*F*	*P*	*M*	*F*	*P*
01- Bidaura	15.59	16.76	17.47	16.10	14.52	15.37	16.85	18.53	18.58	15.27	12.57	15.23	19.70	17.44	18.43	18.87	17.40	17.75
02- Baruwabagh	19.88	18.90	0.54	21.37	18.74	19.62	22.18	2.84	28.82	20.64	20.20	19.85	20.19	19.44	20.21	21.27	20.26	21.29
03- Sadhu Nagar	19.19	17.85	11.73	19.62	18.67	19.11	17.75	18.15	18.19	21.50	18.83	20.39	19.09	18.65	18.87	19.21	18.26	18.89
04- Navi Nagar	13.72	19.37	20.00	20.65	19.43	19.95	21.05	20.98	20.45	20.84	19.14	21.15	22.82	21.15	21.65	19.52	18.78	20.20
05- Behi	22.05	20.11	20.77	22.96	20.45	21.22	20.23	18.52	19.62	21.34	19.33	20.74	24.39	20.83	23.11	20.87	20.89	20.17
06- Charubeta	20.07	19.97	19.76	20.06	20.03	20.19	18.15	16.76	17.50	19.36	25.85	22.90	21.06	22.55	21.37	19.51	20.76	19.94
07-Gohar Patia	20.39	18.77	19.63	20.13	19.41	19.83	20.05	18.26	19.32	19.65	19.39	19.23	20.25	18.48	18.76	20.10	18.87	19.33
08-Khetalsanda Mustajar	19.88	18.38	19.02	20.86	17.47	18.32	19.82	19.60	19.62	20.20	17.91	18.51	20.82	21.60	18.28	20.34	18.96	18.75
09- Mohammadpur	20.08	19.17	19.61	19.64	18.78	19.22	20.25	18.82	19.49	21.23	18.15	19.35	20.31	18.12	19.18	20.29	18.59	19.39
10- Diyan	20.31	20.16	20.29	21.71	19.62	20.12	21.33	20.29	21.55	21.40	19.40	20.18	21.47	20.10	20.79	21.24	19.92	20.57
Grand Total	**19.40**	**18.66**	**18.43**	**20.67**	**18.97**	**19.50**	**20.04**	**18.54**	**20.09**	**20.42**	**19.57**	**25.15**	**21.03**	**19.86**	**20.08**	**20.13**	**19.59**	**19.64**

*Source:*Field Survey,2005-2006 and computed by the author.

TABLE 5.9

Literacy Status of the Tharu Population in the Sample Villages

Sample Villages	Total Population			Population < 7 Yrs			Population 7 Yrs & >			Literate (% of population 7yrs & >)					
	P	M	F	P	M	F	P	M	F	P		M		F	
	No.	No.	No.	% of total			% of total			No.	%	No.	%	No.	%
01- Bidaura	291	149	142	10.3	12.8	7.7	89.7	87.2	92.3	202	77.4	123	94.6	79	60.3
02- Baruwabagh	133	62.0	71	15.0	14.5	15.5	85.0	85.5	84.5	79	69.9	44	83.0	35	58.3
03- Sadhu Nagar	377	198	179	15.9	13.6	18.4	84.1	86.4	81.6	208	65.6	130	76.0	78	53.4
04- Navi Nagar	132	73	59	33.3	37.0	28.8	66.7	63.0	71.2	67	76.1	42	91.3	25	59.5
05- Behi	96	53.0	43	15.6	18.9	11.6	84.4	81.1	88.4	60	74.1	40	93.0	20	52.6
06- Charubeta	192	100	92	10.4	9.0	12.0	89.6	91.0	88.0	123	71.5	81	89.0	42	51.9
07-Gohar Patia	356	183	173	12.4	12.6	12.7	87.6	87.4	87.3	208	66.7	121	75.6	87	57.6
08 -Khetalsanda Mustajar	238	122	116	13.9	16.4	11.2	86.1	83.6	88.8	164	80.0	94	92.2	70	68.0
09- Mohammadpur	462	230	232	13.6	11.7	15.5	86.4	88.3	84.5	290	72.7	184	90.6	106	54.1
10- Diyan	251	130	121	14.3	16.9	11.6	85.7	83.1	88.4	144	67.0	89	82.4	55	51.4
Grand Total	**2528**	**1300**	**1228**	**14.4**	**14.8**	**14.1**	**85.6**	**85.2**	**85.9**	**1545**	**71.4**	**948**	**85.6**	**597**	**56.6**

Source: Field Survey, 2005-2006.

TABLE 5.10

Educational Level of the Tharu Population in the Sample Villages

Sample Villages	Total literate			Educational Level / Standard (% of total literates)														
	P	M	F	Primary			Junior			High School			Intermediate			Higher & Others		
	No.	No.	No.	P	M	F	P	M	F	P	M	F	P	M	F	P	M	F
01- Bidaura	202	123	79	27.2	23.6	32.9	25.7	24.4	27.8	24.8	27.6	20.3	12.9	15.4	8.9	9.4	8.9	10.1
02- Baruwabagh	79	44	35	38.0	19.0	42.9	30.4	25.0	37.1	25.3	31.8	17.1	2.5	4.5	0.0	3.8	4.5	2.9
03- Sadhu Nagar	208	130	78	31.3	17.3	37.2	32.2	31.5	33.3	27.4	30.8	21.8	8.2	8.5	7.7	1.0	1.5	0.0
04- Navi Nagar	67	42	25	9.0	9.0	0.0	49.3	35.7	72.0	37.3	42.9	28.0	4.5	7.1	0.0	0.0	0.0	0.0
05- Behi	60	40	20	55.0	31.7	70.0	35.0	37.5	30.0	10.0	15.0	0.0	0.0	0.0	0.0	0.0	0.0	0.0
06- Charubeta	123	81	42	29.3	13.0	47.6	26.0	32.1	14.3	25.2	28.4	19.0	11.4	12.3	9.5	8.1	7.4	9.6
07-Gohar Patia	208	121	87	34.1	18.3	37.9	32.2	27.3	39.1	26.4	33.9	16.1	4.8	5.0	4.6	2.4	2.5	2.3
08-Khetalsanda Mustajar	164	94	70	42.1	22.6	45.7	25.0	26.6	22.9	21.3	23.4	18.6	10.4	9.6	11.4	1.2	1.1	1.4
09- Mohammadpur	290	184	106	34.1	17.2	46.2	29.3	30.4	27.4	21.7	25.5	15.1	9.0	10.3	6.6	5.9	6.5	4.7
10- Diyan	144	89	55	43.8	24.3	50.9	35.4	39.3	29.1	17.4	16.9	18.2	1.4	2.2	0.0	2.1	2.2	1.8
Grand Total	**1545**	**948**	**597**	**34.1**	**18.2**	**41.2**	**30.6**	**30.3**	**31.2**	**23.8**	**27.4**	**17.9**	**7.6**	**8.5**	**6.0**	**3.9**	**4.1**	**3.7**

Source: Field Survey, 2005-2006.

TABLE 5.11

Reasons For Not Attaining the Education by Tharu Population in the Sample Villages (% of Total Illiterate)

	Illiterate			*Reasons for not attaining the education (% of total Illiterates)*											
	Sample Villages (No.)			*Lack of School*			*Lack of Money*			*To Look Youngers*			*To Look Animals*		
	P	*M*	*F*	*P*	*M*	*F*	*P*	*M*	*F*	*P*	*M*	*F*	*P*	*M*	*F*
01- Bidaura	59	7	52	39.0	14.3	42.3	10.2	42.9	5.8	44.1	14.3	48.1	6.8	28.6	3.8
02- Baruwabagh	34	9	25	26.5	11.1	32.0	32.4	55.6	24.0	26.5	0.0	36.0	14.7	33.3	8.0
03- Sadhu Nagar	109	41	68	45.9	24.4	58.8	16.5	31.7	7.4	21.1	0.0	33.8	16.5	43.9	0.0
04- Navi Nagar	21	4	17	47.6	50.0	47.1	23.8	25.0	23.5	23.8	0.0	29.4	4.8	25.0	0.0
05- Behi	21	3	18	52.4	0.0	61.1	14.3	33.3	11.1	23.8	0.0	27.8	9.5	66.7	0.0
06- Charubeta	49	10	39	44.9	20.0	51.3	8.2	10.0	7.7	32.7	0.0	41.0	14.3	70.0	0.0
07-Gohar Patia	103	39	64	46.6	25.6	59.4	16.5	30.8	7.8	20.4	0.0	32.8	16.5	43.6	0.0
08.-Khetalsanda Mustajar	42	8	34	54.8	75.0	50.0	16.7	0.0	20.6	23.8	0.0	29.4	4.8	25.0	0.0
09- Mohammadpur	109	19	90	53.2	36.8	56.7	12.8	21.1	11.1	26.6	0.0	32.2	7.3	42.1	0.0
10- Diyan	71	19	52	57.7	52.6	59.6	18.3	31.6	13.5	19.7	0.0	26.9	4.2	15.8	0.0
Grand Total	**618**	**159**	**459**	**47.7**	**30.8**	**53.6**	**15.9**	**28.9**	**11.3**	**25.6**	**0.6**	**34.2**	**10.8**	**39.6**	**0.9**

Source: Field Survey, 2005-2006.

cms respectively (Table 5.6). Similarly the mean weight of the surveyed tribal people is 45.8 kg while mean weight for male and female is respectively 48 kg and 44.2 kg (Table 5.7). Average height of the Tharu tribe can be termed as short-statured in general and tribal women can be termed as low weight from pregnancy point of view in particular. It reveals the tribal people are not much healthy due to over workload on the one hand and low nourishment including heavy drinking (liquors) habits on the other.

Body Mass Index (BMI) was calculated using the formula weight (kg)/height^2(m) (James *et al.*, 1988, and Pant, 2002, 2003 and 2004). Average BMI varies from 17.75 in village Bidaura to 21.29 in village Baruwabagh (Table 5.8). Similar trend was seen in the male and female Body Mass Index while the Body Mass Index is very low in the group of very low income and it shows in increasing trend as per increasing income level. About 27.88% Tharus belong to very low income group have BMI below 18.5 which is the criterion (optimum) for Chronic Energy Deficiency (CED) grade I i.e. moderate type of malnutrition. Remaining income groups falls in low weight normal and normal groups.

Education is an important indicator to measure the level of social progress in a society. On an average in the study area 71.4% Tharu population is registered as literate which is higher than the district (63.9%), state (63.2%) and national (47.1.8%) averages (Table 5.3). Literacy varies from the lowest 67% in village Diyan to the highest 80% in village Khetalsanda Mustajar. About 56.6% females are literate while 85.6% males are enumerated as literate (Table 5.9). Table 5.9 shows that 14.4% population considered as below 7 years age. It is considerable that maximum 34.1% of total Tharu literates have an education level up to primary standard while only 4% Tharus have higher and technical education. Likewise 41.2% female Tharus have primary education only. The study shows that decreasing number of literate people with increasing standard of education such as 34.1% literate up to primary standard, 30.6% up to junior, 23.8% up to high school, 7.6% intermediate and 3.9 are literate up to higher education (Table 5.10). Table 5.10 shows the similar trend in all the sample villages. About 28.6% Tharus are still illiterate. Among them 14.4%

are males and illiterate females are three times more than that (43.4%). During the field investigation, it was tried to find the causes behind the illiteracy among the Tharu population. About 48% persons are illiterate due to lack of school, 15.9% due to lack of money, 25.6% due to look after the younger siblings in the family and 10.8% due to animals rearing respectively. It is noticed that the more boys than girls are illiterate due to look animals and more girls than boys are illiterate due to look after the infants. Similar trend is found in all the sample villages (Table 5.11). The study reflects that the dropout rate of tribal girls and boys is more than the non-tribal children. A recent report by the Comptroller and Auditor General says the gap in the gross dropout rate between general category students and SC and students which was 6.7% and 15.1% respectively in 2001-02 went up to 10.4% and 16.6% in 2003-04 (*Hindustan Times*, Aug. 26, 2007).

TABLE 5.12

Migration Pattern in the Tharu Population

Sample Villages	*Total Population (No.)*	*Total Migrants*		*Reason for Out-Migration Labour*	
		(No.)	*% of Total Population*	*(No.)*	*% of Migrants*
01. Bidaura	291	17	5.8	17	100.0
02. Baruwabagh	133	18	13.5	18	100.0
03. Sadhu Nagar	377	27	7.2	27	100.0
04. Navi Nagar	132	11	8.3	11	100.0
05. Behi	96	5	5.2	5	100.0
06. Charubeta	192	12	6.3	12	100.0
07. Gohar Patiya	356	11	3.1	11	100.0
08. Khetalsanda Mustajar	238	18	7.6	18	100.0
09. Mohammadpur	462	22	4.8	22	100.0
10. Diyan	251	15	6.0	15	100.0
Grand Total	**2528**	**156**	**6.2**	**156**	**100.0**

Source: Field Survey, 2005-2006.

Out of the total surveyed Tharu population only 6.2% male Tharus are registered as out-migrants working as labourers out-

TABLE 5.13

Occupational Structure of Tharu Households in the Sample Villages

Sample Villages	Total H.H. No.	Occupational Structure (%of total Household)									
		Agri. only	*Agri. & Labour*	*Agri.,Lab.& Livestock*	*Labour only*	*Agricul. & Livestock*	*Agri., Lab. &.Service*	*Labour & Livestock*	*Agri.,Shop & Livestock*	*Agri., &. Service*	*Agri., Live. &.Service*
01- Bidaura	50	14.0	8.0	18.0	6.0	24.0	2.0	2.0	8.0	6.0	12.0
02- Baruwabagh	23	8.7	4.3	26.1	4.3	39.1	0.0	0.0	8.7	8.7	0.0
03- Sadhu Nagar	70	22.9	4.3	5.7	8.6	50.0	0.0	4.3	0.0	0.0	4.3
04- Navi Nagar	24	16.7	20.8	25.0	12.5	25.0	0.0	0.0	0.0	0.0	0.0
05- Behi	21	0.0	14.3	66.7	9.5	4.8	0.0	4.8	0.0	0.0	0.0
06- Charubeta	40	5.0	30.0	20.0	7.5	25.0	2.5	0.0	0.0	5.0	5.0
07-Gohar Patia	60	3.3	16.7	13.3	21.7	15.0	0.0	20.0	0.0	8.3	1.7
08 -Khetalsanda Mutsjar	38	2.6	18.4	23.7	2.6	39.5	0.0	5.3	2.6	0.0	5.3
09- Mohammadpur	76	10.5	14.5	23.7	6.6	32.9	1.3	2.6	0.0	5.3	2.6
10- Diyan	43	14.0	14.0	9.3	4.7	7.0	0.0	0.0	37.2	14.0	0.0
Grand Total	**445**	**10.8**	**13.9**	**19.3**	**8.8**	**28.1**	**0.7**	**4.7**	**5.2**	**4.9**	**3.6**

Source: Field Survey, 2005-2006.

TABLE 5.14

Per Capita Land of Tharu Households in the Sample Villages

Sample Villages	*Total House-holds*	*Land in Acres (% of total households)*							
		Nil	*< 1.0*	*1.1-3.0*	*3.1-5.0*	*5.1-7.0*	*7.1-9.0*	*9.1-11.0*	*> 11.1*
01- Bidaura	50	8.0	20.0	36.0	16.0	8.0	10.0	0.0	2.0
02- Baruwabagh	23	4.3	21.7	65.2	0.0	4.3	4.3	0.0	0.0
03- Sadhu Nagar	70	15.7	22.9	38.6	17.1	2.9	2.9	0.0	0.0
04- Navi Nagar	24	12.5	0.0	79.2	4.2	0.0	0.0	4.2	0.0
05- Behi	21	14.3	47.6	23.8	14.3	0.0	0.0	0.0	0.0
06- Charubeta	40	7.5	55.0	22.5	10.0	5.0	0.0	0.0	0.0
07-Gohar Patia	60	35.0	25.0	26.7	8.3	3.3	0.0	0.0	1.7
08 -Khetalsanda Mustajar	38	7.9	34.2	34.2	15.8	2.6	2.6	2.6	0.0
09- Mohammadpur	76	10.5	25.0	52.6	7.9	1.3	1.3	0.0	1.3
10- Diyan	43	7.0	27.9	41.9	11.6	4.7	2.3	2.3	2.3
Grand Total	**445**	**13.5**	**27.4**	**40.4**	**11.2**	**3.4**	**2.5**	**0.7**	**0.9**

Source: Field Survey, 2005-2006.

side the study region (Table 5.12).

Agriculture is the basic source of livelihood of the Tharu population. Total surveyed Tharu population has been divided in ten occupational categories. It is worth to mention that the Tharus are engaged in more than one occupation including agriculture only. About 8.8% Tharus are registered as labourer while 10.8% have agriculture as occupation only. Maximum 28.1% have an occupation of cultivation and animal rearing. About 5% Tharus have cultivation including public/private sector tertiary jobs (Table 5.13). As stated that single occupation doesn't provide the self-reliant base. It also highlights the fact by and large all the family members are essentially engaged in their inherent occupations whether their labour is required or not. Thus one can see the latent unemployment scenario in the tribal society. Per capita land point of view total Tharu household categorized into seven groups.

TABLE 5.15

Livestock Holder Households in the Sample Villages (% of Holder)

Sample Villages	*Total House-holds*	*Livestock Holder HH*		*Animals (% of total Holders)*		
		No.	*% of total*	*Milky*	*Draught*	*Both*
01. Bidaura	50	32	64.0	15.6	18.8	65.6
02. Baruwabagh	23	23	100.0	21.7	34.8	43.5
03. Sadhu Nagar	70	57	81.4	22.8	33.3	43.9
04. Navi Nagar	24	24	100.0	41.7	25.0	33.3
05. Behi	21	21	100.0	28.6	23.8	47.6
06. Charubeta	40	19	47.5	31.6	15.8	52.6
07. Gohar Patiya	60	31	51.7	9.7	48.4	41.9
08. Khetalsanda Mustajar	38	29	76.3	6.9	55.2	37.9
09. Mohammadpur	76	47	61.8	27.7	25.5	46.8
10. Diyan	43	28	65.1	60.7	17.9	21.4
Grand Total	**445**	**311**	**69.9**	**25.7**	**30.5**	**43.7**

Source: Field Survey, 2005-2006.

Out of total 445 Tharu households, 13.5% are landless. Maximum 40.4% households have 1.1% to 3.0% acres per capita land while 27.4% have less than 1.0 acres per capita land. About 11.2% households are in the group of 3.1 to 5.0 acres per capita land. Total 7.5% households have more than 5 acres per capita land (Table 5.14).

Due to the changing economic setup of the Tharu society only 69.9% of total 445 Tharu families have animals. Among that 25.7% have only milky animals and 30.5% have draught animals. About 43.7% families have both milky and drought animals (Table 5.15). They cultivate their land with the help of animals and machines. Due to the scarcity of fodder and man-power they are not dependant on animals only.

The economic status of any segments of the society including Tharu tribe certainly depends on the occupational pattern. The net annual income of per household and per capita is worked out often summing up the total output from all sources and subtracts the cost of inputs (expenditures). Out of total income two third incomes is received from the two occupations (cultivation; cultivation and labour) only (Table 5.16). The average per capita and per household's income is Rs. 305 and Rs. 4812 respectively. The study shows that the per capita income is far below from the national poverty line.

Role and Status of Tharu Women

In the present day circumstances, the Tharu women enjoy a very dominant position in their community. They have considerable liberty and wield great influence in the domestic sphere. The significant role of Tharu women in socio-economic and cultural sphere of Tharu life can never be under-estimated. The Tharus were practising various forms of marriage. But now with the integration of the Tharu society and with growing contact with the Hindus and Punjabis, the Tharus have given up some of the older marriage practices.

Table 5.17 shows that out of the total surveyed Tharus 46.8% persons are ever married. Among them 43.6% are males and 46% females. Out of total marriages 99.7% are traditional. Remaining 0.3% Tharus have selected their life partner by choice (love marriage). It shows that regular form of marriage is becoming more common.

TABLE 5.16

Income Sources of Tharu Households in the Sample Villages

Sample Villages	Total Households	Income Sources (% of total households)									
		Agriculture		Agri. & Labour		Labour		Agri. & Shop		Agri.& Service	
	No.	No.	%	No.	%	No.	%	No.	%	No.	%
01. Bidaura	50	17	34.0	14	28.0	4	8.0	5	10.0	10	20.0
02. Baruwabagh	23	11	47.8	7	30.4	1	4.3	2	8.7	2	8.7
03. Sadhu Nagar	70	25	35.7	31	44.3	11	15.7	0	0.0	3	4.3
04. Navi Nagar	24	12	50.0	9	37.5	3	12.5	0	0.0	0	0.0
05. Behi	21	3	14.3	15	71.4	3	14.3	0	0.0	0	0.0
06. Charubeta	40	12	30.0	20	50.0	3	7.5	0	0.0	5	12.5
07. Gohar Patia	60	11	18.3	18	30.0	25	41.7	0	0.0	6	10.0
08. Khetalsanda Mustajar	38	15	39.5	17	44.7	2	5.3	1	2.6	3	7.9
09. Mohammadpur	76	31	40.8	31	40.8	7	9.2	0	0.0	7	9.2
10. Diyan	43	22	51.2	13	30.2	2	4.7	5	11.6	1	2.3
Grand Total	**445**	**159**	**35.7**	**175**	**39.3**	**61**	**13.7**	**13**	**2.9**	**37**	**8.3**

Source: Field Survey, 2005-2006.

TABLE 5.17

Marital Status Among the Tharu Population in the Sample Villages

Sample Villages	*Total Population*			*Ever Married Population (% of total)*			*Marriage Type*	
	P	*M*	*F*	*P*	*M*	*F*	*Traditional*	*Choice*
	No.	*No.*	*No.*	*%*	*%*	*%*	*(% of Married Population)*	
01. Bidaura	291	149	142	46.7	40.9	52.8	100	0.0
02. Baruwabagh	133	62	71	45.1	45.2	45.1	100	0.0
03. Sadhu Nagar	377	198	179	45.4	43.4	47.5	98.8	1.2
04. Navi Nagar	132	73	59	43.2	39.7	47.5	100	0.0
05. Behi	96	53	43	53.1	47.2	60.5	100	0.0
06. Charubeta	192	100	92	50.0	46.0	54.3	100	0.0
07. Gohar Patia	356	183	173	48.9	44.8	53.2	100	0.0
08. Khetalsanda Mustajar	238	122	116	45.0	42.6	47.4	100	0.0
09. Mohammadpur	462	230	232	47.4	45.2	49.6	100	0.0
10. Diyan	251	130	232	44.6	41.5	25.0	98.2	1.8
Grand Total	**2528**	**1300**	**1339**	**46.8**	**43.6**	**46.0**	**99.7**	**0.3**

Source: Field Survey, 2005-2006.

TABLE 5.18

Age at First Marriage of Tharu Population in the Sample Village

Sample Villages	Total Married Population			Age at First Marriage (% of total Married Population)																	
				Below 14			15—16			17—18			19—20			21—22			Above 23		
	P	M	F	P	M	F	P	M	F	P	M	F	P	M	F	P	M	F	P	M	F
01. Bidaura	136	61	75	1.5	0	2.7	22.1	0	40.0	41.2	27.9	52.0	28.7	62.3	1.3	1.5	3.3	0.0	5.1	6.6	4.0
02. Baruwabagh	60	28	32	0.0	0	0.0	10.0	0	18.8	28.3	7.1	46.9	36.7	39.3	34.4	20.0	42.9	0.0	5.0	10.7	0.0
03. Sadhu Nagar	171	86	85	1.2	0	2.4	12.3	4.7	20.0	43.9	16.3	71.8	42.1	79.1	4.7	0.6	0.0	1.2	0.0	0.0	0.0
04. Navi Nagar	57	29	28	0.0	0	0.0	1.8	0.0	3.6	28.1	10.3	46.4	45.6	48.3	42.9	21.1	34.5	7.1	3.5	6.9	0.0
05. Behi	51	25	26	5.9	0	11.5	33.3	12.0	53.8	39.2	44.0	34.6	21.6	44.0	0.0	0.0	0.0	0.0	0.0	0.0	0.0
06. Charubeta	96	46	50	5.2	0	10.0	20.8	2.2	38.0	37.5	30.4	44.0	30.2	54.3	8.0	6.3	13.0	0.0	0.0	0.0	0.0
07. Gohar Patia	174	82	92	8.6	0	16.3	23.0	4.9	39.1	29.3	24.4	33.7	31.0	56.1	8.7	4.6	7.3	2.2	3.4	7.3	0.0
08. Khetalsanda Mustajar	107	52	55	7.5	0	14.5	16.8	3.8	29.1	25.2	15.4	34.5	30.8	42.3	20.0	13.1	25.0	1.8	6.5	13.5	0.0
09. Mohammadpur	219	104	115	9.1	0	17.4	19.6	4.8	33.0	32.0	27.9	35.7	29.7	47.1	13.9	6.8	14.4	0.0	2.7	5.8	0.0
10. Diyan	112	54	58	0.9	0	1.7	11.6	0.0	22.4	33.0	14.8	50.0	41.1	59.3	24.1	11.6	22.2	1.7	1.8	3.7	0.0
Grand Total	**1183**	**567**	**616**	**4.7**	**0**	**9.1**	**17.7**	**3.4**	**30.8**	**34.2**	**22.2**	**45.3**	**33.6**	**55.7**	**13.1**	**7.0**	**13.4**	**1.1**	**2.8**	**5.3**	**0.5**

Source: Field Survey, 2005-2006.

It is tried to find out the average age at first marriage among the Tharus. The Table 5.18 shows the average age at which marriage take place among the Tharus. Child marriage particularly girls is common phenomenon in the Tharu society. Table 5.18 shows that 4.7% persons (among them all are girl), child marriage take place below 14 years of age. About 90% Tharu marriages take place up to 20 years while 85% females got married below 18 years of age which is absolutely against the marriage act. Early marriage provides a safeguard against premarital sexual relationship among the Tharus.

TABLE 5.19

Age at First Child Birth Among the Tharu Married/Fertile Women in the Sample Villages

Sample Villages	*Fertile Women*	*Age Groups (% of Married Women)*					
		<-14	*15-16*	*17-18*	*19-20*	*21-22*	*Above 23*
01. Bidaura	73	0.0	12.3	31.5	31.5	17.8	6.8
02. Baruwabagh	30	0.0	0.0	53.3	26.7	13.3	6.7
03. Sadhu Nagar	80	1.3	6.3	18.8	41.3	17.5	15.0
04. Navi Nagar	26	0.0	0.0	11.5	69.2	19.2	0.0
05. Behi	25	0.0	8.0	56.0	28.0	8.0	0.0
06. Charubeta	50	0.0	8.0	22.0	46.0	14.0	10.0
07. Gohar Patiya	81	0.0	14.8	25.9	30.9	21.0	7.4
08. Khetalsanda Mustajar	51	3.9	9.8	31.4	41.2	9.8	3.9
09. Mohammadpur	108	0.0	13.9	15.7	38.0	25.0	7.4
10. Diyan	58	0.0	1.7	29.3	44.8	17.2	6.9
Grand Total	**582**	**0.5**	**9.1**	**26.3**	**38.7**	**17.9**	**7.6**

Source: Field Survey, 2005-2006.

Note: Out of total married women , 34 women are still infetile in the sample villages.

Table 5.19 shows the average age at first child birth among the Tharus fertile/married women. There are 582 fertile women in the 10 sample villages. Table 5.19 shows that 0.5% women's age was below 14 years when they give a child birth while 35.4%

women give child birth below the age of 18 years. Infantile mortality is very high among the Tharus. These deaths occurred because of early marriage of Tharu girls. Only 7.6% women give birth at the age of 23 years.

Table 5.20 shows that out of the total fertile women 98.3% have given birth normally while only 1.7% deliveries were caesarian. All normal deliveries take place at home through local dais while caesarian cases were handled by qualified doctors at hospitals. About one fourth (24.2%) of the total 582 fertile women have given birth only 1 or 2 times on the date of survey (2006) while 37.3% women produce 3 to 4 times.

TABLE 5.20

Delivery Type in the Sample Villages

Sample Villages	*Total Fertile Women (No.)*	*Delivery (% of total fertile women)*			
		Normal		*Cissorian*	
		(No.)	*%*	*(No.)*	*%*
01. Bidaura	73	71	97.3	2	2.7
02. Baruwabagh	30	30	100.0	0	0.0
03. Sadhu Nagar	80	77	96.3	3	3.8
04. Navi Nagar	26	26	100.0	0	0.0
05. Behi	25	24	96.0	1	4.0
06. Charubeta	50	46	92.0	4	8.0
07. Gohar Patiya	81	81	100.0	0	0.0
08. Khetalsanda Mustajar	51	51	100.0	0	0.0
09. Mohammadpur	108	108	100.0	0	0.0
10. Diyan	58	58	100.0	0	0.0
Grand Total	**582**	**572**	**98.3**	**10**	**1.7**

Source: Field Survey, 2005-2006.

Likewise 26.6%, 10.8% and 0.9% fertile women produce child respectively 5 to 6, 7 to 8, and above 8 times in their whole life (Table 5.21). It shows that the Tharu people are still unaware about the family control.

Study shows that 51% Tharus children are breast feed up to one year while 6.9% fertile women give her milk up to 8 months only (Table 5.21). It is because lack of milk production and ill health of mothers who can not feed regularly. Consequently due to the malnourishment, the health of the both mother and offspring is very weak. Table 5.23 shows the pattern of living children of Tharu fertile women in the sample villages. Unfortunately 1% fertile women's babies could not survive so long while 47.3% women's all babies are still long survived. About 14.1%, 21.6%, 14.9% and 1% Tharu fertile women have living children respectively below 2, 3-4, 5-6 and 7-8 babies.

TABLE 5.21

Reproduction Pattern Among the Tharu Women in the Sample Villages

Sample Villages	*Total Fertile Women*	*Reproduction Frequency (% of total fertile women)*				
		< 2	*3-4*	*5-6*	*7-8*	*> 8*
01. Bidaura	73	21.9	38.4	32.9	6.8	0.0
02. Baruwabagh	30	13.3	30.0	33.3	20.0	3.3
03. Sadhu Nagar	80	17.5	33.8	36.3	12.5	0.0
04. Navi Nagar	26	19.2	46.2	23.1	11.5	0.0
05. Behi	25	32.0	40.0	24.0	4.0	0.0
06. Charubeta	50	26.0	48.0	16.0	10.0	0.0
07. Gohar Patiya	81	29.6	39.5	21.0	7.4	2.5
08. Khetalsanda Mustajar	51	27.5	39.2	27.5	5.9	0.0
09. Mohammadpur	108	26.9	36.1	20.4	14.8	0.9
10. Diyan	58	24.1	27.6	32.8	13.8	1.7
Grand Total	**582**	**24.2**	**37.3**	**26.6**	**10.8**	**0.9**

Source: Field Survey, 2005-2006.

Note: Out of total married women, 34 women are still infertile in the sample villages.

TABLE 5.22

Feeding Periods of Infants in the Sample Villages

Sample Villages	*Total Fertile Women (No.)*	*Feeding Periods in months (% of total)*							
		<8		*9—10*		*11—12*		*Above-13*	
		Breast	*Bottle*	*Breast*	*Bottle*	*Breast*	*Bottle*	*Breast*	*Bottle*
01. Bidaura	73	15.1	0.0	35.6	0.0	42.5	0.0	6.8	100.0
02. Baruwabagh	30	3.3	0.0	16.7	0.0	76.7	0.0	3.3	100.0
03. Sadhu Nagar	80	12.5	0.0	28.8	0.0	42.5	1.3	16.3	100.0
04. Navi Nagar	26	0.0	0.0	34.6	0.0	42.3	0.0	23.1	100.0
05. Behi	25	0.0	0.0	44.0	0.0	44.0	0.0	12.0	100.0
06. Charubeta	50	8.0	0.0	30.0	0.0	34.0	0.0	28.0	100.0
07. Gohar Patiya	81	4.9	0.0	27.2	0.0	45.7	0.0	22.2	100.0
08. Khetalsanda Mustajar	51	3.9	0.0	5.9	0.0	68.6	0.0	21.6	100.0
09. Mohammadpur	108	2.8	0.0	14.8	0.0	56.5	0.0	25.9	100.0
10. Diyan	58	8.6	0.0	6.9	0.0	62.1	0.0	22.4	100.0
Grand Total	**582**	**6.9**	**0.0**	**23.0**	**0.0**	**50.9**	**0.2**	**19.2**	**100.0**

Source: Field Survey, 2005.

Note: Out of total married women, 34 women are still infertile in the sample villages.

Out of total 582 fertile or children bearing women who have given birth to 2551 children, among them 82% were survived and remaining 18% were expired in various stages. Out of total died children 65.5% were expired immediately while 23.7% within one month, 9.2% within 2 months and 2.5% were survived only 3 months or more (Table 5.24). It is primarily due to early marriage of Tharu women and partly due to the extremely hard life and harsh condition of work coupled with malnourishment. Pregnant and lactating women have been widely recognized as a vulnerable section of the society from the health and nutritional point of view. Considerable attention has not been paid to their dietary intake and nutritional status in the tribal society of this region. It is universally accepted that the women needed more nutritious food to feed her offspring. The record about the tribal women and infants care were not uncompleted but also poorly maintained. It is observed during the field works that mostly pregnant women and their offspring were not vaccinated. It is due to lack of health facilities as well as awareness. It is noticed that the percentage of Tharu women who visited a health facility and those who were visited at home by the health workers were very low. Therefore 98.3% normal deliveries took place at home with the help of local untrained dais or mostly relatives or neighbours. Majority of the Tharu women were unaware of antenatal services even 90 tablets of iron and folic acid. A number of primary health centres and sub-centres are running without specialized medical personnel. It is very sad that in spite of large number of trained dais, most deliveries in the study area of the U.S. Nagar district are still being attended by untrained persons. Such type of care at the time of birth has a major role to play in determining the survival of mother and offspring. The living conditions of Tharu women during deliveries were very bad. In most of the tribal families mothers and their new born babies were not allowed to move out from the fixed allocated space of the room. In a sanitation point

TABLE 5.23

Alive Children of Tharu Women in the Sample Villages

Sample Villages	*Total Fertile Women*	*Number of Alive Children (% of Total fertile Women)*					
		Nil	*All*	*< 2*	*3 4*	*5 6*	*7 8*
01. Bidaura	73	1.4	61.6	15.1	15.1	6.8	0.0
02. Baruwabagh	30	0.0	0.0	20.0	40.0	40.0	0.0
03. Sadhu Nagar	80	1.3	47.5	10.0	26.3	15.0	0.0
04. Navi Nagar	26	0.0	19.2	30.8	30.8	19.2	0.0
05. Behi	25	4.0	32.0	20.0	32.0	12.0	0.0
06. Charubeta	50	0.0	50.0	16.0	24.0	8.0	2.0
07. Gohar Patiya	81	3.7	54.3	11.1	17.3	11.1	2.5
08. Khetalsanda Mutsjar	51	0.0	43.1	19.6	27.5	7.8	2.0
09. Mohammadpur	108	0.0	54.6	11.1	11.1	21.3	1.9
10. Diyan	58	0.0	50.0	8.6	24.1	17.2	0.0
Grand Total	**582**	**1.0**	**47.3**	**14.1**	**21.6**	**14.9**	**1.0**

Source: Field Survey, 2005-2006.

Note: Out of total married women, 34 women are still infertile in the sample villages.

TABLE 5.24

Mortality of the Tharu Children in the Sample Villages

Sample Villages	Total Fertile Women	Total Conceived	Status of Children (% of conceived)				Death Duration After Birth (% of total died children)			
			Alive Children		Died Children		Immediate	01 Month	02 Months	> 03 Months
	(No.)	(No.)	(No.)	(%)	(No.)	(%)	(%)	(%)	(%)	(%)
01. Bidaura	73	288	247	85.8	41	14.2	46.3	39.0	7.3	7.3
02. Baruwabagh	30	156	118	75.6	38	24.4	50.0	34.2	13.2	2.6
03. Sadhu Nagar	80	402	313	77.9	79	19.7	48.1	32.9	15.2	3.8
04. Navi Nagar	26	153	132	86.3	21	13.7	61.9	28.6	9.5	0.0
05. Behi	25	94	70	74.5	24	25.5	58.3	29.2	8.3	4.2
06. Charubeta	50	235	202	86.0	33	14.0	69.7	21.2	9.1	0.0
07. Gohar Patia	81	317	261	82.3	56	17.7	71.4	23.2	5.4	0.0
08. Khetalsanda Mutsjar	51	203	161	79.3	42	20.7	76.2	14.3	7.1	2.4
09. Mohammadpur	108	441	378	85.7	61	13.8	91.8	11.5	3.3	0.0
10. Diyan	58	262	210	80.2	52	19.8	75.0	9.6	11.5	3.8
Grand Total	**582**	**2551**	**2092**	**82.0**	**447**	**17.5**	**65.5**	**23.7**	**9.2**	**2.5**

Source: Field Survey, 2005-2006.

Note: Out of total married women, 34 women are still infetile in the sample villages.

of view it is very striking features in the tribal society that both mother and child would bath after a gap of six days of the delivery. As a result mothers and their babies are more vulnerable to suffer various diseases and increased number of mortality and morbidity. However, such data has not been gathered during the field survey because generally women concealed this type of information. It is noticed that one fourth of the total new offspring have normal weight (above 2.5 kg) at the time of birth while 2/3 babies have low weight (below 2.5 kg) at the time of birth. The main cause of low weight birth was poor calorie and protein intake by mothers during the pregnancy on the one hand hard work on the other.

TABLE 5.25

Prevailing Means for Population Control Among the Tharu Women in the Sample Villages

Sample Villages	*Total Married Women (No.)*	*Total Users*		*Prevailing Means (% of Users)*		
		No.	*% of total*	*Operation*	*Tablet*	*Coper-T*
01. Bidaura	75	63	84.0	57.1	30.2	12.7
02. Baruwabagh	32	27	84.4	77.8	22.2	0.0
03. Sadhu Nagar	85	70	82.4	58.6	40.0	1.4
04. Navi Nagar	28	22	78.6	22.7	77.3	0.0
05. Behi	26	21	80.8	33.3	61.9	4.8
06. Charubeta	50	40	80.0	30.0	67.5	2.5
07. Gohar Patiya	92	63	68.5	50.8	47.6	1.6
08. Khetalsanda Mustajar	55	42	76.4	45.2	54.8	0.0
09. Mohammadpur	115	78	67.8	38.5	59.0	2.6
10. Diyan	58	47	81.0	61.7	38.3	0.0
Grand Total	**616**	**473**	**76.8**	**49.0**	**48.0**	**3.0**

Source: Field Survey, 2005-2006.

Out of total ever married women 76.8% were using population control mean-operation, tablets and copper T. Out of total users 49% women have done operations, 48% were using tablets and remaining 3% have selected copper T as a birth control measure (Table 5.25). Among the Tharu society, male population is not interested to adopt the birth control means.

Housing and Environmental Sanitation Pattern in the Sample Villages

The health status of the people in any caste and class in any geographical region largely depends upon the physical quality of the environment. Health is a crucial attribute of human resource and a healthy human population is the most desired national asset. Adequate sanitation and safe potable water are necessary for the prevention of infectious and water borne diseases. Inadequacy of the safe drinking water and improper disposal of night soil solid and liquid waste leading to polluted environmental conditions and lack of personal and food hygiene have been the major causes of many fatal diseases in developing countries including India (Banerji, 1985, anon, 1992 and Pant, 2003). While these elaborate arrangement for housing and sanitation in the urban areas, rural housing and sanitation have been of marginal interest of the policy makers. Health surveys conducted in different parts of the country reveal that about 70% of the morbidity and mortality among rural population can be attributed to the direct and indirect effects of poor environmental conditions in the villages (Santhanam, 1989). Realizing the significance of environmental sanitation, the WHO (1953) expert committee on environmental sanitation recommended provision of adequate supply of water and safe disposal of human excreta (night soil) as essential step for hygienic environmental conditions in rural areas. Even environmental Hygiene Committee of Government of India, as early as in 1984, suggested that measure should be taken to make the provision of safe drinking water supply and sanitation. Moreover, following the recommendation of U N Habitat Conference (1976), U N Water Conference (1977) decided to observe 1981-90 as the "International Drinking Water and Sanitation Decade, " which was finally endorsed by 31st U N General Assembly in 1977. According to the resolution passed in General Assembly, the member states had agreed to provide its population safe drinking water and hygienic waste disposal by the year 1990.

Village-wise data regarding housing and environmental

sanitation is presented in Tables 5.26 to 5.28. In the sample villages 60.9% households have pucca houses while 39.1% households were still living in kuchha houses. About 32.6% households have attached kitchen i.e. a corner of any room is used for this purpose while 67.4% households have separate kitchen either permanent or temporary. In this region Tharu people used a separate thatched for kitchen purpose. It is very serious problem in the sample villages where only 5.2% and 8.5% Tharu households have both the bathroom and toilet facilities in their houses (Table 5.26). Latrines were generally constructed outside the house. It is noticed that only economically sound households have these facilities. As there was no public latrine facility in the villages, majority of the Tharu households (91.5%) have to go in open fields or nearby jungle for latrine. Though it provides manure, the soil get indiscriminately polluted resulting in heavy infestations with helminthes parasites. Clearing the toilets is problematic due to cultural perceptions and this discouraged people from having toilets either inside or outside

TABLE 5.26

House Type and Facilities Available in the Tharu Houses

Sample Villages	*Total Houses (No.)*	*House Type*		*Kitchen*		*Bathroom*	*Toilet*
		Pucca	*Kuchha*	*Attached*	*Separate*	*Available*	*Available*
		(% of total)		*(% of total)*		*(% of total)*	
01. Bidaura	50	80.0	20.0	32.0	68.0	16.0	26.0
02. Baruwabagh	23	47.8	52.2	30.4	69.6	0.0	4.3
03. Sadhu Nagar	70	35.7	64.3	24.3	75.7	2.9	10.0
04. Navi Nagar	24	79.2	20.8	12.5	87.5	0.0	0.0
05. Behi	21	66.7	33.3	28.6	71.4	0.0	0.0
06. Charubeta	40	72.5	27.5	37.5	62.5	17.5	22.5
07. Gohar Patiya	60	63.3	36.7	33.3	66.7	3.3	3.3
08. Khetalsanda Mustajar	38	57.9	42.1	36.8	63.2	2.6	5.3
09. Mohammadpur	76	69.7	30.3	39.5	60.5	2.6	3.9
10. Diyan	43	46.5	53.5	39.5	60.5	2.3	2.3
Grand Total	**445**	**60.9**	**39.1**	**32.6**	**67.4**	**5.2**	**8.5**

Source: Field Survey, 2005-2006.

TABLE 5.27

Housing and Environmental Sanitation Pattern in the Sample Villages

Sample Villages	*Total*	*Satisfactory Conditions (% of total Households)*									
	Households No.	*Potable Water*	*Vantilation Condition*	*Sunlight Condition*	*Space*	*Sanitation Condition*	*Waste Disposal*	*Water Disposal*	*Drains*	*Pest Condition*	*Kitchen Garden*
01. Bidaura	50	34.0	66.0	74.0	60.0	46.0	20.0	24.0	6.0	24.0	64.0
02. Baruwabagh	23	26.1	47.8	56.5	52.2	8.7	30.4	0.0	0.0	21.7	95.7
03. Sadhu Nagar	70	32.9	32.9	55.7	64.3	38.6	37.1	5.7	2.9	28.6	88.6
04. Navi Nagar	24	25.0	25.0	54.2	66.7	20.8	29.2	12.5	8.3	12.5	75.0
05. Behi	21	23.8	42.9	76.2	66.7	0.0	33.3	0.0	0.0	47.6	71.4
06. Charubeta	40	17.5	67.5	80.0	57.5	27.5	15.0	5.0	5.0	47.5	87.5
07. Gohar Patia	60	18.3	60.0	70.0	55.0	20.0	30.0	8.3	0.0	46.7	93.3
08. Khetalsanda Mustajar	38	13.2	42.1	68.4	63.2	28.9	7.9	5.3	5.3	39.5	63.4
09. Mohammadpur	76	17.1	51.3	78.9	65.8	28.9	21.1	5.3	2.6	42.1	84.2
10. Diyan	43	20.9	55.8	76.7	58.1	46.5	18.6	9.3	4.7	62.8	83.7
Grand Total	**445**	**22.9**	**50.3**	**69.9**	**61.1**	**29.9**	**24.3**	**8.1**	**3.4**	**38.4**	**82.2**

Source: Field Survey, 2005-2006.

the house. Generally courtyards were made by mud. Maximum courtyards of the Tharus were in bad conditions in terms of sanitation. In the tribal rural area, along with the type of housing, the quality of houses is also greatly affected by the provision of ventilation, sunlight condition, pest and insects conditions etc. The ventilation conditions of 50.3% houses were satisfactory. The sunlight condition of 69.9% houses were good while 61.2% of the total houses were suffering from pests and insects and 70.1% were in worse sanitation conditions respectively, also effect its inhabitants. It is also observed that few Tharu households used the pesticides and insecticides in their house to protect themselves and their foodgrains from the pests and insects. Open space around the houses also influences the health of its members. About 61% households have enough open space surrounding their house while remaining 39% houses were in very congestion (Table 5.27). It is due to the expansion of the family.

TABLE 5.28

Congestion (Room Density) in Tharu Houses of the Sample Villages

Sample Villages	*Total House-holds*	*Ranges of Rooms/Persons (% of total households)*					
		<0.20	*0.21-0.30*	*0.31-0.40*	*0.41-.050*	*0.51-0.60*	*> 0.61*
01. Bidaura	50	16.0	20.0	22.0	20.0	2.0	20.0
02. Baruwabagh	23	30.4	13.0	39.1	8.7	4.3	4.3
03. Sadhu Nagar	70	17.1	30.0	22.9	10.0	4.3	15.7
04. Navi Nagar	24	20.8	16.7	37.5	8.3	0.0	16.7
05. Behi	21	38.1	19.0	19.0	19.0	0.0	4.8
06. Charubeta	40	0.0	7.5	32.5	32.5	0.0	27.5
07. Gohar Patiya	60	18.3	20.0	18.3	16.7	8.3	18.3
08. Khetalsanda Mustajar	38	18.4	15.8	36.8	21.1	2.6	5.3
09. Mohammadpur	76	15.8	17.1	25.0	17.1	11.8	13.2
10. Diyan	43	20.9	30.2	23.3	9.3	4.7	11.6
Grand Total	**445**	**17.8**	**20.0**	**26.1**	**16.4**	**4.9**	**14.8**

Source: Field Survey, 2005-2006.

In the evaluation of the housing conditions from the health view point, it is not merely the type or quality of house but its size or room density (rooms/person) also plays very important role. As evident from the Table 5.28 the room density about 17.8% of the total Tharu households was 0.2 room/person i.e. five persons in one room, while less than 20% household members have half room per person.

Lack of safe drinking water and indiscriminate defecation are the major source of many serious diseases. It is noticed that the main source of water supply was hand pumps. About 23% households were using safe portable water. It is observed that there were no treatment plants for water purification in the Tharu villages.

The method of waste water disposal in the sample villages was very unhygienic. There was no drainage system in the sample village. There were no drains to carry either the rain or the waste water. The waste water spills around or in front of the houses which promotes the breeding of mosquitoes and flies and spread the diseases. About 91.9% of the total surveyed households disposed of the water in open space while 8.1% have managed to have drain adjacent to their houses. These drains carry the waste water to some distance from where it spills over the open space again.

Refuses includes several substances in it like ashes, rubbish, stable manure, home and street sweeping, garbage, night soil of infants, children, sick persons etc. the method of handling of refuse has a strong bearing on sanitary condition. Majority of Tharu households (75.7%) have dumped the refuse in open space. Remaining 24.3% of the households have put it in the uncovered ditches. It is observed that Tharus were so unaware to sanitation in the villages that not a single household had a proper covered compost pit for dumping the refuse. Tharu has no idea of keeping manure pits and this is responsible for breeding flies, mosquitoes and other germs and making the air impure and unhealthy. A good lot of manure is also lost, because it is washed away during the rains. Streets or paths conditions of the Tharu villages were not satisfactory. Maximum garbage stores were open and closed to the house. Hence, the conditions of environmental sanitation assessed in terms of water and waste disposal have been very unhygienic in the sample villages as a whole without any difference between castes/class.

The habitat of the Tharu tribe is generally marked by compact settlement to the extent that most dwellings have common walls with their neighbours particularly brothers. Such condition facilitates dissemination of communicable diseases. The justa position of house and cattle sheds (thatches), often in single compound or keeping animals in corner of the house, is common feature in the sample villages. This unhealthy practice of keeping animals in close proximity to human being is partly taken to be a safeguard from wild animals and shortage of covered space during the winters. As a result of unsanitary conditions produced by the animal urine and dung carry lot of pathogens. The visible effect of such practices in causing infection is beyond the scope of this study, albeit their contribution in producing unsanitary and unhygienic conditions cannot be connived at. It is noticed that in Tarai and Bhabar region the quality of construction and building materials, the houses are usually built of mud and shaft (tatar) with grass roof and no stone foundation. A defect in their houses seems to be that there is no outlet for the kitchen smoke to escape. The result is that it filters slowly through the roof so that its rafters and articles suspended from it are always thickly coated with soot and cobwebs. Defective thatches and its wall bring the number of the family in contact with several disease agents such as parasites and enteropathogenic bacteria. During the rainy season, the drafty and leaky dwellers often enhance the prevalence of respiratory infections i.e. common colds. The compact layout further restricts air circulation and sunshine in most dwellings. The hot and humid conditions of the study area are ideal for the multiplication of pathogens and several vectors which in turn help in transmitting infectious diseases.

The Tharu people already suffering from minor ailments may thus become potential host to several waterborne diseases, e.g., dysentery, hookworm, hepatitis, typhoid, etc. The open drain can be the dangerous source of disease carrying vectors such as houseflies and mosquitoes. During field study of the sample villages, it is found that most families in the rural areas were generally little conscious of personal hygiene. Use of common towels and drinking cups glass, carelessness about handkerchief, imperfectly washed dishes and hand soiled with nasal secretion were prevalent practices. Diffusion of some infectious diseases could possibly be related to such unhygienic routine habits.

Before a Tharu settles down in a village and builds his house, he tries to grab as much land as possible for a vegetable garden (*bari*) and also for small fields around or nearby his house. About 82.2% households have their courtyards for seasonal vegetables and spices particularly chilly and garlic for their personal consumption (Table 5.27).

Amenities in the Sample Villages

In this chapter few indicators such as schools, post office, hospitals, bus stop, workshop and Government shop have been included. About 30% villages have sub post offices while none of bank situated in the sample villages. Fifty percent villages

TABLE 5.29

Infrastructural Facilities Available in the Sample Villages

Name of Sample Villages	*Post Office*	*Bank*	*Hos-pital*	*Primary School*	*Junior School*	*High School*	*Interme-diate College*	*Govt. Shop*	*Bus Stop*	*Work-shop*
Bidaura	Yes	No	Yes	Yes	Yes	Yes	No	Yes	Yes	Yes
Baruwabagh	Yes	No	No	Yes	Yes	No	No	Yes	Yes	Yes
Sadhu Nagar	No	No	Yes	Yes	Yes	No	No	Yes	No	Yes
Navi Nagar	No	No	No	Yes	Yes	No	No	Yes	No	No
Behi	No	No	No	Yes	Yes	No	No	No	No	No
Charubeta	Yes	No	No	Yes	Yes	No	No	Yes	Yes	Yes
Gohar Patia	No	No	Yes	Yes	No	No	No	Yes	No	No
Khetalsanda Mustajar	No	No	No	Yes	Yes	No	No	No	No	No
Mohammadpur	No	No	Yes	Yes	Yes	No	No	Yes	No	No
Diyan	No	No	Yes	Yes	No	No	No	Yes	No	No
Availability (% of total villages)	**30**	**0**	**50**	**100**	**80**	**10**	**0**	**80**	**30**	**40**

Source: Field Survey, 2005-2006.

have health centres (clinic/PHCs) while none have livestock centres. It is very satisfactory that each and every sample village has a primary school while 80% have junior schools and 10% have high schools. There are no intermediate colleges in the sample villages. About 80% villages have government shops while only 30% villages are situated along state highway. Workshops are available in 40% sample villages for the repairing of agricultural tools, tractors and various types of machines (Table 5.29).

Fuel consumption pattern is also an indicator of level of the society. It is clear from the Table 5.30 that 18% of the total surveyed Tharu households have used cow dung, wood, and kerosene as a fuel while about two third (65%) of total households have supply their fuel demands by electricity, cow dung, wood, and kerosene. Including these means 16.2% households were found using L.P.G. during the field works. Thus study concludes that no one fuel means is not sufficient for the tribal people because of their poor economic conditions.

TABLE 5.30

Fuel Consumption Pattern in the Sample Villages

Sample Villages	*Total Households*	*% of total household*					
		Cowdung, Wood and Kerosene		*Electricity, Cow-dung, Wood and Kerosene*		*L.P.G, Electricity, Cowdung, Wood and Kerosene*	
	No.	*No*	*%*	*No*	*%*	*No*	*%*
01. Bidaura	50	6	12.0	22	44.0	22	44.0
02. Baruwabagh	23	0	0.0	21	91.3	2	8.7
03. Sadhu Nagar	70	18	25.7	45	64.3	7	10.0
04. Navi Nagar	24	3	12.5	20	83.3	1	4.2
05. Behi	21	7	33.3	14	66.7	0	0.0
06. Charubeta	40	10	25.0	17	42.5	13	32.5
07. Gohar Patia	60	17	28.3	35	58.3	8	13.3
08. Khetalsanda Mustajar	38	6	15.8	32	84.2	0	0.0
09. Mohammadpur	76	4	5.3	56	73.7	16	21.1
10. Diyan	43	9	20.9	31	72.1	3	7.0
Grand Total	**445**	**80**	**18.0**	**293**	**65.8**	**72**	**16.2**

Source: Field Survey, 2005-2006.

From the viewpoint of entertainment 51.5% of the total surveyed houscholds has only least one recreation means. Table 5.31 shows that 65.9% households have one recreation means i.e. television, tape, VCD, VCP, DVD, radio, newspaper, dish antenna etc. About 22.3%, 5.2%, and 6.6% households have respectively any two, three, and four entertainment means. It is clear from the table that about half of the total surveyed households are without entertainment means.

TABLE 5.31

Number of Entertainment Means of the Tharu Households in the Sample Villages

Sample Villages	*Total House holds*	*Total Holder*		*No. of Entertainment Means (% of total)*			
		No.	*% of total*	*One*	*Two*	*Three*	*Four*
01. Bidaura	50	30	60.0	46.7	40.0	3.3	10.0
02. Baruwabagh	23	10	43.5	50.0	0.0	10.0	40.0
03. Sadhu Nagar	70	37	52.9	75.7	24.3	0.0	0.0
04. Navi Nagar	24	10	41.7	80.0	10.0	10.0	0.0
05. Behi	21	12	57.1	100.0	0.0	0.0	0.0
06. Charubeta	40	22	55.0	72.7	22.7	4.5	0.0
07. Gohar Patiya	60	28	46.7	71.4	7.1	3.6	17.9
08. Khetalsanda Mustajar	38	26	68.4	69.2	30.8	0.0	0.0
09. Mohammadpur	76	32	42.1	59.4	28.1	12.5	0.0
10. Diyan	43	22	51.2	50.0	22.7	13.6	13.6
Grand Total	**445**	**229**	**51.5**	**65.9**	**22.3**	**5.2**	**6.6**

Source: Field Survey, 2005-2006.

Entertainment Means: T.V., Tape, VCD, VCP, DVD, Radio, News Paper & Dish Antenna.

An attempt has been made here to examine the status of development programmes in the tribal villages. It is clear from the Table 5.32 in which 26.1% of the total households have availed the developmental programmes launched by the government since 1996 to 2006. Maximum 17.1% households got benefit during 2001-05. It is also clear from the table that one fourth households are aware from the government development programmes.

TABLE 5.32

Development Programmes (Number of Beneficiary Households)

Sample Villages	*Total House-holds*	*Number of Beneficiary Households (% of total)*			
		Beneficiary Households	*1990-1995*	*1996-2000*	*2001-2005*
01. Bidaura	50	20.0	4.0	0.0	16.0
02. Baruwabagh	23	47.8	4.3	0.0	43.5
03. Sadhu Nagar	70	8.6	1.4	1.4	5.7
04. Navi Nagar	24	58.3	0.0	4.2	54.2
05. Behi	21	33.3	0.0	14.3	19.0
06. Charubeta	40	37.5	2.5	5.0	30.0
07. Gohar Patiya	60	26.7	3.3	16.7	6.7
08. Khetalsanda Mustajar	38	26.3	0.0	21.1	5.3
09. Mohammadpur	76	25.0	1.3	5.3	18.4
10. Diyan	43	18.6	2.3	4.7	11.6
Grand Total	**445**	**26.1**	**2.0**	**7.0**	**17.1**

Source: Field Survey, 2005-2006.

Hygiene Pattern in the Sample Villages

Sense of hygiene or awareness towards the hygiene plays a significant role to determine the nutria and health status of the people. Awareness generally depends upon the educational status and economic level. To measure the hygiene pattern among the Tharu people of Uttarakhand few indicators such as daily bath, daily brush, washing hands before meals, cutting of nails and cleaning of mattress etc. have been included which were noticed during the door to door survey. Village wise data regarding the personal hygiene is presented in Table 5.33. Out of total surveyed population (2528) 59.5% took bath daily. It varies minimum 21.1% in Baruwabagh village to maximum 85.4% in Gohar Patia village. Likewise bath, 64.6% population have brush their teeth daily. It is also worth to mention that brush means, cleaning of teeth by any means. About 70.8% Tharu were washed their hands before any meal while remaining 29.2% were took food by dirty hands which is absolutely unhygienic. Nearly 32% tribal people were cut their nails monthly. Only

15% Tharus were washing their mattress etc. regularly. The study concludes that the hygienic conditions of the Tharu population are not satisfactory. Majority of the sample Tharus were using soap or washing powder for washing clothes and bathing soap (Table 5.33).

TABLE 5.33

Hygiene Pattern in the Sample Villages

Sample Villages	*Total Population (No.)*	*Percentage of Total Population*				
		Daily Bath	*Daily Brush*	*Wash hands before Meal*	*Cutting Nails*	*Cleaning Mattress etc.*
01. Bidaura	291	35.1	25.8	64.3	17.9	18.9
02. Baruwabagh	133	21.1	16.5	72.9	14.3	8.3
03. Sadhu Nagar	377	50.4	64.7	78.8	25.7	10.3
04. Navi Nagar	132	62.9	50.0	84.1	51.5	21.2
05. Behi	96	76.0	84.4	83.3	29.2	20.8
06. Charubeta	192	67.2	80.7	81.3	41.7	24.0
07. Gohar Patiya	356	85.4	75.0	63.8	23.3	14.0
08. Khetalsanda Mutsjar	238	68.1	78.6	63.4	50.0	24.8
09. Mohammadpur	462	54.3	76.2	62.1	42.0	9.1
10. Diyan	251	72.1	73.7	78.9	29.1	14.7
Grand Total	**2528**	**59.5**	**64.6**	**70.8**	**32.2**	**15.3**

Source: Field Survey, 2005-2006.

Food Intake Pattern

As it is well known fact that food is the main source nourishment for human body, the food is therefore, defined as a substance, which yields heat to energy for building up new tissues and for repairing worn out tissues as well as for the regulation of the body process. Without adequate nutritious food one can not get the desired physical, mental, social and emotional status. The main source of nourishment for a human body is food; it is called nutrients, available in the foods in different amounts. Health, nutritious food and a balance diet are interdependent. Nutrition has to be translated into food to meet the needs of the body. The requirement of nutrition is however different according to the age, sex and occupation. In the present study area "Sitarganj–Khatima Tehsil", the per capita per day energy—2225 k cal requirement has been taken as standard requirement. Food items taken by Tharu people have been converted in to various nutrients—protein, fat, carbohydrates, minerals and vitamins. These nutrients have a specific role of its own to play in the human body such as protein is mainly for growth, minerals salts regulates the function of the body, carbohydrates and fats aid in the production of the heat and energy, each vitamin has a specific relation to certain structure of the body. Therefore nutritious food is of great importance in fostering physical, mental, social and emotional wellbeing of mankind.

Food habits of the people are outcome of the general beliefs which are deeply rooted in the minds of the people of any community about food. Those beliefs have a gradual evolution over generation and are geographical and socio-cultural in origin. When food beliefs become firmly embedded in the society they become taboos. These taboos are mostly harmless and many times are good and useful because these are the product of long experiences.

It is observed that the diets of the Tharu people are mainly limited to cereals with little vegetables. Diets are monotonous and restricted in nature and variety. The dietary habits the sample villages depend mostly upon the production. Generally the Tharu people of the sample villages take their food two/three times a gastronomic day. The main items of the food in any time are chapattis, rice, pulses and vegetables.

Food intake pattern of the sample villages is more or less similar while the preparation method of food items among the Tharu tribe also similar in these sample villages. The food items depend on the availability of raw food while preparation methods of Tharu people depends on their tradition which are now borrowed from the other relatively advance societies.

The main items for breakfast/lunch are chapattis and vegetables while they took their dinner before the sunset. The main items for dinner are rice, pulses, fish etc. Fried food items also prepared during the festivals or any other ceremonial occasions. Milk products consumption also depends on availability and are mostly seasonal (rainy). Fruits intake also depends on its availability and mostly regional and seasonal.

It is noticed that a considerable proportion of the Tharu people is drinkers and smokers. These habits among the Tharu people are traditional. Taking these items not only affects the women's health but also injurious for their offspring. Majority of the sample are non vegetarian. Village wise food pattern is shown in Table 5.34.

Out of total surveyed 445 Tharu households 84% households had their food twice and 16% took thrice in a gastronomic day. Though breakfast includes full meal as they were engaged in strenuous work. As evident from Table 5.34 that 24.7%, 18.2% and 39.9% households had respectively milk, curd and ghee daily while 2.2%, 4.3% and 6.3% had consumed these items occasionally. It is observed during the field study that in food intake pattern, there were no much difference between one village to another and one economic status to other. It is well known fact that milk is most balance and important diet for health particularly for women and children. Since the study indicates that an overwhelming proportion of the sample population was deprived of these items. Thus one can imagine the poor health condition of the Tharus in the study region.

Likewise daily pulse intake accounts for only 1.1% of total surveyed households while 98.8% were taking pulses weekly. Pulses are another important source of nutrients particularly for protein. It is also noticed that a number of total sample households are non-vegetarian. Out of total 57.8% households had flesh, fish etc. weekly while 42.2% consume flesh products occasionally. Since the long years back the Tharus were much more interested in catching the fish but present generation is not so interested because there is lack of time in one hand and private ponds have been disappeared and converted into agricultural fields on the other. It is very considerable that 100% families were taking seasonal vegetables daily. Generally green vegetables have seasonally consumed by the Tharus. Green vegetables are also important source of vitamins, the deficiency of which causes

TABLE 5.34

Food Pattern in the Sample Villages

Sample Villages	Total	Meal		Milk			Curd			Ghee			Pulses			Non-Vege. Vege.	
	H.H. (No.)	Twice	Thrice	Daily	Weekly	Occasionaly	Daily	Weekly	Occasionaly	Daily	Weekly	Occasionaly	Daily	Weekly	Occasionaly	Daily	Weekly
01. Bidaura	50	72.0	28.0	38.0	0.0	0.0	34.0	4.0	0.0	54.0	46.0	0.0	4.0	96.0	52.0	48.0	100.0
02. Baruwabagh	23	78.3	21.7	21.7	0.0	8.7	4.3	4.3	21.7	39.1	43.5	17.4	0.0	100.0	39.1	60.9	100.0
03. Sadhu Nagar	70	81.4	18.6	30.0	17.1	0.0	28.6	18.6	0.0	52.9	44.3	2.9	0.0	100.0	48.6	51.4	100.0
04. Navi Nagar	24	75.0	25.0	33.3	0.0	0.0	20.8	0.0	0.0	33.3	66.7	0.0	0.0	100.0	54.2	45.8	100.0
05. Behi	21	81.0	19.0	23.8	14.3	23.8	9.5	14.3	28.6	28.6	52.4	14.3	0.0	100.0	47.6	52.4	100.0
06. Charubeta	40	87.5	12.5	20.0	12.5	2.5	10.0	17.5	7.5	35.0	62.5	0.0	7.5	92.5	62.5	37.5	100.0
07. Gohar Patia	60	88.3	11.7	10.0	6.7	3.3	6.7	8.3	0.0	23.3	76.7	0.0	0.0	100.0	63.3	36.7	100.0
08. Khetalsanda Mustajar	38	94.7	5.3	21.1	7.9	0.0	18.4	5.3	5.3	26.3	57.9	15.8	0.0	100.0	63.2	36.8	100.0
09. Mohammadpur	76	82.9	17.1	28.9	2.6	0.0	17.1	11.8	2.6	28.9	47.4	11.8	0.0	100.0	60.5	39.5	100.0
10. Diyan	43	95.3	4.7	18.6	4.7	0.0	18.6	2.3	2.3	39.5	51.2	9.3	0.0	100.0	74.4	25.6	100.0
Grand Total	**445**	**84.0**	**16.0**	**24.7**	**7.0**	**2.2**	**18.2**	**9.7**	**4.3**	**36.9**	**54.4**	**6.3**	**1.1**	**98.9**	**57.8**	**42.2**	**100.0**

The column group spanning everything after the Total H.H. column is headed *Frequency of Items (% of total household)*.

Source: Field Survey, 2005-2006.

various nutrition deficiency diseases. It is worth to mention that in rainy season Tharus have consumed green and leafy vegetables twice even thrice a day but not regularly. It is observed that two third of the total households have not milk throughout the year.

The diet survey of the selected households in the sample villages of the study region is carried out through oral questionnaires and weighment methods. In oral questionnaires survey of the raw food consumed the previous day was noted and a weighment methods survey of the food intake has been prepared for the mid day and night were measured in the morning and the evening, respectively. Food items were measured in local units particularly glasses and bowels; and then converted into grams and milligrams. Afterwards, the data collected through both were added and that were analyzed and therefore the possibility of errors was minimum.

The diet of the Tharus is primarily based on cereals. Taking together all the sample villages, approximately the per capita per day cereals intake was 426.3 grams which is 3.1% less than the standard requirement of 440 grams. The cereals intake of 80% villages was found less the standard and 60% villages were found less than the regional average (426.3 grams).

Per head per day cereal intake varies from minimum 393.4 grams in village Behi to the maximum 468.9 grams in village Bidaura (Table 5.35). Behi village is situated far flung from the road or block headquarter while Biduara village is situated along motor road and nearest village of block headquarters or Sitarganj cereals includes rice and wheat only.

Per capita daily intake of pulse was only 26.8 grams which is 40.4% less than the standard requirement of 45 grams. Pulse intake varies from minimum 22.9 grams in village Behi to 30.6 grams in village Charubeta. Charubeta village is also situated in nearby the Khatima block headquarter along the Khatima-Pilibhit highway. However the pulse intake of 50% villages was found less than the regional average (26.8 grams). The per capita daily all vegetable consumption in the region was 63.3 grams which is 66.7% lower than the standard requirement of 190 grams (including leafy root and other vegetables). It varies from 54.1

TABLE 5.35

Average Per Head Per Day Food Intake Pattern in the Sample Villages (in Grams)

Sample Villages	*Rice*	*Wheat Flour*	*Pulses*	*Potato*	*Onion*	*Other Vegetables*	*Cooking Oil*	*Deshi Ghee*	*Spices*	*Milk*	*Flesh*	*Fish*	*Fruits*	*Sugar/ Jaggery*
01. Bidaura	318.9	150.0	27.3	13.6	4.7	40.7	8.9	5.0	8.1	54.1	1.2	9.5	15.1	14.7
02. Baruwabagh	279.6	160.6	25.2	14.5	4.0	43.5	8.5	4.5	8.7	47.2	4.6	9.7	13.1	12.9
03. Sadhu Nagar	298.8	139.6	27.4	12.4	4.6	37.1	8.0	5.0	7.4	41.1	5.0	10.4	16.0	12.8
04. Navi Nagar	289.4	148.2	28.1	15.7	4.2	47.0	10.4	4.7	9.4	43.7	2.5	7.6	11.5	14.2
05. Behi	230.2	163.4	22.9	15.6	4.2	46.8	8.3	7.2	9.4	41.1	3.24	8.8	13.3	16.7
06. Charubeta	282.6	136.4	30.6	14.0	4.1	41.9	11.7	3.2	8.4	72.3	1.3	8.6	16.1	10.8
07. Gohar Patia	276.22	142.36	29.8	15.4	3.8	46.3	6.4	3.7	9.3	52.9	3.4	5.9	10.1	11.4
08. Khetalsanda Mustajar	265.7	154.3	26.6	15.4	2.9	46.2	7.8	2.0	9.2	46.8	2.5	5.7	8.5	9.8
09. Mohammadpur	270.1	141.8	26.3	16.4	3.8	49.1	8.5	4.1	9.8	44.0	2.9	6.7	9.3	7.5
10. Diyan	277.92	137.02	23.8	15.5	3.4	46.5	7.4	4.9	9.3	39.5	2.7	7.8	9.5	13.2
Average	**278.9**	**147.4**	**26.8**	**14.8**	**4.0**	**44.5**	**8.6**	**4.4**	**8.9**	**48.3**	**2.9**	**8.1**	**12.3**	**12.4**

Source: Field Survey, 2005-2006.

grams in village Sadunagar to 69.3 grams in village Mohammadpur. Sadunagar village is situated far away from road and block headquarter at relatively higher elevation. The vegetable intake of 60% villages was found above from that average intake of the region. In the study region, the average consumption of ghee and cooking oil per capita daily was found 13 grams which is 67.5% less than the 40 grams standard requirement. It is because of Tharus poverty and low purchasing capacity. The ghee and cooking oil intake varies from 9.8 grams in village Khetalsanda Mustajar to 15.5 grams in village Behi. Tharus of Behi village have consumed more desi ghee (self prepared). It is because the Behi village boundary is demarcated by the forest and optimum conditions are available for catering the animals. The daily intake of ghee and oil of about 40% villages was found less then the average of the all sample villages (13.0 grams).

The average intake of milk and milk products per capita was found 48.3 grams which is 67.8% lower than the 150 grams standard requirement. The per capita daily consumption of milk varies minimum from 39.5 grams in Diyan village to maximum 72.3% in villages Charubeta. Out of total 70% villages fall below from the average intake of the region (48.3 grams). The consumption of units in the sample villages is seasonal and occasional apart from the fruits produced in the village itself, Tharus are also supplied from nearby markets. The average fruits consumption per capita daily is 12.3 grams. The daily intake of fruits varies from minimum 8.5 grams in village Khetalsanda Mustajar to maximum 16.1 grams in village Charubeta. However the amount of fruit consumption is very small and not much effective from nutrition point of view. The main fruits consumed by Tharus were banana, mango, guava, apple, orange etc. In the sample villages, average intake of the sweet (sugar & jaggery) items per capita per day was 12.4 grams which is 58.7% less than the 30 grams standard requirement. It was generally consumed in tea and porridges.

Mostly Tharus were interested in catching fish but present time there were no permanent ponds for the fishing. Therefore Tharus used to buy fish and flesh from nearby market. Due to their poor purchasing capacity the daily intake of these items was very nominal 8.1 grams flesh and 12.3 grams fish.

The average consumption of condiments and spices per capacity per day was 8.9 grams. It is noticed during the study the consumption of these items were similar in all the sample villages. It is clear from the Table 5.35 that per head per day intake of pulses, flesh, fish, milk, vegetables, sweet, ghee, cooking oil is very inadequate. It is also remarkable that the Tharus were not aware about the essential intake of other food items like pulses, vegetables, fruits etc. Because of this ignorance they consumed more cereals than other items.

Nutrition Status

Food items taken by the Tharus have been converted into various nutrients e.g., energy, protein, fat, carbohydrates, calcium, phosphorus, iron, carotene, thiamin (B1), riboflavin (B2), niacin, vitamin C with the help of food composition tables and then compared with the standard requirement determined by the ICMR experts Gopalan *et al.* 1993 and website of NFI, village wise nutrients intake per capita per day of 2528 Tharus people has been analyzed. Taking together all the sample villages approximately except fat, thiamin and niacin the consumption of all other important nutrients was below the standard requirement (Table 5.36). The pattern of nutrients intake is presented in Tables 5.36 and Figure 5.2).

Out of total energy intake 70-80% is down from cereals. Remaining energy intake depends on other food pulses, vegetables, fruits, milk and which are consumed seasonally and very nominal.

In all the sample villages the average energy intake per capita per day was found 1924.8 k cal which is 13.5% below the standard requirement (2225 k cal). It varies 1806.5 k cal in village Behi to 2090.6 k cal in Bidaura village. The average energy intake in all the villages of the study region was found below the standard requirement. Category-wise energy intake in the sample villages is presented in the Table. About 80% of the total sample villages, the consumption of energy intake was found less than 2000 k cal (Table 5.36).

TABLE 5.36

Average Per Head Per Day Energy, Protein and Fat Intake Pattern in the Sample Villages (% Departure from the (R.D.A.) Recommended Dietary Allowances)

Sample Villages	*Energy(kcal)*			*Protein (gm.)*			*Fat (gm.)*		
	Actual	*Departure from RDA*		*Actual*	*Departure from RDA*		*Actual*	*Departure from RDA*	
	Intake	*Actual*	*%*	*Intake*	*Actual*	*%*	*Intake*	*Actual*	*%*
R.D. A./Day	**2225(kcal)**			**50(g)**			**20(g)**		
01. Bidaura	2090.6	-134.4	-6.0	52.1	2.1	4.2	22.0	2.0	10.2
02. Baruwabagh	1967.8	-257.2	-11.6	50.9	0.9	1.8	21.0	1.0	4.9
03. Sadhu Nagar	1945.8	-279.2	-12.5	49.7	-0.3	-0.6	20.2	0.2	0.8
04. Navi Nagar	2006.2	-218.8	-9.8	50.1	0.1	0.2	22.7	2.7	13.6
05. Behi	1806.5	-418.5	-18.8	47.1	-2.9	-5.8	23.1	3.1	15.5
06. Charubeta	1987.2	-237.8	-10.7	49.7	-0.3	-0.6	24.0	4.0	19.9
07. Gohar Patia	1870.9	-354.1	-15.9	49.3	-0.7	-1.4	18.2	-1.8	-9.1
08. Khetalsanda Mustajar	1872.6	-352.4	-15.8	48.7	-1.3	-2.6	17.6	-2.4	-12.1
09. Mohammadpur	1852.3	-372.7	-16.7	47.7	-2.3	-4.6	20.1	0.1	0.7
10. Diyan	1848.5	-376.5	-16.9	46.8	-3.2	-6.4	19.3	-0.7	-3.3
Average	**1924.8**	**-300.2**	**-13.5**	**49.2**	**-0.8**	**-1.6**	**20.8**	**0.8**	**4.1**

Source: Gopalan et al., 1993 and Web Site of Nutrition Foundation of India, New Delhi.

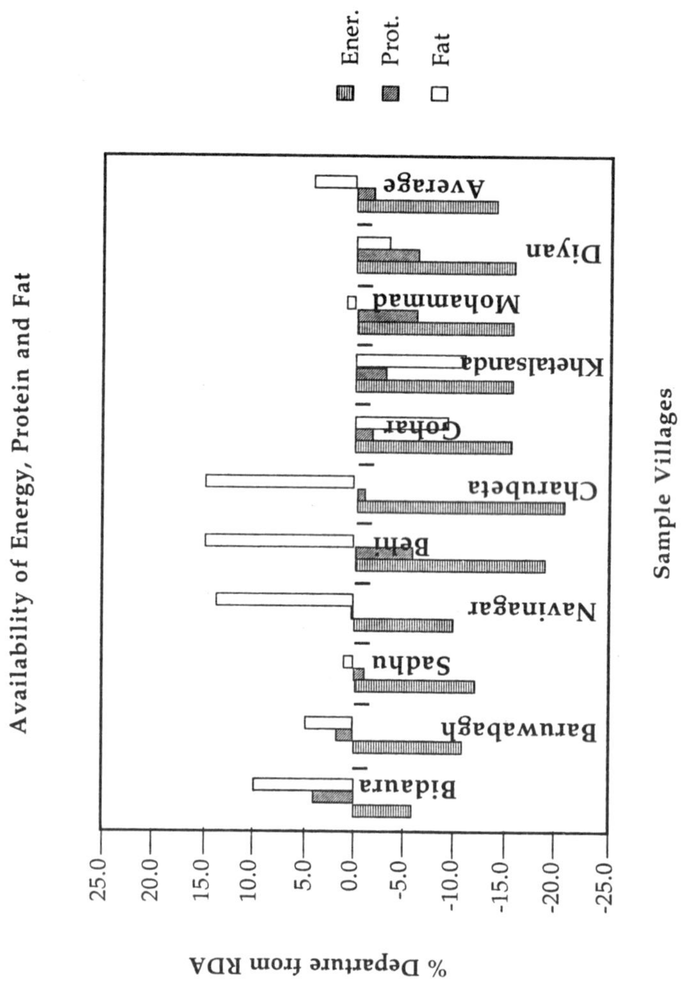
Availability of Energy, Protein and Fat
Ener.
Prot.
Fat
Bidaura
Baruwabagh
Sadhu
Navinagar
Behi
Charubeta
Gohar
Khetalsanda
Mohammad
Diyan
Average
25.0
20.0
15.0
10.0
5.0
0.0
-5.0
-10.0
-15.0
-20.0
-25.0
% Departure from RDA
Sample Villages

FIG. 5.2

The average per capita per day protein intake was found 49.2 grams which is 1.6% less than the standard requirement of 50 grams. It varies from minimum from 46.8 grams in village Diyan to maximum 52.1 grams in village Bidaura. The protein intake of 30% villagers was found slightly above from the standard (Table 5.36 and Figure 5.2).

The average fat intake percentage per day was found 20.8 grams which is 4.1% above the standard requirement of 20 grams. It varies from minimum 17.6 grams in village Khetalsanda Mustajar to 24 grams in Charubeta village. Although only three villages namely Gohar Patia, Khetalsanda and Diyan and Ten fall short from the standard requirement the fat in total of four villages of Khatima Tehsils namely Gohar Patia, Khetalsanda, Mustajar, Mohammadpur and Diyan was found below the average fat consumption of the region (20.8 grams) (Table 5.36).

In the study region, average carbohydrate intake was found 370.5 grams per head/day which 59.5% below the standard requirement of 430 grams. It varies 345.7 gram in village Behi to 406.2 grams in village Bidaura. On an average all the villages were found below the standard requirement out of total 10 villages, the carbohydrates intake of 60% villages was noticed below the regional average (Table 5.37 and Figure 5.3).

The average per capita daily calcium intake was found 337.6 mg in the region this is 62.4% below from the standard requirement of 400 mg. It varies minimum of 312.8 mg in village Diyan to maximum of 385.7 mg in village Charubeta. Table shows that the calcium intake of 70% villages was found below the regional average. However all villages fall short by 14.3% to 87.2% from the normal requirement (Table 5.37).

In the sample villages of the region the average phosphorous intake per head/day was found 1192.3 mg which is 14.8% below the standard requirement of 1400 mg. It varies 1136.7 mg in village Diyan to 1259 mg, in village Bidaura on an average the phosphorous intake of all the sample villages fall short by 10.1% to 18.8% for the normal requirement. About 40% of the total villagers' phosphorous intake was below the regional average

TABLE 5.37

Average Per Head Per Day Carbohydrates, Calcium and Phosphorus Intake Pattern in the Sample Villages (% Departure from the Recommended Dietary Allowances)

Sample Villages	*Carbohydrates (gm)*			*Calcium (mg)*			*Phosphorus (mg)*		
	Actual	*Departure from RDA*		*Actual*	*Departure from RDA*		*Actual*	*Departure from RDA*	
	Intake	*Actual*	*%*	*Intake*	*Actual*	*%*	*Intake*	*Actual*	*%*
R.D. A./Day	**430(g)**			**400(mg)**			**1400(mg)**		
01. Bidaura	406.2	-23.8	-5.5	357.2	-42.8	-10.7	1259.2	-140.8	-10.1
02. Baruwabagh	379.6	-50.4	-11.7	352.3	-47.7	-11.9	1238.4	-161.6	-11.5
03. Sadhu Nagar	379.5	-50.5	-11.7	326.1	-73.9	-18.5	1177.9	-222.1	-15.9
04. Navi Nagar	382.4	-47.6	-11.1	330.2	-69.8	-17.5	1212.2	-187.8	-13.4
05. Behi	345.7	-84.3	-19.6	337.5	-62.5	-15.6	1166.4	-233.6	-16.7
06. Charubeta	367.5	-62.5	-14.5	385.7	-14.3	-3.6	1193.6	-206.4	-14.7
07. Gohar Patia	366.1	-63.9	-14.9	332.8	-67.2	-16.8	1185.7	-214.3	-15.3
08. Khetalsanda Mustajar	361.9	-68.1	-15.8	320.5	-79.5	-19.9	1192.7	-207.3	-14.8
09. Mohammadpur	355.3	-74.7	-17.4	321.4	-78.6	-19.7	1160.0	-240.0	-17.1
10. Diyan	361.3	-68.7	-16.0	312.8	-87.2	-21.8	1136.7	-263.3	-18.8
Average	**370.5**	**-59.5**	**-13.8**	**337.6**	**-62.4**	**-15.6**	**1192.3**	**-207.7**	**-14.8**

Source: Gopalan *et al.*, 1993 and Web Site of Nutrition Foundation of India, New Delhi.

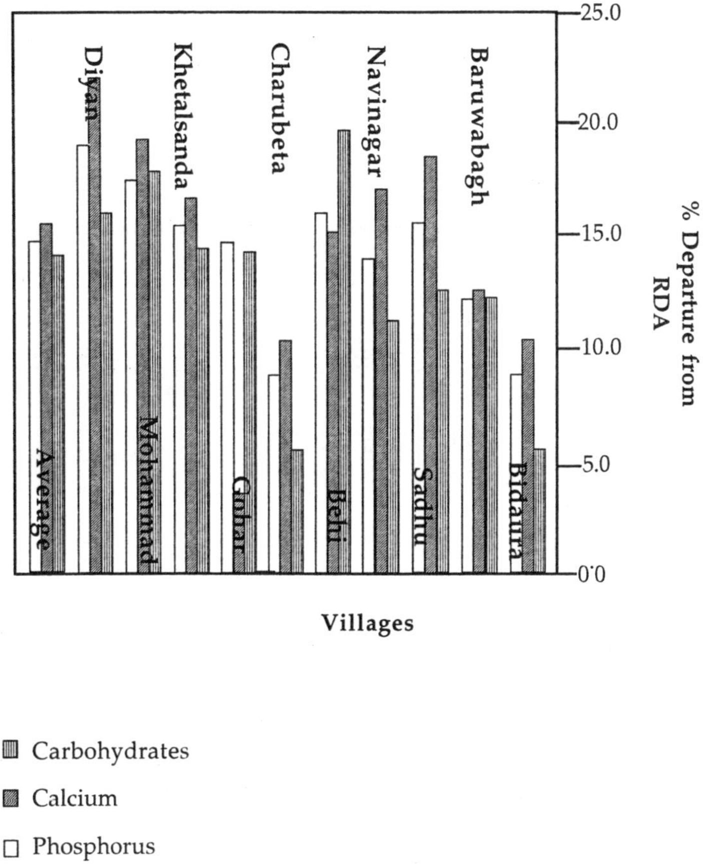

Fig. 5.3 : Availability of Carbohydrates, Calcium and Phosphorous

TABLE 5.38

Average Per Head Per Day Iron, Carotene and Thiamine Intake Pattern in the Sample Villages (% Departure from the (R.D.A.) Recommended Dietary Allowances)

Sample Villages	Iron (mg)			Carotene (μ)			Thiamine (mg)		
	Actual	Departure from RDA		Actual	Departure from RDA		Actual	Departure from RDA	
	Intake	Actual	%	Intake	Actual	%	Intake	Actual	%
R.D.A./Day	**30(mg)**			**750(μ)**			**1.1(mg)**		
01. Bidaura	13.9	-16.1	-53.7	708.2	-41.8	-5.6	1.6	0.5	45.5
02. Baruwabagh	13.9	-16.1	-53.8	645.3	-104.7	-14.0	1.6	0.5	45.5
03. Sadhu Nagar	13.1	-16.9	-56.3	699.8	-50.2	-6.7	1.5	0.4	36.4
04. Navi Nagar	13.6	-16.4	-54.7	606.8	-143.2	-19.1	1.6	0.5	45.5
05. Behi	13.4	-16.6	-55.4	643.6	-106.4	-14.2	1.5	0.4	36.4
06. Charubeta	13.2	-16.8	-56.1	772.3	22.3	3.0	1.5	0.4	36.4
07. Gohar Patia	13.3	-16.7	-55.8	585.5	-164.5	-21.9	1.5	0.4	36.4
08. Khetalsanda Mustajar	13.5	-16.5	-55.1	525.8	-224.2	-29.9	1.5	0.4	36.4
09. Mohammadpur	12.9	-17.1	-56.9	546.3	-203.7	-27.2	1.5	0.4	36.4
10. Diyan	12.6	-17.4	-58.1	531.4	-218.6	-29.1	1.5	0.4	36.4
Average	**13.3**	**-16.7**	**-55.6**	**626.5**	**-123.5**	**-16.5**	**1.5**	**0.4**	**36.4**

Source: Gopalan *et al.*, 1993 and Web Site of N.F.I., New Delhi.

(Table 5.37). The deficiency of phosphorous intake is not much alarming. The main source of phosphorous is cereals which is the main food of the Tharus.

The per head/day iron intake of Tharus population in the sample village was found 13.3 mg which is 55.6% below the standard requirement of 30 mg. It varies minimum 12.6 mg in village Diyan to maximum of 13.9 mg in village Bidaura and Baruwabagh. Per head/day intake of all the villages was found more than 50% from below the standard requirement. It varies from minimum 58.1% to maximum 53.7. Out of total 40% villages falls short from the average intake of the region average (Table 5.38 and Figure 5.4).

The carotene (vitamin A) intake among the Tharus population of the sample village is very unsatisfactory because the consumption of per head/day was 626.5 mg in average which is 16.5% below from the recommended dietary allowances (RDA), a 750 mg. It varies from minimum of 525.8 mg in village Khetalsanda, Mustajar to maximum 772.3 mg in village Charubeta. The per head/day intake of carotene in 90% of the total villages was found short 5.6% to 29.9%. One village Charubeta 3% falls above the standard requirement (Table 5.38).

Thiamine (vitamin B1) intake in the sample villages was 39.6% above the normal requirement of 1.1 mg per capita daily intake of the riboflavin (vitamin B2) in the sample villages was 0.5 mg which was 57.7% below from the standard requirement of 1.3 mg. The intakes of riboflavin in the all sample villages fall short by more than 50%. It varies minimum 53.8% in Bidaura to maximum of in the village Diyan (Table 5.39 Figure 5.5).

In the sample villages, the average niacin (nicotinic acid) intake was found 18.3 mg which is 30.8% above the standard requirement of 14 mg. It varies 17.1 mg in village Behi to 20 mg in village Bidaura. On an average all the sample villages of the region the consumption of niacin was found above the standard requirement (Table 5.39). Green vegetables and fruits are the main source of vitamin C or ascorbic acid. In the study region its average intake was found 34.6 mg which is 86.5% fall short from the standard requirement of 40 mg. The per head/day intake of

TABLE 5.39

Average Per Head Per Day Riboflavin, Niacin and Vitamin C Intake Pattern in the Sample Villages (% Departure from the (R.D.A.) Recommended Dietary Allowances)

Sample Villages	*Riboflavin (mg)*			*Niacin (mg)*			*Vitamin C (mg)*		
	Actual	*Departure from RDA*		*Actual*	*Departure from RDA*		*Actual*	*Departure from RDA*	
	Intake	*Actual*	*%*	*Intake*	*Actual*	*%*	*Intake*	*Actual*	*%*
R.D.A./Day	**1.3 (mg)**			**14(mg)**			**40(mg)**		
01. Bidaura	0.6	-0.7	-53.8	20.0	6.0	42.6	5.8	-34.2	-85.5
02. Baruwabagh	0.6	-0.7	-53.8	18.9	4.9	34.8	5.5	-34.5	-86.3
03. Sadhu Nagar	0.5	-0.8	-61.5	18.7	4.7	33.7	5.6	-34.4	-86.1
04. Navi Nagar	0.6	-0.7	-53.8	18.8	4.8	34.2	5.4	-34.6	-86.5
05. Behi	0.5	-0.8	-61.5	17.1	3.1	22.0	5.7	-34.3	-85.9
06. Charubeta	0.6	-0.7	-53.8	18.1	4.1	29.4	6.1	-33.9	-84.7
07. Gohar Patia	0.5	-0.8	-61.5	18.1	4.1	29.0	5.2	-34.8	-87.0
08. Khetalsanda Mustajar	0.6	-0.7	-53.8	18.1	4.1	29.0	4.8	-35.2	-88.1
09. Mohammadpur	0.5	-0.8	-61.5	17.7	3.7	26.6	5.1	-34.9	-87.2
10. Diyan	0.5	-0.8	-61.5	17.7	3.7	26.7	4.9	-35.1	-87.7
Average	**0.5**	**-0.8**	**-61.5**	**18.3**	**4.3**	**30.8**	**5.4**	**-34.6**	**-86.5**

Source: Gopalan et al., 1993 and Web Site of Nutrition Foundation of India, New Delhi.

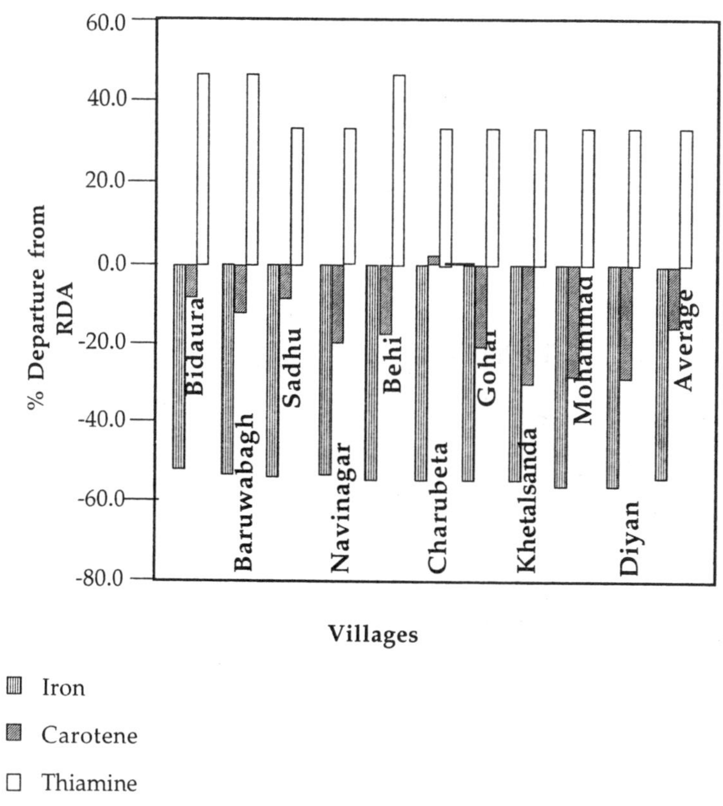

Fig. 5.4 : Availability of Iron, Carotene and Thiamine

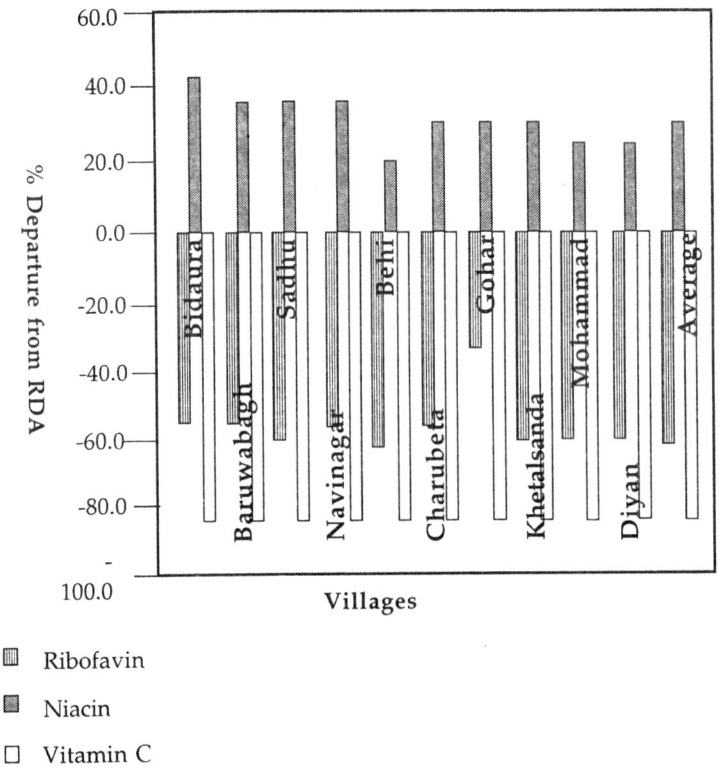

Fig. 5.5 : Availability of Riboflavin, Niacin and Vitamin C

TABLE 5.40

Health Status and Disease Pattern Among the Tharu Population in the Sample Villages

Sample Villages	Total Population			Unhealthy Population (% of total)						Reasons of Unhealthyness (% of total Unhealthy population)											
	P	M	F	P		M		F		Fever			Stomach Related			Eye Related			Waterborn		
	No.			No.	%	No.	%	No.	%	P	M	F	P	M	F	P	M	F	P	M	F
01. Bidaura	291	149	142	17	5.8	7	4.7	10	7.0	52.9	57.1	50.0	29.4	42.9	20.0	5.9	0.0	10.0	5.9	0.0	10.0
02. Baruwabagh	133	62	71	11	8.3	5	8.1	6	8.5	36.4	40.0	33.3	45.5	60.0	33.3	18.2	0.0	33.3	0.0	0.0	0.0
03. Sadhu Nagar	377	198	179	39	10.3	21	10.6	18	10.1	43.6	52.4	33.3	43.6	42.9	44.4	12.8	4.8	22.2	0.0	0.0	0.0
04. Navi Nagar	132	73	59	12	9.1	7	9.6	5	8.5	41.7	57.1	20.0	58.3	42.9	80.0	0.0	0.0	0.0	0.0	0.0	0.0
05. Behi	96	53	43	9	9.4	4	7.5	5	11.6	77.8	75.0	80.0	11.1	25.0	0.0	11.1	0.0	20.0	0.0	0.0	0.0
06. Charubeta	192	100	92	18	9.4	6	6.0	12	13.0	55.6	83.3	41.7	22.2	16.7	25.0	11.1	0.0	16.7	11.1	0.0	16.7
07. Gohar Patia	356	183	173	36	10.1	16	8.7	20	11.6	41.7	43.8	40.0	33.3	43.8	25.0	16.7	6.3	25.0	8.3	6.3	10.0
08. Khetalsanda Mustajar	238	122	116	34	14.3	16	13.1	18	15.5	41.2	43.8	38.9	35.3	50.0	22.2	20.6	0.0	38.9	2.9	6.3	0.0
09. Mohammadpur	462	230	232	47	10.2	20	8.7	27	11.6	36.2	50.0	25.9	34.0	35.0	33.3	27.7	10.0	40.7	2.1	5.0	0.0
10. Diyan	251	130	121	23	9.2	10	7.7	13	10.7	47.8	60.0	38.5	21.7	40.0	7.7	26.1	0.0	46.2	4.3	0.0	7.7
Grand Total	**2528**	**1300**	**1228**	**246**	**9.7**	**112**	**8.6**	**134**	**10.9**	**44.3**	**52.7**	**37.3**	**34.1**	**41.1**	**28.4**	**17.5**	**3.6**	**29.1**	**3.7**	**2.7**	**4.5**

Source: Field Survey, 2005-2006.

TABLE 5.41

Mortality Among Tharu Population 1989-2004

Sample Villages	*Total*	*Periods (% of total Deaths)*							
	Death (No.)	*1989—1990*	*1991-1992*	*1993-1994*	*1995-1996*	*1997-1998*	*1999-2000*	*2001-2002*	*2003-2004*
01. Bidaura	54	18.5	14.8	14.8	13.0	14.8	9.3	7.4	7.4
02. Baruwabagh	32	31.3	28.1	12.5	6.3	6.3	9.4	0.0	6.3
03. Sadhu Nagar	45	26.7	20.0	15.6	15.6	13.3	2.2	0.0	6.7
04. Navi Nagar	27	14.8	14.8	14.8	7.4	25.9	3.7	14.8	3.7
05. Behi	29	27.6	17.2	13.8	6.9	10.3	6.9	10.3	6.9
06. Charubeta	36	38.9	27.8	2.8	13.9	5.6	2.8	2.8	5.6
07. Gohar Patia	70	22.9	20.0	18.6	8.6	12.9	8.6	5.7	2.9
08. Khetalsanda Mustajar	56	21.4	12.5	10.7	12.5	8.9	14.3	8.9	10.7
09. Mohammadpur	94	29.8	19.1	8.5	8.5	11.7	5.3	8.5	8.5
10. Diyan	59	27.1	15.3	13.6	13.6	8.5	10.2	6.8	5.1
Grand Total	**502**	**25.9**	**18.5**	**12.5**	**10.8**	**11.6**	**7.6**	**6.6**	**6.6**

Source: Field Survey, 2005-2006.

TABLE 5.42

Mortality in the Sample Villages During 1989—2004

Sample Villages	Total Death	Age Groups (Percentage of total died persons)														
		< 5	6—10	11—15	16—20	21—25	26—30	31—35	36—40	41—45	46—50	51—55	56—60	61—65	66—70	> 71
01. Bidaura	54	75.9	0.0	1.9	0.0	3.7	0.0	1.9	1.9	1.9	0.0	3.7	1.9	1.9	0.0	5.6
02. Baruwabagh	32	84.4	0.0	0.0	0.0	0.0	0.0	0.0	0.0	0.0	0.0	0.0	0.0	6.3	3.1	6.3
03. Sadhu Nagar	86	91.9	0.0	0.0	0.0	0.0	0.0	0.0	0.0	1.2	0.0	1.2	2.3	2.3	0.0	1.2
04. Navi Nagar	27	77.8	0.0	0.0	0.0	0.0	0.0	3.7	11.1	0.0	0.0	0.0	0.0	3.7	3.7	0.0
05. Behi	29	82.8	0.0	0.0	0.0	0.0	0.0	0.0	0.0	3.4	0.0	3.4	3.4	6.9	0.0	0.0
06. Charubeta	36	91.7	0.0	0.0	0.0	0.0	2.8	0.0	0.0	2.8	0.0	0.0	0.0	0.0	0.0	2.8
07. Gohar Patia	70	80.0	1.4	1.4	0.0	0.0	1.4	0.0	0.0	1.4	0.0	1.4	4.3	1.4	1.4	5.7
08. Khetalsanda Mustajar	56	75.0	0.0	0.0	0.0	0.0	0.0	0.0	0.0	1.8	1.8	7.1	3.6	1.8	1.8	7.1
09. Mohammadpur	94	69.1	1.1	1.1	0.0	1.1	1.1	3.2	1.1	1.1	3.2	2.1	0.0	5.3	3.2	7.4
10. Diyan	59	88.1	0.0	0.0	0.0	0.0	0.0	0.0	0.0	0.0	0.0	3.4	3.4	1.7	1.7	1.7
Grand Total	**543**	**81.0**	**0.4**	**0.6**	**0.0**	**0.6**	**0.6**	**0.9**	**0.9**	**1.3**	**0.7**	**2.4**	**2.0**	**2.9**	**1.5**	**4.2**

Source: Field Survey, 2005-2006.

vitamin C in all the samples village fall short by more than 85%. It varies from 4.8 mg in village Khetalsanda, Mustajar to 6.1 mg in village Charubeta. It is due to fruits and fresh vegetable during the field study and these vitamin C giving items have not been included in the dietary survey (Table 5.39).

There are many other factors that also influence the diet requirement. In the food as nutrients intake pattern much disparity was seen in the regional and category level.

Health Status

Out of the total sample population 97% were found unhealthy in one case to other (Table 5.40). Out of the total ill people 10.9% were females and 8.6% were males. Four came of their unhealthy men have been noticed during the field study. Out of total indisposed persons 44.3% were suffering from fever 34.11% from stomach related problem, 17.5 eyes related and 3.7% were suffering from water borne diseases. Maximum 52.7% and 41.1% males were suffering from fever and stomach while 37.3 and 28.4% female were suffering. Maximum 29.1% & 4.5% women were suffering from eye related and water borne diseases while males were lower than females sufferer from these diseases (Table 5.40).

Mortality in 1989-90 to 2003-04 was also noticed during the field study. Total 502 deaths have been occurred during the specific period (Table 5.41). It is noticed that the annual no. of deaths were decreasing, it means the medical facility and awareness among the Tharus were increased. Another Table 5.42 shows that maximum 81% deaths occurred before the age of five i.e., infant mortality among Tharus is still more due to early marriage of girls one the one hand and poor nutrition intake on the other. Remaining 4.2% deaths occurred above the age of 71 years. The longevity of Tharus people is much higher than the average of India. About 3% persons died between the ages of 61-65 years. Table 5.42 shows the percentage of total died persons.

A particular deficiency disease among the sample with the correlation of a particular deficiency of food nutrients has not been worked out in the present study. However no. of studies done by several authors in various parts of the country indicates the clear relationship between the nutrients intake and deficiency diseases.

Summary

To appraise the socio-economic and nutritional status of the Tharu population, ten villages have been selected from different areas of district U.S. Nagar in Uttarakhand state. Total 50% (445) households from the various income groups of ten sample village (890 households) have been selected. A total 2528 persons of 445 households have been surveyed. Out of total population 1300 are males and 1228 are females. The average household size in the sample villages is 5.7 persons per household. The sex ratio in sample population is 945 females per thousand males. About 50.7% of the total sample population belong the age group below 20 years while 2.9% are above 60 years age. Of these 46% are in working age group. On an average of the sample population 72.2% Tharu are literate while 56.7% females are literate. Among total literates 66.5% have education up to junior standard. Out of total females 74.4% have primary and junior level education. The low level of literacy is because lack of school (47.7%), lack of money (15.9%), to look younger (25.6%) and to look animals (10.8%). Agriculture is the basic source of the Tharu population. It is worth to mention that the Tharu are engaged in more than one occupation because none of occupations provide self-reliant base. Out of total households 28.1% households have agriculture and livestock occupation while 19.3% families are considered as agriculturist, labour and animal herders. Out of total income 35.7%, 39.3%, 13.7%, 2.9% and 8.3% is received from agriculture, agriculture and labour, labour; agriculture and shop and agriculture and service, respectively.

In the sample households 60.9% have pucca houses while 39.1% families are living in kuchha houses. About 47.4% households have separate kitchen either pucca or kuchha while 32.6% attached kitchen i.e. one corner of any room. It is very serious problem in the villages where 94.8% and 91.5% households have not bathroom and toilet facilities respectively. The method of waste water waste disposal in the sample villages is very unhygienic. It is observed that there was no drainage system in the villages. A majority of households have dumped the refuse in open space. The environmental sanitation assessed in terms of water and waste disposal have been very unhygienic in the sample villages as a whole without any differences between castes/class and region. The room density (rooms/persons) is very high. The room density of 37.8% households have below 0.3 rooms/persons while 19.7% has above 0.5 rooms/person i.e. half room per person. About 13.5% households have no land while 67.8% have below 3 acres per capita land. Only 1.6% households have more than 9 acres per capita land. About 69.9% Tharu families have animals. Out of total animals 25.7%, 30.5% and 43.7% households have respectively milky, draught and both type of animals. Out of total married women (582), 35.5% Tharu women get marriage below the age of 18 years i.e. against the law.

Study shows that 0.5% women's age was below 14 years when they give a child birth while 35.4% women give child birth below the age of 18 years. Infantile mortality is very high among the Tharus. These deaths occurred because of early marriage of Tharu girls. Out of total 582 fertile or children bearing women who have given birth to 2551 children, among them 82% were survived and remaining 18% were expired in various stages. Out of total died children 65.5% were expired immediately while 23.7% within one month, 9.2% within 2 months and 2.5% were survived only 3 months or more.

Out of total sample surveyed 64.6%, 59.5%, 70.8% and 32.25 respectively brush their teeth daily, took bath daily, washed their hands before every meals and cut their nails weekly. Food intake pattern of the sample is more or less similar. Out of total sample household 84% had their food twice in a gastronomic day. Tharu families took their dinner before sunset. Low proportion of the total Tharu took milk, curd, ghee, pulse and non-vegetables daily. The diet of the Tharu population is primarily based on cereals. Taking together all the samples, approximately the per capita per day rice, wheat flour, pulses, vegetables, oils/ghee and milk intake is 278.9, 147.4, 26.8, 63.3, 13.0 and 48.3 grams which are below the recommended dietary allowances. The intake pattern is varying from one economic level to another.

Taking together all the sample, the consumption of all nutrients except niacin and thiamine are below the standard requirement. The average per capita per day energy, protein, carbohydrates, calcium, phosphorus, iron, carotene, riboflavin and vitamin C intake is found 1924.8 k cal, 49.2 gm, 370.5 gm, 337.6 mg, 1192.3 mg, 13.3 mg, 625.5 µg, 0.5 mg and 5.4 mg which are respectively 13.5, 1.6, 13.8, 15.6, 14.8, 55.6, 16.5, 61.5 and 85.5 per cent below from the standard requirement except fat, thiamine and niacin which are 4.1, 36.4 and 30.8 per cent above from the recommended dietary allowances. Consequently 9.7% population of the sample is unhealthy. Generally they are suffering from deficiency and other diseases.

Out of the total 2528 sample population 9.7% were found unhealthy by one cause to other. Out of the total ill people 10.9% were females and 8.6% were males. Four causes of their unhealthiness have been noticed during the field study. Out of total indisposed persons 44.3% was suffering from fever, 34.11% from stomach related problem, 17.5% eyes related and 3.7% was suffering from water born diseases. Maximum 52.7% and 41.1% males were suffering form fever and stomach respectively while 37.3% and 28.4% females were suffering in these diseases. Maximum 29.1% and 4.5% women were suffering from eye related and water born diseases while males were lower than the female sufferer from these diseases.

Mortality in 1989-90 to 2003-04 was also noticed during the field study. Total 502 deaths have been occurred during the specific period. It is noticed that the annually average number of deaths were decreasing, it means the medical facility and awareness among the Tharus were increased. Study shows that maximum 81% deaths occurred before the age of five i.e., infant mortality among Tharus still more due to early marriage of girls in one hand and poor nutrition intake on the other. Remaining 4.2% deaths occurred above the age of 71 years. The longevity of Tharus is much higher than the average of India. About 3% persons died between the ages of 61-65 years.

6

Summary and Conclusions

The tribal community and their habitats constitute very significant proportion of backward people and regions of the country respectively. The tribal community encompasses around 18 per cent of country's land and 8.2 per cent of its population. As per 2001 census country's largest tribal population is found in Madhya Pradesh (14.51%). Out of total thirty states; one third (33.33%) have less than 0.5% country's population. But their largest proportion to total state population among all the states is found in Mizoram (94.5%). The average household size of the scheduled tribe in India is 5.1 persons per household which is less than the all castes population average (5.3). The household size varies from 3.9 persons/household in Goa to 6.6 persons/household in Uttar Pradesh. Average sex ratio of the tribal population of India is 978 in 2001 which is higher than the sex ratio of all castes population. Total sex ratio in tribal population ranges between 893 in Goa to 1028 in Dadra and Nagar Haveli in 2001. India has registered 20.34% growth of population during the decade of 1991-2001 which is lower than the total growth of tribal population in the same decade (24.45%). Total sex ratio in tribal population ranges between 893 in Goa to 1028 in Dadra and Nagar Haveli in 2001. The sex ratio below the age of 6 years tribal population in India is registered 973 which are too high from the same segment of total population (927). The sex ratio of this segment varies from minimum 915 in Goa to maximum 1009 in Dadra and Nagar Haveli. As per census 2001 Indian tribal population has registered only 47.1% literacy which is much lower than the literacy of total population at national level (64.8%). The tribal literacy varies minimum from 28.2% in Bihar to maximum 89.3% in Mizoram state. The highest proportion of male tribal literates has been registered in Lakshadweep (92.2%) followed by Mizoram (91.7%). Likewise total tribal literacy the lowest proportion of male tribal literates was recorded in Bihar (39.8%) which is much lower than the national average (59.2%). About 60% states have registered the high male literacy than the national average (59.2%). Average female literacy of India is registered only 34.8% which is too less than the all castes female literacy (53.7%). Bihar has least proportion of female literates (15.5%). It is observed that there are contiguous patches of states with low literacy rates in the tribal population of the country. The states situated in the relatively more rugged topography and adverse climate have also recorded very low literacy rates while states having high literacy associated with comparatively high level of urbanization and high proportion of population in secondary and tertiary jobs. There is an urgent need to improve the quality of education than the quantity of the literates. Average 24.4% points gap between male and female literacy of the total tribal population in the country has been registered in 2001 census which is slightly higher than the all castes population (21.6%). The gap between male and female literacy rate varies from minimum 4.3% in Meghalaya followed by Mizoram (4.8%) to maximum 35.9% in Rajasthan. It is observed that the states with high level of total, male and female literacy have registered fewer gaps between male and female literacy.

The percentage of total workers in tribal population has recorded higher (49.1%) in comparison to the total population (39.1%) in the country as a whole. The percentage of total workers in the tribal population varies from minimum 22.9% in Lakshadweep to maximum 54.9% in Tamilnadu. Similarly the work participation rates of male population varies minimum 38.6% in Lakshadweep to 60.1% in Tamilnadu. About 53% tribal males of India are registered as workers in 2001 census while 51.7% males of all castes population are considered as workers. Out of total tribal female population only 44.8% are considered as workers which are higher than the females of all castes population as 25.6%. The work participation rates of females vary from minimum 7.10% in Lakshadweep to maximum 52.7% in Himachal Pradesh. Out of the total tribal workers of the country 36.9%, 30.3% and 19.8% persons, males and females are respectively registered as agriculture labourers. Less than 3% tribal workers are found in household industries. 4.2%, 3.2% and 6.5% person, males and females of all castes workers are registered in this occupation. Out of the total tribal workers 16.3% person are registered as other workers. Out of the total male workers 20.6% males are considered as other workers which are less than the half of all castes male workers. Similarly about 11.1% female workers are registered in other workers category while 21.71% females of all castes population are found in this category. It reflects that the percentage of female workers in both tribal and non-tribal categories is still very low. Study concludes that the plans for the development of tribal population should be launched at grass root level. Educational and infrastructural facilities should be provided in the tribal areas. There is an urgent need of political will to ensure the grass root people participation the implementation of their welfare programmes.

The tribal population of Uttarakhand is concentrated in the remote/forest areas of Tarai and Bhabar and higher reaches of Pithoragarh, Chamoli, Uttarkashi districts and Jaunsar-Bhabar area of Dehradun district. As per 2001 census it comes to 2,56,129 people constitute about 3% to the total population of the states. Uttarakhand state contributes only 0.83% to total population and 0.3% to the tribal population of India. Among the 13 districts of the states, Udham Singh Nagar with a tribal population of 1,10,220 (43.03%) is at the top followed by Dehradun (99,329 person or 38.78%), Pithoragarh (19,279 person or 7.53%) and Chamoli (4.09%). In fact four districts of Uttarakhand contribute about 93% of total tribal population. But their largest proportion to total population among all the districts is found in U.S. Nagar (8.9%) followed by Dehradun (7.7%), Pithoragarh (4.2%) and Chamoli (2.8%). Proportion of the tribal population to the total population of the remaining districts is found less than 1%.

The average household size of the tribal population in the state is found 6.1 people per family, which is higher than that of the all castes population (5.3) of the state and country (5.1) while the size of family in urban area (4.31) is less than the all castes population (5.2). Arithmetic density of the states as a whole works out to 159 p/km2 in 2001 as against to 132 in 1991 census while the tribal density is 4.79 person in 2001 as against to 3.46 person per km^2 in 1991, which is lower than that of the national average. This means that the total and tribal pressure in the states has increased. The total growth of tribal population of Uttarakhand during 1991-2001 was 20.89% which is higher than the growth of all castes population. The decadal growth rate of tribal population of India and Uttarakhand has increased while the growth rate of all castes population for both the state and country has decreased during decades 1981-1991 to 1991-2001.

Average sex ratio of the tribal total population is 950, which is less than the sex ratio of the all castes population (962) while the sex ratio in below the age of six years population the numerical higher (955) sex ratio is than that of the total population (908). The sex ratio has usually been quite high in the hill districts as compared to districts in plains of Uttarakhand. The total literacy of the Uttarakhand is 71.6% which is higher than the national average (64.8%). Similarly in case of tribal literacy Uttarakhand with 63.2% literates is quite ahead of average literacy registered for the country (47.1%). The Level of male and female literacy among the tribal community of Uttarakhand is higher than that of the country average. The tribal literacy varies to minimum of 46.3% in Hardwar districts to maximum of 93.3% in Almora district while the literacy rate for all castes population is higher than that of tribal population in the state. It is observed that there are some particular regions of the state and districts where the tribal literacy rates are relatively low. The region situated in comparatively more rugged topography and adverse climatic conditions have recorded low literacy rates while the region having high literacy associated with comparatively high level of urbanization and high proportion of population in tertiary and secondary jobs. The low level of total, male and female literacy of the districts particularly Hardwar and Dehradun is associated with tribal traditions in which proper emphasis was not placed on education on the one hand and economically backward on the other.

On an average 27% points gap between male and female literacy of the total tribal population in the state has been registered in 2001 census which is higher than the state's all castes (23.6%)

and country total (21.6%) and tribal (24.4%) population. The gap between male and female literacy rate varies from minimum even minus 9.4% in Tehri to maximum of 29.9% in U.S. Nagar and Hardwar districts. Out of total thirteen districts only 46.2% districts have fewer gaps in male-female literacy rate than state (27.0%) and national (24.4%) averages.

The percentage of total workers in tribal population is registered higher (41.1%) in comparison to the all castes population (36.9%) in state as a whole which figures are respectively lower than the country averages. The percentage of total worker in the tribal population varies from minimum 32.6% in Hardwar to the maximum of 59.5% in Tehri district. About 49.9% tribal males of the state are found as workers in 2001 which is higher than the all castes workers (46.1%). The work participation rate of male tribal population varies from minimum 42.3% in Almora district to maximum of 76% in Tehri district. Out of total tribal female population in the state only 31.9% are considered as workers which are also higher than the females of all castes population (27.3%). Although the percentage of female workers in the Uttarakhand is lower than the average of the nation (44.8%). The work participation rates of females vary from minimum of 10.3% in Tehri to the maximum of 51.3% in Bageshwar districts.

About 63% of the total tribal workers of the state are registered as cultivators which are 10% and 18% points more than the all castes and tribal cultivators of the state and country respectively. The percentage of tribal cultivators in the state varies from 2.2% in Tehri to 71% in Dehradun district followed by 70% in U.S. Nagar. Out of total male and female tribal workers in the state, 61.7% males and 65.3% females are registered as cultivators. Out of total tribal workers in the state, 13.2, 13.1 and 13.3% persons, males and females are respectively registered as agricultural labourers. About 6.2% tribal workers are found in household industries while 2.6% males and 12.1% female workers are found in household industries.

Out of total tribal workers 17.6% persons are registered as other workers i.e. persons engaged in white colour jobs which is higher than the other workers of all castes population (16.3%). The percentage of other workers of tribal total workers varies minimum of 9.8% in U.S. Nagar to maximum 97.6% in Tehri district. Out of total male tribal workers, 22.6% males are considered as other workers which are less than the half of all castes other workers. Similarly about 9.3% female workers are found in this category. It reflects that the percentage of female workers in both tribal and non-tribal categories is still very low.

About 6.2% of the total tribal population is registered as urban population, which is lower than the total population (25.66%) of the state. It reveals that still maximum tribal population resides in their ancestral remote villages. The economic and educational status of the urban tribal population is relatively higher than the rural tribal population.

To appraise the socio-economic and nutritional status of the Tharu population, ten villages have been selected from different areas of district U.S. Nagar in Uttarakhand state. Total 50% (445) households from the various income groups of ten sample villages (890 households) have been selected. A total 2528 persons of 445 households have been surveyed. Out of total population 1300 are males and 1228 are females. The average household size in the sample villages is 5.7 persons per household. The sex ratio in sample population is 945 females per thousand males. About 50.7% of the total sample population belong the age group below 20 years while 2.9% are above 60 years age. Of these 46% are in working age group. On an average of the sample population 72.2% Tharu are literate while 56.7% females are literate. Among total literates 66.5% have education up to junior standard. Out of total females 74.4% have primary and junior level education. The low level of literacy is because lack of school (47.7%), lack of money (15.9%), to look after younger siblings (25.6%) and to look animals (10.8%). Agriculture is the basic income source of the Tharu population. It is worth to mention that the Tharu are engaged in more than one occupation because none of occupations provide self-reliant base. Out of total households 28.1% households have agriculture and livestock occupation while 19.3% families are considered as agriculturist, labourer and animal herders. Out of total income 35.7%, 39.3%, 13.7%, 2.9% and 8.3% is received from agriculture, agriculture and labour, labour; agriculture and shop and agriculture and service, respectively.

In the sample households 60.9% have pucca houses while 39.1% families are living in kuchha houses. About 67.4% households have separate kitchen either pucca or kuchha while 32.6% have attached kitchen i.e. one corner of any room. It is very serious problem in the villages where 94.8% and 91.5% households have not bathroom and toilet facilities respectively. The method of waste water and waste disposal in the sample villages is very unhygienic. It is observed that there was no drainage system in the villages. A majority of households have dumped the refuse in open space. The environmental sanitation assessed in terms of water and waste disposal have been very unhygienic in the sample villages as a whole without any differences between castes/class and region. The room density (rooms/persons) is very high. The room density of 37.8% households has below 0.3 rooms/persons while 19.7% has above 0.5 rooms/person i.e. half room per person. About 13.5% households have no land while 67.8% have below 3 acres per capita land. Only 1.6% households have more than 9 acres per capita land. About 69.9% tharu families have animals. Out of total animals 25.7%, 30.5% and 43.7% households have respectively milky, draught and both type of animals. Out of total married women (582), 35.5% Tharu women were married below the age of 18 years i.e. against the statutory prescription.

Study shows that 0.5% women's age was below 14 years when they give birth to child while 35.4% women give child birth below the age of 18 years. Infantile mortality is very high among the Tharus. These deaths occurred because of early marriage of Tharu girls. Out of total 582 fertile or child bearing women who have given birth to 2551 children, among them 82% were survived and remaining 18% were expired in various stages. Out of total died children 65.5% expired immediately while 23.7% within one month, 9.2% within 2 months and 2.5% survived only 3 months or more.

Out of total sample surveyed 64.6%, 59.5%, 70.8% and 32.25 respectively brush their teeth daily, took bath daily, washed their hands before every meals and cut their nails weekly. Food intake pattern of the sample is more or less similar. Out of total sample household 84% had their food twice in a gastronomic day. Tharu families took their dinner before sunset. Low proportion among Tharus takes milk, curd, ghee, pulse and non-vegetables daily. The diet of the Tharu population is primarily based on cereals. Taking together all the samples, approximately the per capita per day rice, wheat flour, pulses, vegetables, oils / ghee and milk intake is 278.9, 147.4, 26.8, 63.3, 13.0 and 48.3 grams which are below the recommended dietary allowances. The intake pattern is varying from one economic level to another.

Food items taken by the Tharu people have been converted into various nutrients—energy, protein, fat, carbohydrates, minerals, vitamins etc. with the help of food composition tables and then compared with the standard requirement for each economic level. Taking together all the sample, the consumption of all nutrients except niacin and thiamine are below the standard requirement. The average per capita per day energy, protein, carbohydrates, calcium, phosphorus, iron, carotene, riboflavin and vitamin C intake is found 1924.8 k cal, 49.2 gm, 370.5 gm, 337.6 mg, 1192.3 mg, 13.3 mg, 626.5 µg, 0. 5 mg and 5.4 mg which are respectively 13.5, 1.6, 13.8, 15.6, 14.8, 55.6, 16.5, 61.5 and 86.5 percent below from the standard requirement except fat, thiamine and niacin which are 4.1, 36.4 and 30.8 percent above from the recommended dietary allowances. Consequently 9.7% population of the sample is unhealthy. Generally they are suffering from deficiency and other diseases.

Out of the total 2528 sample population 9.7% were found ill by one cause or other. Out of the total ill people 10.9% were females and 8.6% were males. Four causes of their unhealthiness have been noticed during the field study. Out of total indisposed persons 44.3% were suffering from fever, 34.11% from stomach problems, 17.5% eyes related and 3.7% were suffering from water borne diseases. Maximum 52.7% and 41.1% males were suffering from fever and stomach respectively while 37.3% and 28.4% female were suffering in these diseases. Maximum 29.1% & 4.5% women were suffering from eye related and water born diseases while males were lower than the female sufferer from these diseases.

Mortality during 1989-90 to 2003-04 was also noticed during the field study. Total 502 deaths have been occurred during the specific period. It is noticed that the annual average number of deaths were decreasing, it means the medical facility and awareness among the Tharus have increased. Study shows that maximum 81% deaths occurred before the age of five i.e., infant mortality among Tharus still more due to early marriage of girls on one hand and poor nutrition intake on the other. Remaining 4.2% deaths occurred above the age of 71 years. The longevity of Tharus people is much higher than the average of India. About 3% persons died between the ages of 61-65 years.

The study concludes that the major determinants of the nutrition and health status of Tharu population are the education, income and awareness. Measures should be adopted for efficient utilization of available food such as supplementary feeding programmes, reducing the losses, increasing the production, production of other nutritionally essential items etc. To eradicate these problems following remedial measures should be adopted with regular monitoring.

Schooling of Tharu girls up to the age of fourteen should be made compulsory. Minimum age of girls and boys marriage as per Act 18 and 21 years respectively should be strictly observed among Tharu population. Education, health and medical facilities should be increased in the Tharu villages. Developmental and awareness programmes should be launched in the tribal region. There in an urgent need for thorough management of housing, water supply and sanitation in the Tharu villages. No doubt, a meticulous planning on these lines will improve the life of tribal a lot. Let us hope for a better future.

Bibliography

Aggrawal, B.C. and K.S. Mathur, 1973. *Tribe, Caste, Peasantry.* Lucknow Ethnographic and Folk Culture Society.

Ali, S.A., 1972. *Tribal Demography in Madhya Pradesh,* Bhopal, Jai Bharat Publishers House.

Anonymous, 1953. *Reports of Expert Committee on Environmental Sanitation,* World Health Organization, Geneva.

Anonymous, 1982. *Reports of the Task Force for the Study of Eco-Development in the Himalayan Region,* Planning Commission, Govt. of India, New Delhi.

Anonymous, 1992. *Planning Commission, Eight Five Year Plan (1992-1997),* Govt. of India, New Delhi.

Anonymous, 1993. *Surface Water Drainage for Low Income Communities,* World Health Organization, Geneva.

Anonymous, 1998., *World Health Report 1997,* World Health Organization, Reprinted by Bookwell, New Delhi.

Anonymous, 1991. *Census of India SC/ST Population,* Registrar General of India, New Delhi (in C.D.).

Anonymous, 2001 a. *Census of India PCA Totals, SC/ST.* Registrar General of India, New Delhi (in C.D.).

Anonymous, 2001 b. *Census of India for the State of Uttaranchal, Bihar and Jharkhand,* Registrar General of India, New Delhi (in C.D., vol. 04).

Atkinson, E.T., 1886. *The Himalayan Districts of North Western Provinces of India;* Vols. Ist, IInd, IIIrd Gazetteers of North Provinces and Oudh, Allahabad, (Reprint 1973), Cosmo Pub. New Delhi.

Aurora, G.S. 1972. *Tribe –Caste-Class Encounters: Some Aspect of Folk Urban Relations in Alirajpur Tehsils,* Hyderabad: Administrative Staff College of India.

Banerji, D.D., 1985. *Health and Family Planning Services in India : an Epidemiological, Socio Cultural and Political Analysis and a Perspectives,* Lok Prakash, New Delhi.

Berreman, G.D., 1972. Demography, Domestic Economy in Western Himalaya, *Eastern Anthropologist,* 30 (2): 157-193.

Berreman, G.D., 1983. The U.P. Himalaya: Culture and Regionalism, in O.P. Singh (ed.) *The Himalaya: Nature, Man and Culture.* Rajesh Pub. New Delhi: 227-265.

Bhati, J.P., 1972. Innovativeness and Agricultural Performance among (Tharu) Tribal of U.P., in *M.V. Tribal Institute Udaipur* (Raj.) 8 (3&4):22-28.

Bhole, A.S. and S.D. Bhangale, 1999. Role of Immigration of Tribal Population in Utilization of Resources in Jalgaon District. *Geog. Review of India* 61 (1): 89-94.

Bisht, G.S., G.S. Satyal and H. Singh, 1995. Agricultural Economy of the Bhotias in Central Himalaya: Status and Potentialities, in B.R. Pant and M.C. Pant (eds.), *Glimpses of Central Himalaya: A Socio-economic and Ecological Perspective,* Radha Publications, New Delhi, pp. 317-332.

Bose, Ashish, 1990. *Demography of Tribal Development* B.R. Publishing Corporation, New Delhi.

Burrerd S.G., H.H. Hayden and A.M. Hirons, 1933. *A Sketch of Geology and Geography of the Himalaya Mountain and Tibet,* Pt. 1: 5.

Champion, H.G. and S.K. Seth. 1968. *A Revised Survey of the Forest Types of India,* Managers of Publications, Delhi.

Chand, R., 1981. *Rural Settlements in Pithoragarh District.* Ph.D. Thesis, Kumaun University Nainital.

Chand, R., 1989. Socio-economic Structure of Villages in Kumaun Himalaya, *Geog. Review of India,* 51(4): 25-35.

Chand, R., 1989. *Brokpas: The Hidden Highlanders of Bhutan*, Pahar Pothi Nainital.

Chaudhary, A.K. and N.A. Ghatak, 1987. Marriage Distance among the Bhoksas of Dehradun, *Vanyajati*, 35(3) 20-24.

Chib, S.S., 1995. Demographic Dynamics in the Trans-Himalaya Tribal Region of Kinnaur, H.P. Perspective of Socio-economic Implications, *Geog. Review of India*, 57(1): 22-28.

Crook, W., 1896. *The Tribes and Castes of North Western Provinces and Oudh* (in four vols.).

Dash, N.K. and A. Ahmad, 1985. Tribal Literacy in India: Its Determinants and Correlation. *The Geographer*, 48: (2).

Despande, C.D., 1973. The Naga Villages: A Reconnaisa Study. *Geographical Outlook* 9:15-18.

Fernandez, W., 1994. *Tribal Development in India: Myth and Reality*, Vikas Publishing House Pvt. Ltd., New Delhi.

Furer-Haimendorf, C.V., 1909. *Tribes of India: The Struggle for Survival*, University of California Press, Berkeley.

Ghildyal, B.P., 1981. Soils of the Garhwal and Kumaun Himalaya, in J.S. Lal and A.D. Moddie (eds.) *The Himalaya: Aspects of Change*, Oxford University Press, New Delhi: 120-137.

Gopalan, C., B.V. Ramashastry and S.C. Subramanian, Revised and update by Narsingha Rao, Y.G. Deosthale and K.C. Pant, 1993. *Nutritive Value of Indian Foods*, NIN, ICMR, Hyderabad: 156 p.

Goswami, D.B., 1994. Distribution and Development of Tribes in Uttar Pradesh, *Vanyajati*, 42 (2):1-11.

Gupta, H.S. and A. Baghel, 1995. Fertility Pattern among the Scheduled Tribes of Raipur District. *Annals of the NAGI*, 15 (2): 36-54.

Hasan, A., 1990. The Tharu of Uttar Pradesh, *Vanyajati*, 38

(3):10-18.

Hazra, M., 1981. Some Aspects of Cultural Life of Bhotias of Garbyang, *Vanyajati*, 29 (4): 19-24.

Hedin Seven, 1913. *Southern Tibet Discoveries in Farmer Times Compared to My Own Research*, 12 Vols.. London.

Jafri, S.S.A. and A. Lanu Imchen, 1994. Socio-Cultural Village, *Geog. Review of India*, 56(4): 58.

Jain, C.K., 1992. Transformation of Agriculture in Tribal Madhya Pradesh, in N. Mohammad (ed.) *New Dimensions in Agricultural Geography*, Vol. 5, Concept, New Delhi: 209-220.

Jalal, D.S., B.R. Pant and R.C. Joshi, 2001. *Environmental Study in Himalayan Region*, Anmol Publication Pvt. Ltd. New Delhi.

James, W.P.T., L. Anna Ferro and J.C. Waterlow, 1988. Definition Chronic Energy Deficiency in Adults, *European Journal of Clinical Nutrition*, 42:969.

Joshi, Hemlata, 1996. Demographic Profile of Banswara—A Predominantly Tribal District of Rajasthan, *Geog. Review of India*, 58(3): 219-230.

Lall, Panna, 1911. An Inquiry in to the Birth and Marriage Customs of the Khasa and the Bhotias of Almora District, *Indian Antiquary*, 46: 190-199.

Majumdar, D.N., 1942. Tharus and their Blood Groups, *Journal of Royal Asiatic Society of Bengal*, vol. VIII, No. 1.

Majumdar, D.N. and T.N. Madan, 1970. *An Introduction to Social Anthropology*, Asia Publishing House, Bombay.

Majumdar, Kumkum, 1973. Distribution of Tribal Population in Eastern Gujarat, *NGJI*, 19 (3&4): 177-192.

Mookerji, S., 1986. Ecology and Tribals: A Process of Human Adjustment with Environment, *The Geographer*, 50 (2).

Mukerji, A.B., 1979. Tribe, in Moonis Raza (ed.) *ICSSR Survey of Research in Geography*, 1969-72. Allied Pub. New Delhi:

97-107.

Nevill, H.R., 1922. *Nainital: A District Gazetteer*, Govt. Printing Press. Allahabad.

Pande, G.C., 1988. *Indian Tribes: The Habitat, Society, Economy and Change*. Anmol Publication, New Delhi.

Pant, B.R., 1994. *Food and Nutrition: A Study of Himalayan Region*, Anmol Publication Pvt. Ltd., New Delhi, 195 p.

Pant, B.R., 1995. The Central Himalaya: Geographical Outlook, in B.R. Pant and M.C. Pant (eds.), *Glimpses of Central Himalaya: A Socio Economic and Ecological Perspective*, Radha Publications, New Delhi, pp. 3-86.

Pant, B.R., 1998. *Geo- Economic Environment and Nutrition: A Study of Kumaun Himalaya*, Anmol Publication Pvt. Ltd., New Delhi, 173 p.

Pant, B.R., 2002. Drudgery and Nutrition Status of the Rural Women in the Central Himalaya (Uttarakhand Himalaya), *The Indonesian Journal of Geography*, 34(1&2):1-16.

Pant, B.R., 2003 a. Mal Nutritional Problem in the Himalayan Women, *Man in India*: 83 (1&2):29-48.

Pant, B.R., 2003 b. Housing and Environmental Sanitation Pattern in the Himalayan Villages, *Geog. Review of India*, 65 (4): 403-407.

Pant, B.R., 2003c. Environmental Degradation and Demographic Structure of Himalaya, *ENVIS BULLETIN*: 11 (1):23-34.

Pant, B.R., 2003d. Women and nutrition in Himalayan Region: A case study from Uttarakhand. *Geographer*, 50(2): 22-29.

Pant, B.R., 2004. *Women and Nutrition in Himalaya*, Anmol Publication Pvt. Ltd., New Delhi: 227 p.

Pant, B.R., 2005. A Study of Socio Economic and Nutritional Status of Tharu Tribe in Uttaranchal, Project Report First submitted to the U.G.C., New Delhi, 44 p. (Mimeo.)

Pant, B.R., 2006a. A Study of Socio Economic and Nutritional Status of Tharu Tribe in Uttaranchal, Project Report Second submitted to the U.G.C. New Delhi: 141 p. (Mimeo.).

Pant, B.R. 2006b. Gender Gap in Literacy Rates among the Indian Scheduled Tribes, Paper accepted for the presentation in the 1st International Geography Congress 2006 Osmania University, Hyderabad.

Pant, B.R (in press) Tribal Demography of India. *Man in India*, Serials Publication New Delhi.

Pant B.R. and R. Chand (in press.) Demographic Structure of S.T. Population in India, *Annals of the NAGI.*

Pant, S.D., 1937. *Social Economy of Himalayas*, George Allen & Unwin, London: 267.

Parizanganeh, A.H., and V. Rangaswamy, 1991. Tribal Environment of Chhota Udaipur Region in Gujarat, *Transaction I.I.G.*, 13(1):65-72.

Pathak, C.R., 2001. Impact of Development on the Tribal Community in Jharkhand State, *Geog. Review of India*, 63 (4): 305-316.

Pati, R.N., 1991. *Tribal Development in India*, Ashish Publishing House, New Delhi.

Patnaik, N., *Tribes and their Development: A Study of Two Tribals Development Blocks in Orissa*, NICD, Hyderabad.

Pranavanand, Swami, 1950. *Exploration in Tibet*, Govt. Press Allahabad.

Pranavanand, Swami, 1953. *Kailas Mansarovar* (Hindi Translation).

Prasad, R.R. and A.R. Kapoor, 1982. Obstetrical Practice Among the Bhotia Tribals, *Vanyajati*, 30(4): 7-8.

Pratap, D.R., 1975. *Tribes of Andhra Pradesh*, World Telugu Conference Office, Hyderabad.

Raghaviah, R., 1972. *Tribes of India*, Vol. I & II, Bharatiya

Adimjati Sevak Sangh, New Delhi.

Ram, Pati, 1911. *Garhwal: Ancient and Modern*, Army Press, Shimla.

Raza, Mehdi, 1973. Genre Devie: A Case Study, *The Geographer*, 20 (1) 49-54.

Raza, Moonis, 1979. Defining the Area of Social Geography, in Moonis Raza (ed.), *ICSSR Survey of Research in Geography*, Allied Publishers, Delhi.

Raza, Moonis, and A. Ahmad, 1984. Social Geography : Tribes, Caste, Literacy, Religion, in Shah Manjoor Alam (ed.) *ICSSR Survey of Research in Geography 1972-75*, Concept, Delhi, pp. 70-72.

Raza, Moonis, and A. Ahmad, 1985. *Tribal Atlas of India*. New Delhi.

Roy Burman, B.K., 1972. Distribution of S.T. Population of India; An Exploratory Geocultural Appraisal in Census of India, 1971. Economic and Socio-Cultural Dimension of Regionalization : An Indo- U.S.S.R. Collaboration Study.

Samal, P.K., 1993. The Status of Women in Central Himalaya: A Cultural Interpretation, *Man in India*, 73 (1):87-95.

Santhanan, M., 1989. Community Participation and Rural Water Supply and Sanitation Programme, *Social Change*, 19 (1): 53-58.

Satyal, G.S., K. Kumar and D.S. Rawat, 1999. Sustainable Use of Natural Resources: A Case Study of Tribal Village in the Kumaun Himalaya, *Geog. Review of India*, 61 (2): 183-195.

Shafi, Mohammad and A. Aziz, 1989. *Food Systems of the World*, Rawat Publication, Jaipur, 526 p.

Sherring, C.A., 1906. *Western Tibet and British Border Land*, Enwardamold, London, Notes on the Bhotia of Almora and British Garhwal, Asiatic Society of Bengal, Calcutta.

Singh, K.S., (ed.) 1972. *Tribal Situation of India*, Indian Institute of Advanced Study, Shimla.

Singh, L.R., 1956. The Tharus: A Study in Human Ecology, *NGJI* (3):153-166.

Singh, L.R., 1965. *The Tarai Region of U.P.: A Study in Human Geography*, Ram Narayan Lal Beni, Allahabad.

Srivastava, R.P., 1953. Rangbhang in the Changing Bhotia of Almora District. *The Anthropologist*, 1:22-23.

Srivastava, S.K., 1958. *The Tharus: A Study in Culture Dynamics*, Agra University Press, Agra.

Tiwari, S.C. 1953. The Rajis of Askot District Almora, U.P. *Vanyajati*, 1 (3) : 52-58.

Trail, G.W., 1832. Statistical Report on the Bhotia Mahal of Kumaun, *Asiatic Research*, 17:1-50.

Upreti, H.C., 1968. The Social Life of Bhotias, *Vanyajati*, 16 (2): 15-20.

Upreti, R.P., 1967. The Social Geography of Bhotias, *Uttarakhand Bharti*, IV: 115-129.

Upreti, R.P., 1968. *Bhotias of Uttarakhand: A Study of Anthropogeography Studies*, V: 115-124.

Valdiya, K.S., 1980. *Geology of Kumaun Lesser Himalaya*, W.I.H.G. Dehradun.: 301.

Valdiya, K.S., 1988. Geology of Kumaun: An Outline, in K.S. Valdiya (ed.) *Kumaun: Land and People*, Gyanodaya Prakashan, Nainital: 37-72.

Vankataraman, S.R., 1972. Socio-Economic Study of Himalayan Border Tribe (Boksha), *Vanyajati*, 20 (1): 5-10.

Verma, R.S.P. 1972. Mundas in Changing Environment, *Indian Geographical Studies*, 5: 50-55.

Vidyarthi, L.P., 1974. Tribal Development in Independent India and its Future, *Man in India*, LIV (1):45-79.

Index

Connectivity in Tharu villages.

Traditional *Chulha* of Tharu woman in Charubeta.

Firewood collection.

Interior of the Tharu House Khetalsanda village.

Mr. Govind Singh Rana Tharu in Khetalsanda.

Old generation in Tharu.

Author interviewed Mr. Dan Singh Tharu in Goharpatia.

Author in Charubeta with Rishipal Singh Ran.

Paddy Nursery.

Paddy plantation in Gohar Patia.

Tharu houses.

Tharu with pucca house.